Reflections on the Life of King David

by David Mills

Reflections on the Life of King David
by David Mills

ISBN: 978-1-105-75402-9

Table of Contents

Introduction

Three sections

The revised edition of **Reflections on the Life of King David** is divided into three sections. The first section is the Bible (English Standard Version) narrative of David's life taken from 1 & 2 Samuel arranged in chronological order with supplementary material from 1 Chronicles. This new section was created primarily because the chronology suggested in Crockett's **Harmony of the Books of Samuel, Kings, and Chronicles** is unacceptable in many places. Although it is apparent that more than one document is incorporated into the Scriptural account of David's life, it is assumed that those documents were not extensively edited or altered but are preserved essentially as they were written. Although some parts of the story overlap with one another, no documentary hypothesis was considered in making the chronology. A basic chronology, which generally follows the Biblical order, can be inferred from what is written in Scripture. It should be noted, however, that Part Six does not follow Part Five but runs parallel to it.

The second section of the book is a revised and expanded version the earlier reflections. The discussion questions, however, have been omitted. The reflections, which follow the chronological order in the first section, are based on the conviction that the Scripture presents an accurate account of the character and career of David. Although he was not a perfect man, he was not an outlaw and traitor whose criminal behavior was masked by religious editors who significantly altered the story to create a hero who never existed. The reflections have nothing in common with the theories of Steven L. McKenzie (2000, **King David: A Biography**) or Baruch Halpern (2001, **David's Secret Demons: Messiah, Murderer, Traitor, King**) who claim to have discovered the historical David whom they say was an ambitious and vicious tyrant. On the contrary, the reflections understand David to be a model of faith, devotion, repentance, and gratitude to a merciful God. Further, the reflections consider his reign to have been important in developing the hope for a Messiah.

The third section of the book explains how the chronology and the dates for each part of David's life were determined.

Supplemental material from Chronicles

Where Samuel and Chronicles are parallel, the text of Samuel is the primary text. Chronicles may modify details, omit details, or add details. Where those differences are significant, they have been noted in the following manner:

- Modification: <Samuel text> [Chronicles text]
- Omission: <Samuel text> [0]
- Addition: [+ Chronicles text]

Here is an example from 1 Sam. 21:19, which is parallel with 1 Chron. 20:5.

> [19] And there was again war with the Philistines <at Gob> [0], and Elhanan the son of <Jaare-oregim, the Bethlehemite> [Jair], struck down [+ Lahmi the brother of] Goliath the Gittite, the shaft of whose spear was like a weaver's beam.

In this passage, Chronicles omits "at Gob," the location of the battle, modifies the identity of Elhanan's father, and adds that the giant was Lahmi the brother of Goliath, not Goliath himself.

In many places, the Chronicles text has no parallel in Samuel. These supplemental passages appear separate from the Samuel text but in the appropriate places.

Useful commentaries

Alter, R. 1999. *The David Story*.

Bergen, R.D. 1996. New American Commentary, Vol. 7: *1, 2 Samuel*. Elec. ed.

Payne, J.B. 1988. "1, 2 Chronicles" in *Expositor's Bible Commentary, Vol. 4*. Elec. ed.

Smith, J.E. 2000. The College Press NIV Commentary: *1 & 2 Samuel*. Elec. ed.

Youngblood, R.F. 1992. "1, 2 Samuel" in *Expositor's Bible Commentary, Vol. 3*. Elec. ed.

Other works

Alter, R. 1981. *The Art of Biblical Narrative*.

Briggs, C.A. 1886. *Messianic Prophecy*.

Cabal, T., et al. 2007. *The Apologetics Study Bible*. Elec. ed..

Crockett, W.D. 1964. *A Harmony of the Books of Samuel, Kings, and Chronicles*.

Smith, H.P. 1898. The International Critical Commentary: *A Critical and Exegetical Commentary on the Books of Samuel*.

Lexicons

BDAG. 2000. *A Greek-English Lexicon of the New Testament and Other Early Christian Literature*. Elec. ed.

BDB. 2000. *Enhanced Brown-Driver-Briggs Hebrew and English Lexicon*. Elec. ed.

TWOT. 1999. *Theological Wordbook of the Old Testament*. Elec. ed.

Table of Dates in David's Life

Event	Date B.C.	Age	Regnal Year
Birth	1040	Newborn	
Saul's court	1023-1016	17-24	
Outcast in Judah	1016-1012	24-28	
Refuge in Philistia	1011-1010	29-30	
Hebron	1009-1003	31-37	1-7
Jerusalem	1002-994	38-46	8-16
Military conquests	1002-994	38-46	8-16
Favor & Forgiveness	992-990	47-50	17-20
Family trouble	989-977	51-63	21-33
National problems	976-973	64-67	34-37
Transfer of power	972-970	68-70	38-40

The Life of King David

Part One: Saul's Court

1023–1016 B.C.; age 17-24

Samuel anoints David to replace Saul
1 Sam. 16:1-13

16 The LORD said to Samuel, "How long will you grieve over Saul, since I have rejected him from being king over Israel? Fill your horn with oil, and go. I will send you to Jesse the Bethlehemite, for I have provided for myself a king among his sons." **2** And Samuel said, "How can I go? If Saul hears it, he will kill me." And the LORD said, "Take a heifer with you and say, 'I have come to sacrifice to the LORD.' **3** And invite Jesse to the sacrifice, and I will show you what you shall do. And you shall anoint for me him whom I declare to you." **4** Samuel did what the LORD commanded and came to Bethlehem. The elders of the city came to meet him trembling and said, "Do you come peaceably?" **5** And he said, "Peaceably; I have come to sacrifice to the LORD. Consecrate yourselves, and come with me to the sacrifice." And he consecrated Jesse and his sons and invited them to the sacrifice.

6 When they came, he looked on Eliab and thought, "Surely the LORD's anointed is before him." **7** But the LORD said to Samuel, "Do not look on his appearance or on the height of his stature, because I have rejected him. For the LORD sees not as man sees: man looks on the outward appearance, but the LORD looks on the heart." **8** Then Jesse called Abinadab and made him pass before Samuel. And he said, "Neither has the LORD chosen this one." **9** Then Jesse made Shammah pass by. And he said, "Neither has the LORD chosen this one." **10** And Jesse made seven of his sons pass before Samuel. And Samuel said to Jesse, "The LORD has not chosen these." **11** Then Samuel said to Jesse, "Are all your sons here?" And he said, "There remains yet the youngest, but behold, he is keeping the sheep." And Samuel said to Jesse, "Send and get him, for we will not sit down till he comes here." **12** And he sent and brought him in. Now he was ruddy and had beautiful eyes and was handsome. And the LORD said, "Arise, anoint him, for this is he." **13** Then Samuel took the horn of oil and anointed him in the midst of his brothers. And the Spirit of the LORD rushed upon David from that day forward. And Samuel rose up and went to Ramah.

Goliath insults the Israelite army
1 Sam. 17:1-11

17 Now the Philistines gathered their armies for battle. And they were gathered at Socoh, which belongs to Judah, and encamped between Socoh and Azekah, in Ephes-dammim. **2** And Saul and the men of Israel were gathered, and encamped in the Valley of Elah, and drew up in line of battle against the Philistines. **3** And the Philistines stood on the mountain on the one side, and Israel stood on the mountain on the other side, with a valley between them. **4** And there came out from the camp of the Philistines a champion named Goliath of Gath, whose height was six cubits and a span. **5** He had a helmet of bronze on his head, and he was armed with a coat of mail, and the weight of the coat was five thousand shekels of bronze. **6** And he had bronze armor on his legs, and a javelin of bronze slung between his shoulders. **7** The shaft of his spear was like a weaver's beam, and his spear's head weighed six hundred shekels of iron. And his shield-bearer went before him. **8** He stood and shouted to the ranks of Israel, "Why have you come out to draw up for battle? Am I not a Philistine, and are you not servants of Saul? Choose a man for yourselves, and let him come down to me. **9** If he is able to fight with me and kill me, then we will be your servants. But if I prevail against him and kill him, then you shall be our servants and serve us." **10** And the Philistine said, "I defy the ranks of Israel this day. Give me a man, that we may fight together." **11** When Saul and all Israel heard these words of the Philistine, they were dismayed and greatly afraid.

David enters the Israelite camp
1 Sam. 17:12-31

12 Now David was the son of an Ephrathite of Bethlehem in Judah, named Jesse, who had eight sons. In the days of Saul the man was already old and advanced in years. **13** The three oldest sons of Jesse had followed Saul to the battle. And the names of his three sons who went to the battle were Eliab the firstborn, and next to him Abinadab, and the third Shammah. **14** David was the youngest. The three eldest followed Saul, **15** but David went back and forth from Saul to feed his father's sheep at Bethlehem. **16** For forty days the Philistine came forward and took his stand, morning and evening.

17 And Jesse said to David his son, "Take for your brothers an ephah of this parched grain, and these ten loaves, and carry them quickly to the camp to your brothers. **18** Also take these ten cheeses to the commander of their thousand. See if your brothers are well, and bring some token from them."

19 Now Saul and they and all the men of Israel were in the Valley of Elah, fighting with the Philistines. **20** And David rose early in the morning and left the sheep with a keeper and took the provisions and went, as Jesse had commanded him. And he came to the encampment as the host was going out to the battle line, shouting the war cry. **21** And Israel and the Philistines drew up for battle, army against army. **22** And David left the things in charge of the keeper of the baggage and ran to the ranks and went and greeted his brothers. **23** As he talked with them, behold, the champion, the Philistine of Gath, Goliath by name, came up out of the ranks of the Philistines and spoke the same words as before. And David heard him.

24 All the men of Israel, when they saw the man, fled from him and were much afraid. **25** And the men of Israel said, "Have you seen this man who has come up? Surely he has come up to defy Israel. And the king will enrich the man who kills him with great riches and will give him his daughter and make his father's house free in Israel." **26** And David said to the men who stood by him, "What shall be done for the man who kills this Philistine and takes away the reproach from Israel? For who is this uncircumcised Philistine, that he should defy the armies of the living God?" **27** And the people answered him in the same way, "So shall it be done to the man who kills him."

28 Now Eliab his eldest brother heard when he spoke to the men. And Eliab's anger was kindled against David, and he said, "Why have you come down? And with whom have you left those few sheep in the wilderness? I know your presumption and the evil of your heart, for you have come down to see the battle." **29** And David said, "What have I done now? Was it not but a word?" **30** And he turned away from him toward another, and spoke in the same way, and the people answered him again as before.

31 When the words that David spoke were heard, they repeated them before Saul, and he sent for him.

David prepares for battle
1 Sam. 17:32-40

32 And David said to Saul, "Let no man's heart fail because of him. Your servant will go and fight with this Philistine." **33** And Saul said to David, "You are not able to go against this Philistine to fight with him, for you are but a youth, and he has been a man of war from his youth." **34** But David said to Saul, "Your servant used to keep sheep for his father. And when there came a lion, or a bear, and took a lamb from the flock, **35** I went after him and struck him and delivered it out of his mouth. And if he arose against me, I caught him by his beard and struck him and killed him. **36** Your servant has struck down both lions and bears, and this uncircumcised Philistine shall be like one of them, for he has defied the armies of the living God." **37** And David said, "The LORD who delivered me from the paw of the lion and from the paw of the bear will deliver me from the hand of this Philistine." And Saul said to David, "Go, and the LORD be with you!"

38 Then Saul clothed David with his armor. He put a helmet of bronze on his head and clothed him with a coat of mail, **39** and David strapped his sword over his armor. And he tried in vain to go, for he had not tested them. Then David said to Saul, "I cannot go with these, for I have not tested them." So David put them off. **40** Then he took his staff in his hand and chose five smooth stones from the brook and put them in his shepherd's pouch. His sling was in his hand, and he approached the Philistine.

David kills Goliath
1 Sam. 17:41-54

41 And the Philistine moved forward and came near to David, with his shield-bearer in front of him. **42** And when the Philistine looked and saw David, he disdained him, for he was but a youth, ruddy and handsome in appearance. **43** And the Philistine said to David, "Am I a dog, that you come to me with sticks?" And the Philistine cursed David by his gods. **44** The Philistine said to David, "Come to me, and I will give your flesh to the birds of the air and to the beasts of the field." **45** Then David said to the Philistine, "You come to me with a sword and with a spear and with a javelin, but I come to you in the name of the LORD of hosts, the God of the armies of Israel, whom you have defied. **46** This day the LORD will deliver you into my hand, and I will strike you down and cut off your head. And I will give the dead bodies of the host of the Philistines this day to the birds of the air and to the wild beasts of the earth, that all the earth may know that there is a God in Israel, **47** and that all this assembly may know that the LORD saves not with sword and spear. For the battle is the LORD's, and he will give you into our hand."

48 When the Philistine arose and came and drew near to meet David, David ran quickly toward the battle line to meet the Philistine. **49** And David put his hand in his bag and took out a stone and slung it and struck the Philistine on his forehead. The stone sank into his forehead, and he fell on his face to the ground.

50 So David prevailed over the Philistine with a sling and with a stone, and struck the Philistine and killed him. There was no sword in the hand of David. **51** Then David ran and stood over the Philistine and took his sword and drew it out of its sheath and killed him and cut off his head with it. When the Philistines saw that their champion was dead, they fled. **52** And the men of Israel and Judah rose with a shout and pursued the Philistines as far as Gath and the gates of Ekron, so that the wounded Philistines fell on the way from Shaaraim as far as Gath and Ekron. **53** And the people of Israel came back from chasing the Philistines, and they plundered their camp. **54** And David took the head of the Philistine and brought it to Jerusalem, but he put his armor in his tent.

Saul inquires about David
1 Sam. 17:55 – 18:1

55 As soon as Saul saw David go out against the Philistine, he said to Abner, the commander of the army, "Abner, whose son is this youth?" And Abner said, "As your soul lives, O king, I do not know." **56** And the king said, "Inquire whose son the boy is." **57** And as soon as David returned from the striking down of the Philistine, Abner took him, and brought him before Saul with the head of the Philistine in his hand. **58** And Saul said to him, "Whose son are you, young man?" And David answered, "I am the son of your servant Jesse the Bethlehemite."

18 As soon as he had finished speaking to Saul, the soul of Jonathan was knit to the soul of David, and Jonathan loved him as his own soul.

David arouses Saul's jealousy
1 Sam. 18:6-9

6 As they were coming home, when David returned from striking down the Philistine, the women came out of all the cities of Israel, singing and dancing, to meet King Saul, with tambourines, with songs of joy, and with musical instruments. **7** And the women sang to one another as they celebrated,

> "Saul has struck down his thousands,
>   and David his ten thousands."

8 And Saul was very angry, and this saying displeased him. He said, "They have ascribed to David ten thousands, and to me they have ascribed thousands, and what more can he have but the kingdom?" **9** And Saul eyed David from that day on.

Saul sends for David
1 Sam. 16:14-23 [18:2]

14 Now the Spirit of the LORD departed from Saul, and a harmful spirit from the LORD tormented him. **15** And Saul's servants said to him, "Behold now, a harmful spirit from God is tormenting you. **16** Let our lord now command your servants who are before you to seek out a man who is skillful in playing the lyre, and when the harmful spirit from God is upon you, he will play it, and you will be well." **17** So Saul said to his servants, "Provide for me a man who can play well and bring him to me." **18** One of the young men answered, "Behold, I have seen a son of Jesse the Bethlehemite, who is skillful in playing, a man of valor, a man of war, prudent in speech, and a man of good presence, and the LORD is with him." **19** Therefore Saul sent messengers to Jesse and said, "Send me David your son, who is with the sheep." **20** And Jesse took a donkey laden with bread and a skin of wine and a young goat and sent them by David his son to Saul. **21** And David came to Saul and entered his service. And Saul loved him greatly, and he became his armor-bearer. <**22** And Saul sent to Jesse, saying, "Let David remain in my service, for he has found favor in my sight."> [And Saul took him that day and would not let him return to his father's house.] **23** And whenever the harmful spirit from God was upon Saul, David took the lyre and played it with his hand. So Saul was refreshed and was well, and the harmful spirit departed from him.

Jonathan makes a covenant with David
1 Sam. 18:3-5

3 Then Jonathan made a covenant with David, because he loved him as his own soul. **4** And Jonathan stripped himself of the robe that was on him and gave it to David, and his armor, and even his sword and his bow and his belt. **5** And David went out and was successful wherever Saul sent him, so that Saul set him over the men of war. And this was good in the sight of all the people and also in the sight of Saul's servants.

David eludes Saul and becomes successful
1 Sam. 18:10-16

10 The next day a harmful spirit from God rushed upon Saul, and he raved within his house while David was playing the lyre, as he did day by day. Saul had his spear in his hand. **11** And Saul hurled the spear, for he thought, "I will pin David to the wall." But David evaded him twice.

12 Saul was afraid of David because the LORD was with him but had departed from Saul. **13** So Saul removed him from his presence and made him a commander of a thousand. And he went out and came in before the people. **14** And David had success in all his undertakings, for the LORD was with him. **15** And when Saul saw that he had great success, he stood in fearful awe of him. **16** But all Israel and Judah loved David, for he went out and came in before them.

David marries Michal
1 Sam. 18:17-30

17 Then Saul said to David, "Here is my elder daughter Merab. I will give her to you for a wife. Only be valiant for me and fight the LORD's battles." For Saul thought, "Let not my hand be against him, but let the hand of the Philistines be against him." **18** And David said to Saul, "Who am I, and who are my relatives, my father's clan in Israel, that I should be son-in-law to the king?" **19** But at the time when Merab, Saul's daughter, should have been given to David, she was given to Adriel the Meholathite for a wife.

20 Now Saul's daughter Michal loved David. And they told Saul, and the thing pleased him. **21** Saul thought, "Let me give her to him, that she may be a snare for him and that the hand of the Philistines may be against him." Therefore Saul said to David a second time, "You shall now be my son-in-law." **22** And Saul commanded his servants, "Speak to David in private and say, 'Behold, the king has delight in you, and all his servants love you. Now then become the king's son-in-law.' " **23** And Saul's servants spoke those words in the ears of David. And David said, "Does it seem to you a little thing to become the king's son-in-law, since I am a poor man and have no reputation?" **24** And the servants of Saul told him, "Thus and so did David speak." **25** Then Saul said, "Thus shall you say to David, 'The king desires no bride-price except a hundred foreskins of the Philistines, that he may be avenged of the king's enemies.' " Now Saul thought to make David fall by the hand of the Philistines. **26** And when his servants told David these words, it pleased David well to be the king's son-in-law. Before the time had expired, **27** David arose and went, along with his men, and killed two hundred of the Philistines. And David brought their foreskins, which were given in full number to the king, that he might become the king's son-in-law. And Saul gave him his daughter Michal for a wife. **28** But when Saul saw and knew that the LORD was with David, and that Michal, Saul's daughter, loved him, **29** Saul was even more afraid of David. So Saul was David's enemy continually.

30 Then the commanders of the Philistines came out to battle, and as often as they came out David had more success than all the servants of Saul, so that his name was highly esteemed.

Jonathan intercedes for David
1 Sam. 19:1-7

19 And Saul spoke to Jonathan his son and to all his servants, that they should kill David. But Jonathan, Saul's son, delighted much in David. **2** And Jonathan told David, "Saul my father seeks to kill you. Therefore be on your guard in the morning. Stay in a secret place and hide yourself. **3** And I will go out and stand beside my father in the field where you are, and I will speak to my father about you. And if I learn anything I will tell you." **4** And Jonathan spoke well of David to Saul his father and said to him, "Let not the king sin against his servant David, because he has not sinned against you, and because his deeds have brought good to you. **5** For he took his life in his hand and he struck down the Philistine, and the LORD worked a great salvation for all Israel. You saw it, and rejoiced. Why then will you sin against innocent blood by killing David without cause?" **6** And Saul listened to the voice of Jonathan. Saul swore, "As the LORD lives, he shall not be put to death." **7** And Jonathan called David, and Jonathan reported to him all these things. And Jonathan brought David to Saul, and he was in his presence as before.

David flees for his life
1 Sam. 19:8-17

[8] And there was war again. And David went out and fought with the Philistines and struck them with a great blow, so that they fled before him. [9] Then a harmful spirit from the LORD came upon Saul, as he sat in his house with his spear in his hand. And David was playing the lyre. [10] And Saul sought to pin David to the wall with the spear, but he eluded Saul, so that he struck the spear into the wall. And David fled and escaped that night.

[11] Saul sent messengers to David's house to watch him, that he might kill him in the morning. But Michal, David's wife, told him, "If you do not escape with your life tonight, tomorrow you will be killed." [12] So Michal let David down through the window, and he fled away and escaped. [13] Michal took an image and laid it on the bed and put a pillow of goats' hair at its head and covered it with the clothes. [14] And when Saul sent messengers to take David, she said, "He is sick." [15] Then Saul sent the messengers to see David, saying, "Bring him up to me in the bed, that I may kill him." [16] And when the messengers came in, behold, the image was in the bed, with the pillow of goats' hair at its head. [17] Saul said to Michal, "Why have you deceived me thus and let my enemy go, so that he has escaped?" And Michal answered Saul, "He said to me, 'Let me go. Why should I kill you?'"

David finds refuge with Samuel
1 Sam. 19:18-24

[18] Now David fled and escaped, and he came to Samuel at Ramah and told him all that Saul had done to him. And he and Samuel went and lived at Naioth. [19] And it was told Saul, "Behold, David is at Naioth in Ramah." [20] Then Saul sent messengers to take David, and when they saw the company of the prophets prophesying, and Samuel standing as head over them, the Spirit of God came upon the messengers of Saul, and they also prophesied. [21] When it was told Saul, he sent other messengers, and they also prophesied. And Saul sent messengers again the third time, and they also prophesied. [22] Then he himself went to Ramah and came to the great well that is in Secu. And he asked, "Where are Samuel and David?" And

one said, "Behold, they are at Naioth in Ramah." **23** And he went there to Naioth in Ramah. And the Spirit of God came upon him also, and as he went he prophesied until he came to Naioth in Ramah. **24** And he too stripped off his clothes, and he too prophesied before Samuel and lay naked all that day and all that night. Thus it is said, "Is Saul also among the prophets?"

Part Two: Outcast in Judah

1016–1012 B.C.; age 24-28

David fails to renew Saul's favor
1 Sam. 20:1-42

20 Then David fled from Naioth in Ramah and came and said before Jonathan, "What have I done? What is my guilt? And what is my sin before your father, that he seeks my life?" **2** And he said to him, "Far from it! You shall not die. Behold, my father does nothing either great or small without disclosing it to me. And why should my father hide this from me? It is not so." **3** But David vowed again, saying, "Your father knows well that I have found favor in your eyes, and he thinks, 'Do not let Jonathan know this, lest he be grieved.' But truly, as the LORD lives and as your soul lives, there is but a step between me and death." **4** Then Jonathan said to David, "Whatever you say, I will do for you." **5** David said to Jonathan, "Behold, tomorrow is the new moon, and I should not fail to sit at table with the king. But let me go, that I may hide myself in the field till the third day at evening. **6** If your father misses me at all, then say, 'David earnestly asked leave of me to run to Bethlehem his city, for there is a yearly sacrifice there for all the clan.' **7** If he says, 'Good!' it will be well with your servant, but if he is angry, then know that harm is determined by him. **8** Therefore deal kindly with your servant, for you have brought your servant into a covenant of the LORD with you. But if there is guilt in me, kill me yourself, for why should you bring me to your father?" **9** And Jonathan said, "Far be it from you! If I knew that it was determined by my father that harm should come to you, would I not tell you?" **10** Then David said to Jonathan, "Who will tell me if your father answers you roughly?" **11** And Jonathan said to David, "Come, let us go out into the field." So they both went out into the field.

12 And Jonathan said to David, "The LORD, the God of Israel, be witness! When I have sounded out my father, about this time tomorrow, or the third day, behold, if he is well disposed toward David, shall I not then send and disclose it to you? **13** But should it please my father to do you harm, the LORD do so to Jonathan and more also if I do not disclose it to you and send you away, that you may go in safety. May the LORD be with you, as he has been with my father. **14** If I am still alive, show me the steadfast love of the LORD, that I may not die; **15** and do not cut off your steadfast love from my house forever, when the LORD cuts off every one of the enemies of David from the face of the earth." **16** And Jonathan made a covenant with the house of David, saying, "May the LORD take vengeance on David's enemies." **17** And Jonathan made David swear again by his love for him, for he loved him as he loved his own soul.

18 Then Jonathan said to him, "Tomorrow is the new moon, and you will be missed, because your seat will be empty. **19** On the third day go down quickly to the place where you hid yourself when the matter was in hand, and remain beside the stone heap. **20** And I will shoot three arrows to the side of it, as though I shot at a mark. **21** And behold, I will send the boy, saying, 'Go, find the arrows.' If I say to the boy, 'Look, the arrows are on this side of you, take them,' then you are to come, for, as the LORD lives, it is safe for you and there is no danger. **22** But if I say to the youth, 'Look, the arrows are beyond you,' then go, for the LORD has sent you away. **23** And as for the matter of which you and I have spoken, behold, the LORD is between you and me forever."

24 So David hid himself in the field. And when the new moon came, the king sat down to eat food. **25** The king sat on his seat, as at other times, on the seat by the wall. Jonathan sat opposite, and Abner sat by Saul's side, but David's place was empty.

26 Yet Saul did not say anything that day, for he thought, "Something has happened to him. He is not clean; surely he is not clean." **27** But on the second day, the day after the new moon, David's place was empty. And Saul said to Jonathan his son, "Why has not the son of Jesse come to the meal, either yesterday or today?" **28** Jonathan answered Saul, "David earnestly asked leave of me to go to Bethlehem. **29** He said, 'Let me go, for our clan holds a sacrifice in the city, and my brother has commanded me to be there. So now, if I have found favor in your eyes, let me get away and see my brothers.' For this reason he has not come to the king's table."

30 Then Saul's anger was kindled against Jonathan, and he said to him, "You son of a perverse, rebellious woman, do I not know that you have chosen the son of Jesse to your own shame, and to the shame of your mother's nakedness? **31** For as long as the son of Jesse lives on the earth, neither you nor your kingdom shall be established. Therefore send and bring him to me, for he shall surely die." **32** Then Jonathan answered Saul his father, "Why should he be put to death? What has he done?" **33** But Saul hurled his spear at him to strike him. So Jonathan knew that his father was determined to put David to death. **34** And Jonathan rose from the table in fierce anger and ate no food the second day of the month, for he was grieved for David, because his father had disgraced him.

35 In the morning Jonathan went out into the field to the appointment with David, and with him a little boy. **36** And he said to his boy, "Run and find the arrows that I shoot." As the boy ran, he shot an arrow beyond him. **37** And when the boy came to the place of the arrow that Jonathan had shot, Jonathan called after the boy and said, "Is not the arrow beyond you?" **38** And Jonathan called after the boy, "Hurry! Be quick! Do not stay!" So Jonathan's boy gathered up the arrows and came to his master. **39** But the boy knew nothing. Only Jonathan and David knew the matter. **40** And Jonathan gave his weapons to his boy and said to him, "Go and carry them to the city." **41** And as soon as the boy had gone, David rose from beside the stone heap and fell on his face to the ground and bowed three times. And they kissed one another and wept with one another, David weeping the most. **42** Then Jonathan said to David, "Go in peace, because we have sworn both of us in the name of the LORD, saying, 'The LORD shall be between me and you, and between my offspring and your offspring, forever.'" And he rose and departed, and Jonathan went into the city.

David obtains supplies from priests at Nob
1 Sam. 21:1-9

21 Then David came to Nob to Ahimelech the priest. And Ahimelech came to meet David trembling and said to him, "Why are you alone, and no one with you?" **2** And David said to Ahimelech the priest, "The king has charged me with a matter and said to me, 'Let no one know anything of the matter about which I send you, and with which I have charged you.' I have made an appointment with the young men for such and such a place. **3** Now then, what do you have on hand? Give me five loaves of bread, or whatever is here." **4** And the priest answered David, "I have no common bread on hand, but there is holy bread—if the young men have kept themselves from women." **5** And David answered the priest, "Truly women have been kept from us as always when I go on an expedition. The vessels of the young men are holy even when it is an ordinary journey. How much more today will their vessels be holy?" **6** So the priest gave him the holy bread, for there was no bread there but the bread of the Presence, which is removed from before the LORD, to be replaced by hot bread on the day it is taken away.

[7] Now a certain man of the servants of Saul was there that day, detained before the LORD. His name was Doeg the Edomite, the chief of Saul's herdsmen.

[8] Then David said to Ahimelech, "Then have you not here a spear or a sword at hand? For I have brought neither my sword nor my weapons with me, because the king's business required haste." [9] And the priest said, "The sword of Goliath the Philistine, whom you struck down in the Valley of Elah, behold, it is here wrapped in a cloth behind the ephod. If you will take that, take it, for there is none but that here." And David said, "There is none like that; give it to me."

David flees to Gath temporarily
1 Sam. 21:10-15

[10] And David rose and fled that day from Saul and went to Achish the king of Gath. [11] And the servants of Achish said to him, "Is not this David the king of the land? Did they not sing to one another of him in dances,

> 'Saul has struck down his thousands,
> and David his ten thousands'?"

[12] And David took these words to heart and was much afraid of Achish the king of Gath. [13] So he changed his behavior before them and pretended to be insane in their hands and made marks on the doors of the gate and let his spittle run down his beard. [14] Then Achish said to his servants, "Behold, you see the man is mad. Why then have you brought him to me? [15] Do I lack madmen, that you have brought this fellow to behave as a madman in my presence? Shall this fellow come into my house?"

David becomes a leader of the oppressed
1 Sam. 22:1-5

22 David departed from there and escaped to the cave of Adullam. And when his brothers and all his father's house heard it, they went down there to him. [2] And everyone who was in distress, and everyone who was in debt, and everyone who was bitter in soul, gathered to him. And he became commander over them. And there were with him about four hundred men.

³ And David went from there to Mizpeh of Moab. And he said to the king of Moab, "Please let my father and my mother stay with you, till I know what God will do for me." ⁴ And he left them with the king of Moab, and they stayed with him all the time that David was in the stronghold. ⁵ Then the prophet Gad said to David, "Do not remain in the stronghold; depart, and go into the land of Judah." So David departed and went into the forest of Hereth.

David gathers soldiers
1 Chron. 12:8-18

⁸ From the Gadites there went over to David at the stronghold in the wilderness mighty and experienced warriors, expert with shield and spear, whose faces were like the faces of lions and who were swift as gazelles upon the mountains: ⁹ Ezer the chief, Obadiah second, Eliab third, ¹⁰ Mishmannah fourth, Jeremiah fifth, ¹¹ Attai sixth, Eliel seventh, ¹² Johanan eighth, Elzabad ninth, ¹³ Jeremiah tenth, Machbannai eleventh. ¹⁴ These Gadites were officers of the army; the least was a match for a hundred men and the greatest for a thousand. ¹⁵ These are the men who crossed the Jordan in the first month, when it was overflowing all its banks, and put to flight all those in the valleys, to the east and to the west.

¹⁶ And some of the men of Benjamin and Judah came to the stronghold to David. ¹⁷ David went out to meet them and said to them, "If you have come to me in friendship to help me, my heart will be joined to you; but if to betray me to my adversaries, although there is no wrong in my hands, then may the God of our fathers see and rebuke you." ¹⁸ Then the Spirit clothed Amasai, chief of the thirty, and he said,

> "We are yours, O David,
>   and with you, O son of Jesse!
> Peace, peace to you,
>   and peace to your helpers!
>   For your God helps you."

Then David received them and made them officers of his troops.

David gives refuge to Abiathar the priest
1 Sam. 22:6-23

6 Now Saul heard that David was discovered, and the men who were with him. Saul was sitting at Gibeah under the tamarisk tree on the height with his spear in his hand, and all his servants were standing about him. **7** And Saul said to his servants who stood about him, "Hear now, people of Benjamin; will the son of Jesse give every one of you fields and vineyards, will he make you all commanders of thousands and commanders of hundreds, **8** that all of you have conspired against me? No one discloses to me when my son makes a covenant with the son of Jesse. None of you is sorry for me or discloses to me that my son has stirred up my servant against me, to lie in wait, as at this day." **9** Then answered Doeg the Edomite, who stood by the servants of Saul, "I saw the son of Jesse coming to Nob, to Ahimelech the son of Ahitub, **10** and he inquired of the LORD for him and gave him provisions and gave him the sword of Goliath the Philistine."

11 Then the king sent to summon Ahimelech the priest, the son of Ahitub, and all his father's house, the priests who were at Nob, and all of them came to the king. **12** And Saul said, "Hear now, son of Ahitub." And he answered, "Here I am, my lord." **13** And Saul said to him, "Why have you conspired against me, you and the son of Jesse, in that you have given him bread and a sword and have inquired of God for him, so that he has risen against me, to lie in wait, as at this day?" **14** Then Ahimelech answered the king, "And who among all your servants is so faithful as David, who is the king's son-in-law, and captain over your bodyguard, and honored in your house? **15** Is today the first time that I have inquired of God for him? No! Let not the king impute anything to his servant or to all the house of my father, for your servant has known nothing of all this, much or little." **16** And the king said, "You shall surely die, Ahimelech, you and all your father's house." **17** And the king said to the guard who stood about him, "Turn and kill the priests of the LORD, because their hand also is with David, and they knew that he fled and did not disclose it to me." But the servants of the king would not put out their hand to strike the priests of the LORD. **18** Then the king said to Doeg, "You turn and strike the priests." And Doeg the Edomite turned and struck down the priests, and he killed on that day eighty-five persons who wore the linen ephod. **19** And Nob, the city of the priests, he put to the sword; both man and woman, child and infant, ox, donkey and sheep, he put to the sword.

20 But one of the sons of Ahimelech the son of Ahitub, named Abiathar, escaped and fled after David. **21** And Abiathar told David that Saul had killed the priests of the LORD. **22** And David said to Abiathar, "I knew on that day, when Doeg the Edomite was there, that he would surely tell Saul. I have occasioned the death of all the persons of your father's house. **23** Stay with me; do not be afraid, for he who seeks my life seeks your life. With me you shall be in safekeeping."

David saves Keilah
1 Sam. 23:1-13

23 Now they told David, "Behold, the Philistines are fighting against Keilah and are robbing the threshing floors." **2** Therefore David inquired of the LORD, "Shall I go and attack these Philistines?" And the LORD said to David, "Go and attack the Philistines and save Keilah." **3** But David's men said to him, "Behold, we are afraid here in Judah; how much more then if we go to Keilah against the armies of the Philistines?" **4** Then David inquired of the LORD again. And the LORD answered him, "Arise, go down to Keilah, for I will give the Philistines into your hand." **5** And David and his men went to Keilah and fought with the Philistines and brought away their livestock and struck them with a great blow. So David saved the inhabitants of Keilah.

6 When Abiathar the son of Ahimelech had fled to David to Keilah, he had come down with an ephod in his hand. **7** Now it was told Saul that David had come to Keilah. And Saul said, "God has given him into my hand, for he has shut himself in by entering a town that has gates and bars." **8** And Saul summoned all the people to war, to go down to Keilah, to besiege David and his men. **9** David knew that Saul was plotting harm against him. And he said to Abiathar the priest, "Bring the ephod here." **10** Then David said, "O LORD, the God of Israel, your servant has surely heard that Saul seeks to come to Keilah, to destroy the city on my account. **11** Will the men of Keilah surrender me into his hand? Will Saul come down, as your servant has heard? O LORD, the God of Israel, please tell your servant." And the LORD said, "He will come down." **12** Then David said, "Will the men of Keilah surrender me and my men into the hand of Saul?" And the LORD said, "They will surrender you." **13** Then David and his men, who were about six hundred, arose and departed from Keilah, and they went wherever they could go. When Saul was told that David had escaped from Keilah, he gave up the expedition.

David avoids Saul
1 Sam. 23:14-29

[14] And David remained in the strongholds in the wilderness, in the hill country of the wilderness of Ziph. And Saul sought him every day, but God did not give him into his hand.

[15] David saw that Saul had come out to seek his life. David was in the wilderness of Ziph at Horesh. [16] And Jonathan, Saul's son, rose and went to David at Horesh, and strengthened his hand in God. [17] And he said to him, "Do not fear, for the hand of Saul my father shall not find you. You shall be king over Israel, and I shall be next to you. Saul my father also knows this." [18] And the two of them made a covenant before the LORD. David remained at Horesh, and Jonathan went home.

[19] Then the Ziphites went up to Saul at Gibeah, saying, "Is not David hiding among us in the strongholds at Horesh, on the hill of Hachilah, which is south of Jeshimon? [20] Now come down, O king, according to all your heart's desire to come down, and our part shall be to surrender him into the king's hand." [21] And Saul said, "May you be blessed by the LORD, for you have had compassion on me. [22] Go, make yet more sure. Know and see the place where his foot is, and who has seen him there, for it is told me that he is very cunning. [23] See therefore and take note of all the lurking places where he hides, and come back to me with sure information. Then I will go with you. And if he is in the land, I will search him out among all the thousands of Judah." [24] And they arose and went to Ziph ahead of Saul.

Now David and his men were in the wilderness of Maon, in the Arabah to the south of Jeshimon. [25] And Saul and his men went to seek him. And David was told, so he went down to the rock and lived in the wilderness of Maon. And when Saul heard that, he pursued after David in the wilderness of Maon. [26] Saul went on one side of the mountain, and David and his men on the other side of the mountain. And David was hurrying to get away from Saul. As Saul and his men were closing in on David and his men to capture them, [27] a messenger came to Saul, saying, "Hurry and come, for the Philistines have made a raid against the land." [28] So Saul returned from pursuing after David and went against the Philistines. Therefore that place was called the Rock of Escape. [29] And David went up from there and lived in the strongholds of Engedi.

David spares Saul's life near Engedi
1 Sam. 24:1-22

24 When Saul returned from following the Philistines, he was told, "Behold, David is in the wilderness of Engedi." **2** Then Saul took three thousand chosen men out of all Israel and went to seek David and his men in front of the Wildgoats' Rocks. **3** And he came to the sheepfolds by the way, where there was a cave, and Saul went in to relieve himself. Now David and his men were sitting in the innermost parts of the cave. **4** And the men of David said to him, "Here is the day of which the LORD said to you, 'Behold, I will give your enemy into your hand, and you shall do to him as it shall seem good to you.'" Then David arose and stealthily cut off a corner of Saul's robe. **5** And afterward David's heart struck him, because he had cut off a corner of Saul's robe. **6** He said to his men, "The LORD forbid that I should do this thing to my lord, the LORD's anointed, to put out my hand against him, seeing he is the LORD's anointed." **7** So David persuaded his men with these words and did not permit them to attack Saul. And Saul rose up and left the cave and went on his way.

8 Afterward David also arose and went out of the cave, and called after Saul, "My lord the king!" And when Saul looked behind him, David bowed with his face to the earth and paid homage. **9** And David said to Saul, "Why do you listen to the words of men who say, 'Behold, David seeks your harm'? **10** Behold, this day your eyes have seen how the LORD gave you today into my hand in the cave. And some told me to kill you, but I spared you. I said, 'I will not put out my hand against my lord, for he is the LORD's anointed.' **11** See, my father, see the corner of your robe in my hand. For by the fact that I cut off the corner of your robe and did not kill you, you may know and see that there is no wrong or treason in my hands. I have not sinned against you, though you hunt my life to take it. **12** May the LORD judge between me and you, may the LORD avenge me against you, but my hand shall not be against you. **13** As the proverb of the ancients says, 'Out of the wicked comes wickedness.' But my hand shall not be against you. **14** After whom has the king of Israel come out? After whom do you pursue? After a dead dog! After a flea! **15** May the LORD therefore be judge and give sentence between me and you, and see to it and plead my cause and deliver me from your hand."

16 As soon as David had finished speaking these words to Saul, Saul said, "Is this your voice, my son David?" And Saul lifted up his voice and wept. **17** He said to David, "You are more righteous than I, for you have repaid me good, whereas I have repaid you evil. **¹⁸** And you have declared this day how you have dealt well with me, in that you did not kill me when the LORD put me into your hands. **¹⁹** For if a man finds his enemy, will he let him go away safe? So may the LORD reward you with good for what you have done to me this day. **²⁰** And now, behold, I know that you shall surely be king, and that the kingdom of Israel shall be established in your hand. **²¹** Swear to me therefore by the LORD that you will not cut off my offspring after me, and that you will not destroy my name out of my father's house." **²²** And David swore this to Saul. Then Saul went home, but David and his men went up to the stronghold.

Samuel dies
1 Sam. 25:1a

25 Now Samuel died. And all Israel assembled and mourned for him, and they buried him in his house at Ramah.

Nabal insults David
1 Sam. 25:1b-13

Then David rose and went down to the wilderness of Paran. **²** And there was a man in Maon whose business was in Carmel. The man was very rich; he had three thousand sheep and a thousand goats. He was shearing his sheep in Carmel. **³** Now the name of the man was Nabal, and the name of his wife Abigail. The woman was discerning and beautiful, but the man was harsh and badly behaved; he was a Calebite. **⁴** David heard in the wilderness that Nabal was shearing his sheep. **⁵** So David sent ten young men. And David said to the young men, "Go up to Carmel, and go to Nabal and greet him in my name. **⁶** And thus you shall greet him: 'Peace be to you, and peace be to your house, and peace be to all that you have. **⁷** I hear that you have shearers. Now your shepherds have been with us, and we did them no harm, and they missed nothing all the time they were in Carmel. **⁸** Ask your young men, and they will tell you. Therefore let my young men find favor in your eyes, for we come on a feast day. Please give whatever you have at hand to your servants and to your son David.' "

⁹ When David's young men came, they said all this to Nabal in the name of David, and then they waited. **¹⁰** And Nabal answered David's servants, "Who is David? Who is the son of Jesse? There are many servants these days who are breaking away from their masters. **¹¹** Shall I take my bread and my water and my meat that I have killed for my shearers and give it to men who come from I do not know where?" **12** So David's young men turned away and came back and told him all this. **13** And David said to his men, "Every man strap on his sword!" And every man of them strapped on his sword. David also strapped on his sword. And about four hundred men went up after David, while two hundred remained with the baggage.

Abigail intercedes for Nabal
1 Sam. 25:14-35

14 But one of the young men told Abigail, Nabal's wife, "Behold, David sent messengers out of the wilderness to greet our master, and he railed at them. **15** Yet the men were very good to us, and we suffered no harm, and we did not miss anything when we were in the fields, as long as we went with them. **16** They were a wall to us both by night and by day, all the while we were with them keeping the sheep. **17** Now therefore know this and consider what you should do, for harm is determined against our master and against all his house, and he is such a worthless man that one cannot speak to him."

18 Then Abigail made haste and took two hundred loaves and two skins of wine and five sheep already prepared and five seahs of parched grain and a hundred clusters of raisins and two hundred cakes of figs, and laid them on donkeys. **19** And she said to her young men, "Go on before me; behold, I come after you." But she did not tell her husband Nabal. **20** And as she rode on the donkey and came down under cover of the mountain, behold, David and his men came down toward her, and she met them. **21** Now David had said, "Surely in vain have I guarded all that this fellow has in the wilderness, so that nothing was missed of all that belonged to him, and he has returned me evil for good. **22** God do so to the enemies of David and more also, if by morning I leave so much as one male of all who belong to him."

23 When Abigail saw David, she hurried and got down from the donkey and fell before David on her face and bowed to the ground. **24** She fell at his feet and said, "On me alone, my lord, be the guilt. Please let your servant speak in your ears, and hear the words of your servant. **25** Let not my lord regard this worthless fellow, Nabal, for as his name is, so is he. Nabal is his name, and folly is with him. But I your servant did not see the young men of my lord, whom you sent. **26** Now then, my lord, as the LORD lives, and as your soul lives, because the LORD has restrained you from bloodguilt and from saving with your own hand, now then let your enemies and those who seek to do evil to my lord be as Nabal. **²⁷** And now let this present that your servant has brought to my lord be given to the young men who follow my lord. **²⁸** Please forgive the trespass of your servant. For the LORD will certainly make my lord a sure house, because my lord is fighting the battles of the LORD, and evil shall not be found in you so long as you live. **²⁹** If men rise up to pursue you and to seek your life, the life of my lord shall be bound in the bundle of the living in the care of the LORD your God. And the lives of your enemies he shall sling out as from the hollow of a sling. **³⁰** And when the LORD has done to my lord according to all the good that he has spoken concerning you and has appointed you prince over Israel, **³¹** my lord shall have no cause of grief or pangs of conscience for having shed blood without cause or for my lord working salvation himself. And when the LORD has dealt well with my lord, then remember your servant."

³² And David said to Abigail, "Blessed be the LORD, the God of Israel, who sent you this day to meet me! **³³** Blessed be your discretion, and blessed be you, who have kept me this day from bloodguilt and from working salvation with my own hand! **³⁴** For as surely as the LORD, the God of Israel, lives, who has restrained me from hurting you, unless you had hurried and come to meet me, truly by morning there had not been left to Nabal so much as one male." **³⁵** Then David received from her hand what she had brought him. And he said to her, "Go up in peace to your house. See, I have obeyed your voice, and I have granted your petition."

David marries Abigail
1 Sam. 25:36-44

³⁶ And Abigail came to Nabal, and behold, he was holding a feast in his house, like the feast of a king. And Nabal's heart was merry within him, for he was very drunk. So she told him nothing at all until the morning light. **³⁷** In the morning, when the wine had gone out of Nabal, his wife told him these things, and his heart died within him, and he became as a stone. **³⁸** And about ten days later the LORD struck Nabal, and he died.

³⁹ When David heard that Nabal was dead, he said, "Blessed be the LORD who has avenged the insult I received at the hand of Nabal, and has kept back his servant from wrongdoing. The LORD has returned the evil of Nabal on his own head." Then David sent and spoke to Abigail, to take her as his wife. **⁴⁰** When the servants of David came to Abigail at Carmel, they said to her, "David has sent us to you to take you to him as his wife."

⁴¹ And she rose and bowed with her face to the ground and said, "Behold, your handmaid is a servant to wash the feet of the servants of my lord." ⁴² And Abigail hurried and rose and mounted a donkey, and her five young women attended her. She followed the messengers of David and became his wife.

⁴³ David also took Ahinoam of Jezreel, and both of them became his wives. ⁴⁴ Saul had given Michal his daughter, David's wife, to Palti the son of Laish, who was of Gallim.

David spares Saul's life in the Desert of Ziph
1 Sam. 26:1-25

26 Then the Ziphites came to Saul at Gibeah, saying, "Is not David hiding himself on the hill of Hachilah, which is on the east of Jeshimon?" ² So Saul arose and went down to the wilderness of Ziph with three thousand chosen men of Israel to seek David in the wilderness of Ziph. ³ And Saul encamped on the hill of Hachilah, which is beside the road on the east of Jeshimon. But David remained in the wilderness. When he saw that Saul came after him into the wilderness, ⁴ David sent out spies and learned that Saul had indeed come. ⁵ Then David rose and came to the place where Saul had encamped. And David saw the place where Saul lay, with Abner the son of Ner, the commander of his army. Saul was lying within the encampment, while the army was encamped around him.

⁶ Then David said to Ahimelech the Hittite, and to Joab's brother Abishai the son of Zeruiah, "Who will go down with me into the camp to Saul?" And Abishai said, "I will go down with you." ⁷ So David and Abishai went to the army by night. And there lay Saul sleeping within the encampment, with his spear stuck in the ground at his head, and Abner and the army lay around him. ⁸ Then Abishai said to David, "God has given your enemy into your hand this day. Now please let me pin him to the earth with one stroke of the spear, and I will not strike him twice." ⁹ But David said to Abishai, "Do not destroy him, for who can put out his hand against the LORD's anointed and be guiltless?" ¹⁰ And David said, "As the LORD lives, the LORD will strike him, or his day will come to die, or he will go down into battle and perish. ¹¹ The LORD forbid that I should put out my hand against the LORD's anointed. But take now the spear that is at his head and the jar of water, and let us go." ¹² So David took the spear and the jar of water from Saul's head, and they went away. No man saw it or

knew it, nor did any awake, for they were all asleep, because a deep sleep from the LORD had fallen upon them.

13 Then David went over to the other side and stood far off on the top of the hill, with a great space between them. **14** And David called to the army, and to Abner the son of Ner, saying, "Will you not answer, Abner?" Then Abner answered, "Who are you who calls to the king?" **15** And David said to Abner, "Are you not a man? Who is like you in Israel? Why then have you not kept watch over your lord the king? For one of the people came in to destroy the king your lord. **16** This thing that you have done is not good. As the LORD lives, you deserve to die, because you have not kept watch over your lord, the LORD's anointed. And now see where the king's spear is and the jar of water that was at his head."

17 Saul recognized David's voice and said, "Is this your voice, my son David?" And David said, "It is my voice, my lord, O king." **18** And he said, "Why does my lord pursue after his servant? For what have I done? What evil is on my hands? **19** Now therefore let my lord the king hear the words of his servant. If it is the LORD who has stirred you up against me, may he accept an offering, but if it is men, may they be cursed before the LORD, for they have driven me out this day that I should have no share in the heritage of the LORD, saying, 'Go, serve other gods.' **20** Now therefore, let not my blood fall to the earth away from the presence of the LORD, for the king of Israel has come out to seek a single flea like one who hunts a partridge in the mountains."

21 Then Saul said, "I have sinned. Return, my son David, for I will no more do you harm, because my life was precious in your eyes this day. Behold, I have acted foolishly, and have made a great mistake." **22** And David answered and said, "Here is the spear, O king! Let one of the young men come over and take it. **23** The LORD rewards every man for his righteousness and his faithfulness, for the LORD gave you into my hand today, and I would not put out my hand against the LORD's anointed. **24** Behold, as your life was precious this day in my sight, so may my life be precious in the sight of the LORD, and may he deliver me out of all tribulation." **25** Then Saul said to David, "Blessed be you, my son David! You will do many things and will succeed in them." So David went his way, and Saul returned to his place.

Part Three: Refuge in Philistia

1011–1010 B.C.; age 29-30

David flees to Philistia
1 Sam. 27:1-12

27 Then David said in his heart, "Now I shall perish one day by the hand of Saul. There is nothing better for me than that I should escape to the land of the Philistines. Then Saul will despair of seeking me any longer within the borders of Israel, and I shall escape out of his hand." **2** So David arose and went over, he and the six hundred men who were with him, to Achish the son of Maoch, king of Gath. **3** And David lived with Achish at Gath, he and his men, every man with his household, and David with his two wives, Ahinoam of Jezreel, and Abigail of Carmel, Nabal's widow. **4** And when it was told Saul that David had fled to Gath, he no longer sought him.

5 Then David said to Achish, "If I have found favor in your eyes, let a place be given me in one of the country towns, that I may dwell there. For why should your servant dwell in the royal city with you?" **6** So that day Achish gave him Ziklag. Therefore Ziklag has belonged to the kings of Judah to this day. **7** And the number of the days that David lived in the country of the Philistines was a year and four months.

8 Now David and his men went up and made raids against the Geshurites, the Girzites, and the Amalekites, for these were the inhabitants of the land from of old, as far as Shur, to the land of Egypt. **9** And David would strike the land and would leave neither man nor woman alive, but would take away the sheep, the oxen, the donkeys, the camels, and the garments, and come back to Achish. **10** When Achish asked, "Where have you made a raid today?" David would say, "Against the Negeb of Judah," or, "Against the Negeb of the Jerahmeelites," or, "Against the Negeb of the Kenites." **11** And David would leave neither man nor woman alive to bring news to Gath, thinking, "lest they should tell about us and say, 'So David has done.'" Such was his custom all the while he lived in the country of the Philistines. **12** And Achish trusted David, thinking, "He has made himself an utter stench to his people Israel; therefore he shall always be my servant."

Mighty men join David in Ziklag
1 Chron. 12:1-7

12 Now these are the men who came to David at Ziklag, while he could not move about freely because of Saul the son of Kish. And they were among the mighty men who helped him in war. [2] They were bowmen and could shoot arrows and sling stones with either the right or the left hand; they were Benjaminites, Saul's kinsmen. [3] The chief was Ahiezer, then Joash, both sons of Shemaah of Gibeah; also Jeziel and Pelet, the sons of Azmaveth; Beracah, Jehu of Anathoth, [4] Ishmaiah of Gibeon, a mighty man among the thirty and a leader over the thirty; Jeremiah, Jahaziel, Johanan, Jozabad of Gederah, [5] Eluzai, Jerimoth, Bealiah, Shemariah, Shephatiah the Haruphite; [6] Elkanah, Isshiah, Azarel, Joezer, and Jashobeam, the Korahites; [7] And Joelah and Zebadiah, the sons of Jeroham of Gedor.

David conscripted into the Philistine army
1 Sam. 28:1-2

28 In those days the Philistines gathered their forces for war, to fight against Israel. And Achish said to David, "Understand that you and your men are to go out with me in the army." [2] David said to Achish, "Very well, you shall know what your servant can do." And Achish said to David, "Very well, I will make you my bodyguard for life."

Saul consults a medium at En-dor
1 Sam. 28:3-14

[3] Now Samuel had died, and all Israel had mourned for him and buried him in Ramah, his own city. And Saul had put the mediums and the necromancers out of the land. [4] The Philistines assembled and came and encamped at Shunem. And Saul gathered all Israel, and they encamped at Gilboa. [5] When Saul saw the army of the Philistines, he was afraid, and his heart trembled greatly. [6] And when Saul inquired of the LORD, the LORD did not answer him, either by dreams, or by Urim, or by prophets. [7] Then Saul said to his servants, "Seek out for me a woman who is a medium, that I may go to her and inquire of her." And his servants said to him, "Behold, there is a medium at En-dor."

8 So Saul disguised himself and put on other garments and went, he and two men with him. And they came to the woman by night. And he said, "Divine for me by a spirit and bring up for me whomever I shall name to you." **9** The woman said to him, "Surely you know what Saul has done, how he has cut off the mediums and the necromancers from the land. Why then are you laying a trap for my life to bring about my death?" **10** But Saul swore to her by the LORD, "As the LORD lives, no punishment shall come upon you for this thing." **11** Then the woman said, "Whom shall I bring up for you?" He said, "Bring up Samuel for me." **12** When the woman saw Samuel, she cried out with a loud voice. And the woman said to Saul, "Why have you deceived me? You are Saul." **13** The king said to her, "Do not be afraid. What do you see?" And the woman said to Saul, "I see a god coming up out of the earth." **14** He said to her, "What is his appearance?" And she said, "An old man is coming up, and he is wrapped in a robe." And Saul knew that it was Samuel, and he bowed with his face to the ground and paid homage.

Samuel's words fill Saul with fear
1 Sam. 28:15-25

15 Then Samuel said to Saul, "Why have you disturbed me by bringing me up?" Saul answered, "I am in great distress, for the Philistines are warring against me, and God has turned away from me and answers me no more, either by prophets or by dreams. Therefore I have summoned you to tell me what I shall do." **16** And Samuel said, "Why then do you ask me, since the LORD has turned from you and become your enemy? **17** The LORD has done to you as he spoke by me, for the LORD has torn the kingdom out of your hand and given it to your neighbor, David. **18** Because you did not obey the voice of the LORD and did not carry out his fierce wrath against Amalek, therefore the LORD has done this thing to you this day. **19** Moreover, the LORD will give Israel also with you into the hand of the Philistines, and tomorrow you and your sons shall be with me. The LORD will give the army of Israel also into the hand of the Philistines."

20 Then Saul fell at once full length on the ground, filled with fear because of the words of Samuel. And there was no strength in him, for he had eaten nothing all day and all night. **21** And the woman came to Saul, and when she saw that he was terrified, she said to him, "Behold, your servant has obeyed you. I have taken my life in my hand and have listened to what you have said to me. **22** Now therefore, you also obey your servant. Let me set a morsel of bread before you; and eat, that you may have strength when you go on your way." **23** He refused and said, "I will not eat." But his servants, together with the woman, urged him, and he listened to their words. So he arose from the earth and sat on the bed. **24** Now the woman had a fattened calf in the house, and she quickly killed it, and she took flour and kneaded it and baked unleavened bread of it, **25** and she put it before Saul and his servants, and they ate. Then they rose and went away that night.

David is excluded from the Philistine army
1 Sam. 29:1-11

29 Now the Philistines had gathered all their forces at Aphek. And the Israelites were encamped by the spring that is in Jezreel. **2** As the lords of the Philistines were passing on by hundreds and by thousands, and David and his men were passing on in the rear with Achish, **3** the commanders of the Philistines said, "What are these Hebrews doing here?" And Achish said to the commanders of the Philistines, "Is this not David, the servant of Saul, king of Israel, who has been with me now for days and years, and since he deserted to me I have found no fault in him to this day." **4** But the commanders of the Philistines were angry with him. And the commanders of the Philistines said to him, "Send the man back, that he may return to the place to which you have assigned him. He shall not go down with us to battle, lest in the battle he become an adversary to us. For how could this fellow reconcile himself to his lord? Would it not be with the heads of the men here? **5** Is not this David, of whom they sing to one another in dances,

> 'Saul has struck down his thousands,
> and David his ten thousands'?"

6 Then Achish called David and said to him, "As the LORD lives, you have been honest, and to me it seems right that you should march out and in with me in the campaign. For I have found nothing wrong in you from the day of your coming to me to this day. Nevertheless, the lords do not approve of you. **7** So go back now; and go peaceably, that you may not displease the lords of the Philistines." **8** And David said to Achish, "But what have I done? What have you found in your servant from the day I entered your service until now, that I may not go and fight against the enemies of my lord the king?" **9** And Achish answered David and said, "I know that you are as blameless in my sight as an angel of God. Nevertheless, the commanders of the Philistines have said, 'He shall not go up with us to the battle.' **10** Now then rise early in the morning with the servants of your lord who came with you, and start early in the morning, and depart as soon as you have light." **11** So David set out with his men early in the morning to return to the land of the Philistines. But the Philistines went up to Jezreel.

David receives defectors from Saul's army
1 Chron. 12:19-22

19 Some of the men of Manasseh deserted to David when he came with the Philistines for the battle against Saul. (Yet he did not help them, for the rulers of the Philistines took counsel and sent him away, saying, "At peril to our heads he will desert to his master Saul.") **20** As he went to Ziklag, these men of Manasseh deserted to him: Adnah, Jozabad, Jediael, Michael, Jozabad, Elihu, and Zillethai, chiefs of thousands in Manasseh. **21** They helped David against the band of raiders, for they were all mighty men of valor and were commanders in the army. **22** For from day to day men came to David to help him, until there was a great army, like an army of God.

David finds Ziklag plundered and burned
1 Sam. 30:1-6

30 Now when David and his men came to Ziklag on the third day, the Amalekites had made a raid against the Negeb and against Ziklag. They had overcome Ziklag and burned it with fire **2** and taken captive the women and all who were in it, both small and great. They killed no one, but carried them off and went their way. **3** And when David and his men came to the city, they found it burned with fire, and their wives and sons and daughters taken captive. **4** Then David and the people who were with him raised their voices and wept until they had no more strength to weep. **5** David's two wives also had been taken captive, Ahinoam of Jezreel and Abigail the widow of Nabal of Carmel. **6** And David was greatly distressed, for the people spoke of stoning him, because all the people were bitter in soul, each for his sons and daughters. But David strengthened himself in the LORD his God.

David rescues his family from the Amalekites
1 Sam. 30:7-20

7 And David said to Abiathar the priest, the son of Ahimelech, "Bring me the ephod." So Abiathar brought the ephod to David. **8** And David inquired of the LORD, "Shall I pursue after this band? Shall I overtake them?" He answered him, "Pursue, for you shall surely overtake and shall surely rescue." ⁹ So David set out, and the six hundred men who were with him, and they came to the brook Besor, where those who were left behind stayed. ¹⁰ But David pursued, he and four hundred men. Two hundred stayed behind, who were too exhausted to cross the brook Besor.

¹¹ They found an Egyptian in the open country and brought him to David. And they gave him bread and he ate. They gave him water to drink, ¹² and they gave him a piece of a cake of figs and two clusters of raisins. And when he had eaten, his spirit revived, for he had not eaten bread or drunk water for three days and three nights. ¹³ And David said to him, "To whom do you belong? And where are you from?" He said, "I am a young man of Egypt, servant to an Amalekite, and my master left me behind because I fell sick three days ago. ¹⁴ We had made a raid against the Negeb of the Cherethites and against that which belongs to Judah and against the Negeb of Caleb, and we burned Ziklag with fire." ¹⁵ And David said to him, "Will you take me down to this band?" And he said, "Swear to me by God that you will not kill me or deliver me into the hands of my master, and I will take you down to this band."

¹⁶ And when he had taken him down, behold, they were spread abroad over all the land, eating and drinking and dancing, because of all the great spoil they had taken from the land of the Philistines and from the land of Judah. ¹⁷ And David struck them down from twilight until the evening of the next day, and not a man of them escaped, except four hundred young men, who mounted camels and fled. ¹⁸ David recovered all that the Amalekites had taken, and David rescued his two wives. ¹⁹ Nothing was missing, whether small or great, sons or daughters, spoil or anything that had been taken. David brought back all. ²⁰ David also captured all the flocks and herds, and the people drove the livestock before him, and said, "This is David's spoil."

David shares the spoil
1 Sam. 30:21-31

²¹ Then David came to the two hundred men who had been too exhausted to follow David, and who had been left at the brook Besor. And they went out to meet David and to meet the people who were with him. And when David came near to the people he greeted them. ²² Then all the wicked and worthless fellows among the men who had gone with David said, "Because they did not go with us, we will not give them any of

the spoil that we have recovered, except that each man may lead away his wife and children, and depart." **²³** But David said, "You shall not do so, my brothers, with what the LORD has given us. He has preserved us and given into our hand the band that came against us. **²⁴** Who would listen to you in this matter? For as his share is who goes down into the battle, so shall his share be who stays by the baggage. They shall share alike." **²⁵** And he made it a statute and a rule for Israel from that day forward to this day.

²⁶ When David came to Ziklag, he sent part of the spoil to his friends, the elders of Judah, saying, "Here is a present for you from the spoil of the enemies of the LORD." **²⁷** It was for those in Bethel, in Ramoth of the Negeb, in Jattir, **²⁸** in Aroer, in Siphmoth, in Eshtemoa, **²⁹** in Racal, in the cities of the Jerahmeelites, in the cities of the Kenites, **³⁰** in Hormah, in Bor-ashan, in Athach, **³¹** in Hebron, for all the places where David and his men had roamed.

Saul dies in battle
1 Sam. 31:1-13 [1 Chron. 10:1-14]

31 Now the Philistines were fighting against Israel, and the men of Israel fled before the Philistines and fell slain on Mount Gilboa. **²** And the Philistines overtook Saul and his sons, and the Philistines struck down Jonathan and Abinadab and Malchi-shua, the sons of Saul. **³** The battle pressed hard against Saul, and the archers found him, and he was badly wounded by the archers. **⁴** Then Saul said to his armor-bearer, "Draw your sword, and thrust me through with it, lest these uncircumcised come and thrust me through, and mistreat me." But his armor-bearer would not, for he feared greatly. Therefore Saul took his own sword and fell upon it. **⁵** And when his armor-bearer saw that Saul was dead, he also fell upon his sword and died with him. **⁶** Thus Saul died, and his three sons, and his armor-bearer, and all his <men> [house], on the same day together. **⁷** And when the men of Israel who were on the other side of the valley and those beyond the Jordan saw that the men of Israel had fled and that Saul and his sons were dead, they abandoned their cities and fled. And the Philistines came and lived in them.

⁸ The next day, when the Philistines came to strip the slain, they found Saul and his three sons fallen on Mount Gilboa. **⁹** <So they cut off his head and stripped off his armor> [And they stripped him and took his head and his armor] and sent messengers throughout the land of the Philistines, to carry the good news to the house of their idols and to the people. **10** They put his armor in the temple of <Ashtaroth>, [their gods] and they fastened <his body to the wall of Beth-shan> [his head in the temple of Dagon]. **11** But when the inhabitants of Jabesh-gilead heard what the Philistines had done to Saul, **12** all the valiant men arose and went all night and took the body of Saul and the bodies of his sons from the wall of Beth-shan, and <they came to Jabesh and burned them there> [brought them to Jabesh]. **13** And they <took their bones and> [0] buried them under the <tamarisk tree> [oak] in Jabesh and fasted seven days.

David receives news of Saul's death
2 Sam. 1:1-16

1 After the death of Saul, when David had returned from striking down the Amalekites, David remained two days in Ziklag. **2** And on the third day, behold, a man came from Saul's camp, with his clothes torn and dirt on his head. And when he came to David, he fell to the ground and paid homage. **3** David said to him, "Where do you come from?" And he said to him, "I have escaped from the camp of Israel." **4** And David said to him, "How did it go? Tell me." And he answered, "The people fled from the battle, and also many of the people have fallen and are dead, and Saul and his son Jonathan are also dead." **5** Then David said to the young man who told him, "How do you know that Saul and his son Jonathan are dead?" **6** And the young man who told him said, "By chance I happened to be on Mount Gilboa, and there was Saul leaning on his spear, and behold, the chariots and the horsemen were close upon him. **7** And when he looked behind him, he saw me, and called to me. And I answered, 'Here I am.' **8** And he said to me, 'Who are you?' I answered him, 'I am an Amalekite.' **9** And he said to me, 'Stand beside me and kill me, for anguish has seized me, and yet my life still lingers.' **10** So I stood beside him and killed him, because I was sure that he could not live after he had fallen. And I took the crown that was on his head and the armlet that was on his arm, and I have brought them here to my lord."

11 Then David took hold of his clothes and tore them, and so did all the men who were with him. **12** And they mourned and wept and fasted until evening for Saul and for Jonathan his son and for the people of the LORD and for the house of Israel, because they had fallen by the sword. **13** And David said to the young man who told him, "Where do you come from?" And he answered, "I am the son of a sojourner, an Amalekite." **14** David said to him, "How is it you were not afraid to put out your hand to destroy the LORD's anointed?" **15** Then David called one of the young men and said, "Go, execute him." And he struck him down so that he died. ¹⁶ And David said to him, "Your blood be on your head, for your own mouth has testified against you, saying, 'I have killed the LORD's anointed.' "

David mourns for Saul and Jonathan
2 Sam. 1:17-27

¹⁷ And David lamented with this lamentation over Saul and Jonathan his son, ¹⁸ and he said it should be taught to the people of Judah; behold, it is written in the Book of Jashar. He said:

> ¹⁹ "Your glory, O Israel, is slain on your high places!
>> How the mighty have fallen!
> ²⁰ Tell it not in Gath,
>> publish it not in the streets of Ashkelon,
> lest the daughters of the Philistines rejoice,
>> lest the daughters of the uncircumcised exult.
> ²¹ "You mountains of Gilboa,
>> let there be no dew or rain upon you,
>> nor fields of offerings!
> For there the shield of the mighty was defiled,
>> the shield of Saul, not anointed with oil.
> ²² "From the blood of the slain,
>> from the fat of the mighty,
> the bow of Jonathan turned not back,
>> and the sword of Saul returned not empty.
> ²³ "Saul and Jonathan, beloved and lovely!
>> In life and in death they were not divided;
> they were swifter than eagles;
>> they were stronger than lions.
> ²⁴ "You daughters of Israel, weep over Saul,
>> who clothed you luxuriously in scarlet,
>> who put ornaments of gold on your apparel.
> ²⁵ "How the mighty have fallen
>> in the midst of the battle!
> "Jonathan lies slain on your high places.
> ²⁶ I am distressed for you, my brother Jonathan;
> very pleasant have you been to me;
>> your love to me was extraordinary,
>> surpassing the love of women.

27 "How the mighty have fallen,
and the weapons of war perished!"

Part Four: Hebron

1009–1003 B.C.; age 31-37; regnal years 1-7

David is proclaimed king over Judah in Hebron
2 Sam. 2:1-7

2 In the course of time, David inquired of the LORD. "Shall I go up to one of the towns of Judah?" he asked.

The LORD said, "Go up."

David asked, "Where shall I go?"

"To Hebron," the LORD answered.

2 So David went up there with his two wives, Ahinoam of Jezreel and Abigail, the widow of Nabal of Carmel. 3 David also took the men who were with him, each with his family, and they settled in Hebron and its towns. 4 Then the men of Judah came to Hebron and there they anointed David king over the house of Judah.

When David was told that it was the men of Jabesh Gilead who had buried Saul, 5 he sent messengers to the men of Jabesh Gilead to say to them, "The LORD bless you for showing this kindness to Saul your master by burying him. 6 May the LORD now show you kindness and faithfulness, and I too will show you the same favor because you have done this. 7 Now then, be strong and brave, for Saul your master is dead, and the house of Judah has anointed me king over them."

David fathers sons in Hebron
2 Sam. 3:2-5 [1 Chron. 3:1-4]

2 And sons were born to David at Hebron: his firstborn was Amnon, of Ahinoam of Jezreel; **3** and his second, <Chileab> [Daniel], of Abigail the widow of Nabal of Carmel; and the third, Absalom the son of Maacah the daughter of Talmai king of Geshur; **4** and the fourth, Adonijah the son of Haggith; and the fifth, Shephatiah the son of Abital; **5** and the sixth, Ithream, of Eglah, David's wife. These were born to David in Hebron [+ where he reigned for seven years and six months].

David is opposed by Ish-bosheth
2 Sam. 2:8-11

8 But Abner the son of Ner, commander of Saul's army, took Ish-bosheth the son of Saul and brought him over to Mahanaim, **9** and he made him king over Gilead and the Ashurites and Jezreel and Ephraim and Benjamin and all Israel. **10** Ish-bosheth, Saul's son, was forty years old when he began to reign over Israel, and he reigned two years. But the house of Judah followed David. **11** And the time that David was king in Hebron over the house of Judah was seven years and six months.

David wins initial victory at Gibeon
2 Sam. 2:12 - 3:1

12 Abner the son of Ner, and the servants of Ish-bosheth the son of Saul, went out from Mahanaim to Gibeon. **13** And Joab the son of Zeruiah and the servants of David went out and met them at the pool of Gibeon. And they sat down, the one on the one side of the pool, and the other on the other side of the pool. **14** And Abner said to Joab, "Let the young men arise and compete before us." And Joab said, "Let them arise." **15** Then they arose and passed over by number, twelve for Benjamin and Ish-bosheth the son of Saul, and twelve of the servants of David. **16** And each caught his opponent by the head and thrust his sword in his opponent's side, so they fell down together. Therefore that place was called Helkath-hazzurim, which is at Gibeon. **17** And the battle was very fierce that day. And Abner and the men of Israel were beaten before the servants of David.

18 And the three sons of Zeruiah were there, Joab, Abishai, and Asahel. Now Asahel was as swift of foot as a wild gazelle. **19** And Asahel pursued Abner, and as he went, he turned neither to the right hand nor to the left from following Abner. **20** Then Abner looked behind him and said, "Is it you, Asahel?" And he answered, "It is I." **21** Abner said to him, "Turn aside to your right hand or to your left, and seize one of the young men and take his spoil." But Asahel would not turn aside from following him. **22** And Abner said again to Asahel, "Turn aside from following me. Why should I strike you to the ground? How then could I lift up my face to your brother Joab?" **23** But he refused to turn aside. Therefore Abner struck him in the stomach with the butt of his spear, so that the spear came out at his back. And he fell there and died where he was. And all who came to the place where Asahel had fallen and died, stood still.

24 But Joab and Abishai pursued Abner. And as the sun was going down they came to the hill of Ammah, which lies before Giah on the way to the wilderness of Gibeon. **25** And the people of Benjamin gathered themselves together behind Abner and became one group and took their stand on the top of a hill. **26** Then Abner called to Joab, "Shall the sword devour forever? Do you not know that the end will be bitter? How long will it be before you tell your people to turn from the pursuit of their brothers?" **27** And Joab said, "As God lives, if you had not spoken, surely the men would not have given up the pursuit of their brothers until the morning." **28** So Joab blew the trumpet, and all the men stopped and pursued Israel no more, nor did they fight anymore.

29 And Abner and his men went all that night through the Arabah. They crossed the Jordan, and marching the whole morning, they came to Mahanaim. **30** Joab returned from the pursuit of Abner. And when he had gathered all the people together, there were missing from David's servants nineteen men besides Asahel. **31** But the servants of David had struck down of Benjamin 360 of Abner's men. **32** And they took up Asahel and buried him in the tomb of his father, which was at Bethlehem. And Joab and his men marched all night, and the day broke upon them at Hebron.

3 There was a long war between the house of Saul and the house of David. And David grew stronger and stronger, while the house of Saul became weaker and weaker.

David accepts Abner's offer
2 Sam. 3:6-21

6 While there was war between the house of Saul and the house of David, Abner was making himself strong in the house of Saul. **7** Now Saul had a concubine whose name was Rizpah, the daughter of Aiah. And Ish-bosheth said to Abner, "Why have you gone in to my father's concubine?" **8** Then Abner was very angry over the words of Ish-bosheth and said, "Am I a dog's head of Judah? To this day I keep showing steadfast love to the house of Saul your father, to his brothers, and to his friends, and have not given you into the hand of David. And yet you charge me today with a fault concerning a woman. **9** God do so to Abner and more also, if I do not accomplish for David what the LORD has sworn to him, **10** to transfer the kingdom from the house of Saul and set up the throne of David over Israel and over Judah, from Dan to

Beersheba." **11** And Ish-bosheth could not answer Abner another word, because he feared him.

12 And Abner sent messengers to David on his behalf, saying, "To whom does the land belong? Make your covenant with me, and behold, my hand shall be with you to bring over all Israel to you." **13** And he said, "Good; I will make a covenant with you. But one thing I require of you; that is, you shall not see my face unless you first bring Michal, Saul's daughter, when you come to see my face." **14** Then David sent messengers to Ish-bosheth, Saul's son, saying, "Give me my wife Michal, for whom I paid the bridal price of a hundred foreskins of the Philistines." **15** And Ish-bosheth sent and took her from her husband Paltiel the son of Laish. **16** But her husband went with her, weeping after her all the way to Bahurim. Then Abner said to him, "Go, return." And he returned.

17 And Abner conferred with the elders of Israel, saying, "For some time past you have been seeking David as king over you. **18** Now then bring it about, for the LORD has promised David, saying, 'By the hand of my servant David I will save my people Israel from the hand of the Philistines, and from the hand of all their enemies.' " **19** Abner also spoke to Benjamin. And then Abner went to tell David at Hebron all that Israel and the whole house of Benjamin thought good to do.

20 When Abner came with twenty men to David at Hebron, David made a feast for Abner and the men who were with him. **21** And Abner said to David, "I will arise and go and will gather all Israel to my lord the king, that they may make a covenant with you, and that you may reign over all that your heart desires." So David sent Abner away, and he went in peace.

Joab kills Abner
2 Sam. 3:22-27

22 Just then the servants of David arrived with Joab from a raid, bringing much spoil with them. But Abner was not with David at Hebron, for he had sent him away, and he had gone in peace. **23** When Joab and all the army that was with him came, it was told Joab, "Abner the son of Ner came to the king, and he has let him go, and he has gone in peace." **24** Then Joab went to the king and said, "What have you done? Behold, Abner came to you. Why is it that you have sent him away, so that he is gone? **25** You know that Abner the son of Ner came to deceive you and to know your going out and your coming in, and to know all that you are doing."

²⁶ When Joab came out from David's presence, he sent messengers after Abner, and they brought him back from the cistern of Sirah. But David did not know about it. ²⁷ And when Abner returned to Hebron, Joab took him aside into the midst of the gate to speak with him privately, and there he struck him in the stomach, so that he died, for the blood of Asahel his brother.

David curses Joab and honors Abner
2 Sam. 3:28-39

²⁸ Afterward, when David heard of it, he said, "I and my kingdom are forever guiltless before the LORD for the blood of Abner the son of Ner. ²⁹ May it fall upon the head of Joab and upon all his father's house, and may the house of Joab never be without one who has a discharge or who is leprous or who holds a spindle or who falls by the sword or who lacks bread!" ³⁰ So Joab and Abishai his brother killed Abner, because he had put their brother Asahel to death in the battle at Gibeon.

³¹ Then David said to Joab and to all the people who were with him, "Tear your clothes and put on sackcloth and mourn before Abner." And King David followed the bier. ³² They buried Abner at Hebron. And the king lifted up his voice and wept at the grave of Abner, and all the people wept. ³³ And the king lamented for Abner, saying,

> "Should Abner die as a fool dies?
> ³⁴ Your hands were not bound;
>   your feet were not fettered;
> as one falls before the wicked
>   you have fallen."

And all the people wept again over him. ³⁵ Then all the people came to persuade David to eat bread while it was yet day. But David swore, saying, "God do so to me and more also, if I taste bread or anything else till the sun goes down!" ³⁶ And all the people took notice of it, and it pleased them, as everything that the king did pleased all the people. ³⁷ So all the people and all Israel understood that day that it had not been the king's will to put to death Abner the son of Ner. ³⁸ And the king said to his servants, "Do you not know that a prince and a great man has fallen this day in Israel? ³⁹ And I was gentle today, though anointed king. These men, the sons of Zeruiah, are more severe than I. The LORD repay the evildoer according to his wickedness!"

David punishes Ish-bosheth's murderers
2 Sam. 4:1-12

4 When Ish-bosheth, Saul's son, heard that Abner had died at Hebron, his courage failed, and all Israel was dismayed. **2** Now Saul's son had two men who were captains of raiding bands; the name of the one was Baanah, and the name of the other Rechab, sons of Rimmon a man of Benjamin from Beeroth (for Beeroth also is counted part of Benjamin; **3** the Beerothites fled to Gittaim and have been sojourners there to this day).

4 Jonathan, the son of Saul, had a son who was crippled in his feet. He was five years old when the news about Saul and Jonathan came from Jezreel, and his nurse took him up and fled, and as she fled in her haste, he fell and became lame. And his name was Mephibosheth.

5 Now the sons of Rimmon the Beerothite, Rechab and Baanah, set out, and about the heat of the day they came to the house of Ish-bosheth as he was taking his noonday rest. **6** And they came into the midst of the house as if to get wheat, and they stabbed him in the stomach. Then Rechab and Baanah his brother escaped. **7** When they came into the house, as he lay on his bed in his bedroom, they struck him and put him to death and beheaded him. They took his head and went by the way of the Arabah all night, **8** and brought the head of Ish-bosheth to David at Hebron. And they said to the king, "Here is the head of Ish-bosheth, the son of Saul, your enemy, who sought your life. The LORD has avenged my lord the king this day on Saul and on his offspring." **9** But David answered Rechab and Baanah his brother, the sons of Rimmon the Beerothite, "As the LORD lives, who has redeemed my life out of every adversity, **10** when one told me, 'Behold, Saul is dead,' and thought he was bringing good news, I seized him and killed him at Ziklag, which was the reward I gave him for his news. **11** How much more, when wicked men have killed a righteous man in his own house on his bed, shall I not now require his blood at your hand and destroy you from the earth?" **12** And David commanded his young men, and they killed them and cut off their hands and feet and hanged them beside the pool at Hebron. But they took the head of Ish-bosheth and buried it in the tomb of Abner at Hebron.

David is proclaimed king of all Israel
2 Sam. 5:1-5; [1 Chron. 11:1-3]

5 Then all the tribes of Israel came to David at Hebron and said, "Behold, we are your bone and flesh. **2** In times past, when Saul was king over us, it was you who led out and brought in Israel. And the LORD said to you, 'You shall be shepherd of my people Israel, and you shall be prince over Israel.'" **3** So all the elders of Israel came to the king at Hebron, and King David made a covenant with them at Hebron before the LORD, and they anointed David king over Israel [+ according to the word of the LORD by Samuel]. **4** David was thirty years old when he began to reign, and he reigned forty years. **5** At Hebron he reigned over Judah seven years and six months, and at Jerusalem he reigned over all Israel and Judah thirty-three years.

Armed men gather to David
1 Chron. 12:23-40

23 These are the numbers of the divisions of the armed troops who came to David in Hebron to turn the kingdom of Saul over to him, according to the word of the LORD. **24** The men of Judah bearing shield and spear were 6,800 armed troops. **25** Of the Simeonites, mighty men of valor for war, 7,100. **26** Of the Levites 4,600. **27** The prince Jehoiada, of the house of Aaron, and with him 3,700. **28** Zadok, a young man mighty in valor, and twenty-two commanders from his own fathers' house. **29** Of the Benjaminites, the kinsmen of Saul, 3,000, of whom the majority had to that point kept their allegiance to the house of Saul. **30** Of the Ephraimites 20,800, mighty men of valor, famous men in their fathers' houses. **31** Of the half-tribe of Manasseh 18,000, who were expressly named to come and make David king. **32** Of Issachar, men who had understanding of the times, to know what Israel ought to do, 200 chiefs, and all their kinsmen under their command. **33** Of Zebulun 50,000 seasoned troops, equipped for battle with all the weapons of war, to help David with singleness of purpose. **34** Of Naphtali 1,000 commanders with whom were 37,000 men armed with shield and spear. **35** Of the Danites 28,600 men equipped for battle. **36** Of Asher 40,000 seasoned troops ready for battle. **37** Of the Reubenites and Gadites and the half-tribe of Manasseh from beyond the Jordan, 120,000 men armed with all the weapons of war.

38 All these, men of war, arrayed in battle order, came to Hebron with a whole heart to make David king over all Israel. Likewise, all the rest of

Israel were of a single mind to make David king. [39] And they were there with David for three days, eating and drinking, for their brothers had made preparation for them. [40] And also their relatives, from as far as Issachar and Zebulun and Naphtali, came bringing food on donkeys and on camels and on mules and on oxen, abundant provisions of flour, cakes of figs, clusters of raisins, and wine and oil, oxen and sheep, for there was joy in Israel.

Part Five: Jerusalem

1002 – 994 B.C.; age 38-46; regnal years 8-16

David conquers Jerusalem
2 Sam. 5:6-10 [1 Chron. 11:4-9]

6 And the king and his men went to Jerusalem against the Jebusites, the inhabitants of the land, who said to David, "You will not come in here, <but the blind and the lame will ward you off"—thinking, "David cannot come in here."> [0] **7** Nevertheless, David took the stronghold of Zion, that is, the city of David. **8** And David said on that day, <"Whoever would strike the Jebusites, let him get up the water shaft to attack 'the lame and the blind,' who are hated by David's soul." Therefore it is said, "The blind and the lame shall not come into the house."> ["Whoever strikes the Jebusites first shall be chief and commander." And Joab the son of Zeruiah went up first, so he became chief.] **9** And David lived in the stronghold and called it the city of David. And David built the city all around from the Millo inward [+ and Joab repaired the rest of the city]. **10** And David became greater and greater, for the LORD, the God of hosts, was with him.

David builds a palace
2 Sam. 5:11-12 [1 Chron. 14:1-2]

11 And Hiram king of Tyre sent messengers to David, and cedar trees, also carpenters and masons who built David a house. **12** And David knew that the LORD had established him king over Israel, and that he had exalted his kingdom for the sake of his people Israel.

David fathers other sons in Jerusalem
2 Sam. 5:13-16 [1 Chr. 14:3-7] [[1 Chr. 3:5-9]]

13 And David took more concubines and wives from Jerusalem, after he came from Hebron, and more sons and daughters were born to David. **14** And these are the names of those who were born to him in Jerusalem: Shammua, Shobab, Nathan, Solomon, [[four by Bath-shua, the daughter of Ammiel;]] **15** Ibhar, Elishua, [+ Elpelet, Nogah,] Nepheg, Japhia, **16** Elishama, <Eliada> [Beeliada], and Eliphelet.

David defeats the Philistines in the Valley of Rephaim
2 Sam. 5:17-25 [1 Chron. 14:8-17]

[17] When the Philistines heard that David had been anointed king over Israel, all the Philistines went up to search for David. But David heard of it and went down to the stronghold. [18] Now the Philistines had come and spread out in the Valley of Rephaim. [19] And David inquired of the LORD, "Shall I go up against the Philistines? Will you give them into my hand?" And the LORD said to David, "Go up, for I will certainly give the Philistines into your hand." [20] And David came to Baal-perazim, and David defeated them there. And he said, "The LORD has broken through my enemies <before me like a breaking flood> [by my hand]." Therefore the name of that place is called Baal-perazim. [21] And the Philistines left their idols there, and <David and his men carried them away> [David gave command, and they were burned].

[22] And the Philistines came up yet again and spread out in the Valley of Rephaim. [23] And when David inquired of the LORD, he said, "You shall not go up; go around to their rear, and come against them opposite the balsam trees. [24] And when you hear the sound of marching in the tops of the balsam trees, <then rouse yourself> [then go out to battle], for then the LORD has gone out before you to strike down the army of the Philistines." [25] And David did as the LORD commanded him, and struck down the Philistines from <Geba> [Gibeon] to Gezer. [+ And the fame of David went out into all lands, and the LORD brought the fear of him upon all nations.]

David makes plans to bring the ark of God to Jerusalem
1 Chron. 13:1-4

13 David consulted with the commanders of thousands and of hundreds, with every leader. [2] And David said to all the assembly of Israel, "If it seems good to you and from the LORD our God, let us send abroad to our brothers who remain in all the lands of Israel, as well as to the priests and Levites in the cities that have pasturelands, that they may be gathered to us. [3] Then let us bring again the ark of our God to us, for we did not seek it in the days of Saul." [4] All the assembly agreed to do so, for the thing was right in the eyes of all the people.

David's procession is abruptly halted
2 Sam. 6:1-11 [1 Chron. 13:5-14]

6 <David again gathered all the chosen men of Israel, thirty thousand.> [So David assembled all Israel from the Nile of Egypt to Lebo-hamath, to bring the ark of God from Kiriath-jearim.] **2** And David arose and went with all the people who were with him from Baale-judah to bring up from there the ark of God, which is called by the name of the LORD of hosts who sits enthroned on the cherubim. **3** And they carried the ark of God on a new cart and brought it out of the house of Abinadab, which was on the hill. And Uzzah and Ahio, the sons of Abinadab, were driving the new cart, **4** with the ark of God, and Ahio went before the ark.

5 And David and all the house of Israel were celebrating before the LORD, with songs and lyres and harps and tambourines and castanets and cymbals. **6** And when they came to the threshing floor of <Nacon> [Chidon], Uzzah put out his hand to the ark of God and took hold of it, for the oxen stumbled. **7** And the anger of the LORD was kindled against Uzzah, and God struck him down there <because of his error> [because he put out his hand to the ark], and he died there beside the ark of God. **8** And David was angry because the LORD had broken out against Uzzah. And that place is called Perez-uzzah to this day. **9** And David was afraid of the LORD that day, and he said, "How can the ark of the LORD come to me?" **10** So David was not willing to take the ark of the LORD into the city of David. But David took it aside to the house of Obed-edom the Gittite. **11** And the ark of the LORD remained in the house of Obed-edom the Gittite three months, and the LORD blessed Obed-edom and all his household.

David consecrates Levites to carry the ark
1 Chron. 15:1-16

15 David built houses for himself in the city of David. And he prepared a place for the ark of God and pitched a tent for it. **2** Then David said that no one but the Levites may carry the ark of God, for the LORD had chosen them to carry the ark of the LORD and to minister to him forever. **3** And David assembled all Israel at Jerusalem to bring up the ark of the LORD to its place, which he had prepared for it. **4** And David gathered together the sons of Aaron and the Levites: **5** of the sons of Kohath, Uriel the chief, with 120 of his brothers; **6** of the sons of Merari, Asaiah the chief, with 220 of his brothers; **7** of the sons of Gershom, Joel the chief, with 130 of his brothers; **8** of the sons of Elizaphan, Shemaiah the chief, with 200 of his brothers; **9** of the sons of Hebron, Eliel the chief, with 80 of his brothers; **10** of the sons of Uzziel, Amminadab the chief, with 112 of his brothers. **11** Then David summoned the priests Zadok and Abiathar, and the Levites Uriel, Asaiah, Joel, Shemaiah, Eliel, and Amminadab, **12** and said to them, "You are the heads of the fathers' houses of the Levites. Consecrate yourselves, you and your brothers, so that you may bring up the ark of the LORD, the God of Israel, to the place that I have prepared for it. **13** Because you did not carry it the first time, the LORD our God broke out against us, because we did not seek him according to the rule." **14** So the priests and the Levites consecrated themselves to bring up the ark of the LORD, the God of Israel. **15** And the Levites carried the ark of God on their shoulders with the poles, as Moses had commanded according to the word of the LORD.

16 David also commanded the chiefs of the Levites to appoint their brothers as the singers who should play loudly on musical instruments, on harps and lyres and cymbals, to raise sounds of joy. (The list of names of musicians and gatekeepers continues through verse 24.)

David brings the ark to Jerusalem
2 Sam. 6:12-19a [1 Chron. 15:25 – 16:3]

12 And it was told King David, "The LORD has blessed the household of Obed-edom and all that belongs to him, because of the ark of God." So David [+ and the elders of Israel and the commanders of thousands] went and brought up the ark of God from the house of Obed-edom to the city of David with rejoicing. **13** And <when those who bore the ark of the LORD had gone six steps> [because God helped the Levites who were carrying the ark of the covenant of the LORD], <he sacrificed an ox and a fattened animal> [they sacrificed seven bulls and seven rams]. **14** <And David danced before the LORD with all his might. And David was wearing a linen ephod.> [David was clothed with a robe of fine linen, as also were all the Levites who were carrying the ark, and the singers and Chenaniah the leader of the music of the singers.] **15** So David and all the house of Israel brought up the ark of the LORD with shouting and with the sound of the horn [+ trumpets, and cymbals, and made loud music on harps and lyres.]

16 As the ark of the LORD came into the city of David, Michal the daughter of Saul looked out of the window and saw King David <leaping

and dancing before the LORD> [dancing and celebrating], and she despised him in her heart. ¹⁷ And they brought in the ark of the LORD and set it in its place, inside the tent that David had pitched for it. And David offered burnt offerings and peace offerings before the LORD. ¹⁸ And when David had finished offering the burnt offerings and the peace offerings, he blessed the people in the name of the LORD of hosts ¹⁹ and distributed among all the people, the whole multitude of Israel, both men and women, a cake of bread, a portion of meat, and a cake of raisins to each one.

David gives thanks to God
1 Chron. 16:4-43 [2 Sam. 6:19b-20a]

⁴ Then he appointed some of the Levites as ministers before the ark of the LORD, to invoke, to thank, and to praise the LORD, the God of Israel. ⁵ Asaph was the chief, and second to him were Zechariah, Jeiel, Shemiramoth, Jehiel, Mattithiah, Eliab, Benaiah, Obed-edom, and Jeiel, who were to play harps and lyres; Asaph was to sound the cymbals, ⁶ and Benaiah and Jahaziel the priests were to blow trumpets regularly before the ark of the covenant of God. ⁷ Then on that day David first appointed that thanksgiving be sung to the LORD by Asaph and his brothers.

⁸ Oh give thanks to the LORD; call upon his name;
    make known his deeds among the peoples!
⁹ Sing to him, sing praises to him;
    tell of all his wondrous works!
¹⁰ Glory in his holy name;
    let the hearts of those who seek the LORD rejoice!
¹¹ Seek the LORD and his strength;
    seek his presence continually!
¹² Remember the wondrous works that he has done,
    his miracles and the judgments he uttered,
¹³ O offspring of Israel his servant,
    children of Jacob, his chosen ones!
¹⁴ He is the LORD our God;
    his judgments are in all the earth.
¹⁵ Remember his covenant forever,
    the word that he commanded, for a thousand
        generations,
¹⁶ the covenant that he made with Abraham,
    his sworn promise to Isaac,
¹⁷ which he confirmed to Jacob as a statute,

to Israel as an everlasting covenant,
18 saying, "To you I will give the land of Canaan,
    as your portion for an inheritance."
19 When you were few in number,
    of little account, and sojourners in it,
20 wandering from nation to nation,
    from one kingdom to another people,
21 he allowed no one to oppress them;
    he rebuked kings on their account,
22 saying, "Touch not my anointed ones,
    do my prophets no harm!"
23 Sing to the LORD, all the earth!
    Tell of his salvation from day to day.
24 Declare his glory among the nations,
    his marvelous works among all the peoples!
25 For great is the LORD, and greatly to be praised,
    and he is to be feared above all gods.
26 For all the gods of the peoples are worthless idols,
    but the LORD made the heavens.
27 Splendor and majesty are before him;
    strength and joy are in his place.
28 Ascribe to the LORD, O families of the peoples,
    ascribe to the LORD glory and strength!
29 Ascribe to the LORD the glory due his name;
    bring an offering and come before him!
Worship the LORD in the splendor of holiness;
30   tremble before him, all the earth;
    yes, the world is established; it shall never be moved.
31 Let the heavens be glad, and let the earth rejoice,
    and let them say among the nations, "The LORD
    reigns!"
32 Let the sea roar, and all that fills it;
    let the field exult, and everything in it!
33 Then shall the trees of the forest sing for joy
    before the LORD, for he comes to judge the earth.
34 Oh give thanks to the LORD, for he is good;
    for his steadfast love endures forever!
35 Say also:
"Save us, O God of our salvation,
    and gather and deliver us from among the nations,
that we may give thanks to your holy name
    and glory in your praise.

36 Blessed be the LORD, the God of Israel,
from everlasting to everlasting!"

Then all the people said, "Amen!" and praised the LORD.

37 So David left Asaph and his brothers there before the ark of the covenant of the LORD to minister regularly before the ark as each day required, **38** and also Obed-edom and his sixty-eight brothers, while Obed-edom, the son of Jeduthun, and Hosah were to be gatekeepers. **39** And he left Zadok the priest and his brothers the priests before the tabernacle of the LORD in the high place that was at Gibeon **40** to offer burnt offerings to the LORD on the altar of burnt offering regularly morning and evening, to do all that is written in the Law of the LORD that he commanded Israel. **41** With them were Heman and Jeduthun and the rest of those chosen and expressly named to give thanks to the LORD, for his steadfast love endures forever. **42** Heman and Jeduthun had trumpets and cymbals for the music and instruments for sacred song. The sons of Jeduthun were appointed to the gate.

43 Then all the people departed each to his house, and David went home to bless his household.

David argues with Michal
2 Sam. 6:20-23

20 And David returned to bless his household. But Michal the daughter of Saul came out to meet David and said, "How the king of Israel honored himself today, uncovering himself today before the eyes of his servants' female servants, as one of the vulgar fellows shamelessly uncovers himself!" **21** And David said to Michal, "It was before the LORD, who chose me above your father and above all his house, to appoint me as prince over Israel, the people of the LORD—and I will celebrate before the LORD. **22** I will make myself yet more contemptible than this, and I will be abased in your eyes. But by the female servants of whom you have spoken, by them I shall be held in honor." **23** And Michal the daughter of Saul had no child to the day of her death.

David rules with justice and righteousness
2 Sam. 8:15-18 [1 Chron. 18:14-17]
(cf. 2 Sam. 20:23-26)

15 So David reigned over all Israel. And David administered justice and equity to all his people. **16** Joab the son of Zeruiah was over the army, and Jehoshaphat the son of Ahilud was recorder, **17** and Zadok the son of Ahitub and Ahimelech the son of Abiathar were priests, and <Seraiah> [Shavsha] was secretary, **18** and Benaiah the son of Jehoiada was over the Cherethites and the Pelethites, and David's sons were <priests> [the chief officials in the service of the king].

David shows kindness to Mephibosheth
2 Sam. 9:1-13

9 And David said, "Is there still anyone left of the house of Saul, that I may show him kindness for Jonathan's sake?" **2** Now there was a servant of the house of Saul whose name was Ziba, and they called him to David. And the king said to him, "Are you Ziba?" And he said, "I am your servant." **3** And the king said, "Is there not still someone of the house of Saul, that I may show the kindness of God to him?" Ziba said to the king, "There is still a son of Jonathan; he is crippled in his feet." **4** The king said to him, "Where is he?" And Ziba said to the king, "He is in the house of Machir the son of Ammiel, at Lo-debar." **5** Then King David sent and brought him from the house of Machir the son of Ammiel, at Lo-debar. **6** And Mephibosheth the son of Jonathan, son of Saul, came to David and fell on his face and paid homage. And David said, "Mephibosheth!" And he answered, "Behold, I am your servant." **7** And David said to him, "Do not fear, for I will show you kindness for the sake of your father Jonathan, and I will restore to you all the land of Saul your father, and you shall eat at my table always." **8** And he paid homage and said, "What is your servant, that you should show regard for a dead dog such as I?"

9 Then the king called Ziba, Saul's servant, and said to him, "All that belonged to Saul and to all his house I have given to your master's grandson. **10** And you and your sons and your servants shall till the land for him and shall bring in the produce, that your master's grandson may have bread to eat. But Mephibosheth your master's grandson shall always eat at my table." Now Ziba had fifteen sons and twenty servants. **11** Then Ziba said to the king, "According to all that my lord the king commands his servant, so will your servant do." So Mephibosheth ate at David's table, like one of the king's sons. ¹² And Mephibosheth had a young son, whose name was Mica. And all who lived in Ziba's house became Mephibosheth's servants. ¹³ So Mephibosheth lived in Jerusalem, for he ate always at the king's table. Now he was lame in both his feet.

David appeases the Gibeonites
2 Sam. 21:1-14

21 Now there was a famine in the days of David for three years, year after year. And David sought the face of the LORD. And the LORD said, "There is bloodguilt on Saul and on his house, because he put the Gibeonites to death." ² So the king called the Gibeonites and spoke to them. Now the Gibeonites were not of the people of Israel but of the remnant of the Amorites. Although the people of Israel had sworn to spare them, Saul had sought to strike them down in his zeal for the people of Israel and Judah. ³ And David said to the Gibeonites, "What shall I do for you? And how shall I make atonement, that you may bless the heritage of the LORD?" ⁴ The Gibeonites said to him, "It is not a matter of silver or gold between us and Saul or his house; neither is it for us to put any man to death in Israel." And he said, "What do you say that I shall do for you?" ⁵ They said to the king, "The man who consumed us and planned to destroy us, so that we should have no place in all the territory of Israel, ⁶ let seven of his sons be given to us, so that we may hang them before the LORD at Gibeah of Saul, the chosen of the LORD." And the king said, "I will give them."

⁷ But the king spared Mephibosheth, the son of Saul's son Jonathan, because of the oath of the LORD that was between them, between David and Jonathan the son of Saul. ⁸ The king took the two sons of Rizpah the daughter of Aiah, whom she bore to Saul, Armoni and Mephibosheth; and the five sons of Merab the daughter of Saul, whom she bore to Adriel the son of Barzillai the Meholathite; ⁹ and he gave them into the hands of the Gibeonites, and they hanged them on the mountain before the LORD, and the seven of them perished together. They were put to death in the first days of harvest, at the beginning of barley harvest.

¹⁰ Then Rizpah the daughter of Aiah took sackcloth and spread it for herself on the rock, from the beginning of harvest until rain fell upon them from the heavens. And she did not allow the birds of the air to come upon them by day, or the beasts of the field by night. ¹¹ When David was told what Rizpah the daughter of Aiah, the concubine of Saul,

had done, ¹² David went and took the bones of Saul and the bones of his son Jonathan from the men of Jabesh-gilead, who had stolen them from the public square of Beth-shan, where the Philistines had hanged them, on the day the Philistines killed Saul on Gilboa. ¹³ And he brought up from there the bones of Saul and the bones of his son Jonathan; and they gathered the bones of those who were hanged. ¹⁴ And they buried the bones of Saul and his son Jonathan in the land of Benjamin in Zela, in the tomb of Kish his father. And they did all that the king commanded. And after that God responded to the plea for the land.

Part Six: Military Conquests

1002–994 B.C.; age 38-46; regnal years 8-16

David defeats the Philistines at Metheg Ammah
2 Sam. 8:1 [1 Chron. 18:1]

8 After this David defeated the Philistines and subdued them, and <David took Metheg-ammah> [he took Gath and its villages] out of the hand of the Philistines.

David conquers the Moabites
2 Sam. 8:2 [1 Chron. 18:2]

2 And he defeated Moab and <he measured them with a line, making them lie down on the ground. Two lines he measured to be put to death, and one full line to be spared. And> [0] the Moabites became servants to David and brought tribute.

The Ammonites insult David's messengers
2 Sam. 10:1-5 [1 Chron. 19:1-5]

10 After this [+Nahash] the king of the Ammonites died, and Hanun his son reigned in his place. **2** And David said, "I will deal <loyally> [kindly] with Hanun the son of Nahash, as his father dealt <loyally> [kindly] with me." So David sent by his servants to console him concerning his father. And David's servants came into the land of the Ammonites [+ to Hanun to console him]. **3** But the princes of the Ammonites said to Hanun their lord, "Do you think, because David has sent comforters to you, that he is honoring your father? Has not David sent his servants to you to search the city and to spy it out and to overthrow it?" **4** So Hanun took David's servants and shaved off half the beard of each and cut off their garments in the middle, at their hips, and sent them away. **5** When it was told David, he sent [+ messengers] to meet them, for the men were greatly ashamed. And the king said, "Remain at Jericho until your beards have grown and then return."

David's army prevails over Ammon's allies
2 Sam. 10:6-14 [1 Chron. 19:6-15]

6 When the Ammonites saw that they had become a stench to David, <the Ammonites sent and hired the Syrians of Beth-rehob, and the Syrians of Zobah, 20,000 foot soldiers, and the king of Maacah with 1,000 men, and the men of Tob, 12,000 men> [Hanun and the Ammonites sent 1,000 talents of silver to hire chariots and horsemen from Mesopotamia, from Aram-maacah, and from Zobah. **7** They hired 32,000 chariots and the king of Maacah with his army, who came and encamped before Medeba. And the Ammonites were mustered from their cities and came to battle.]. **7** And when David heard of it, he sent Joab and all the host of the mighty men. **8** And the Ammonites came out and drew up in battle array at the entrance of the gate, and <the Syrians of Zobah and of Rehob and the men of Tob and Maacah> [the kings who had come] were by themselves in the open country.

9 When Joab saw that the battle was set against him both in front and in the rear, he chose some of the best men of Israel and arrayed them against the Syrians. **10** The rest of his men he put in the charge of Abishai his brother, and he arrayed them against the Ammonites. **11** And he said, "If the Syrians are too strong for me, then you shall help me, but if the Ammonites are too strong for you, then I will come and help you. **12** Be of good courage, and let us be courageous for our people, and for the cities of our God, and may the LORD do what seems good to him." **13** So Joab and the people who were with him drew near to battle against the Syrians, and they fled before him. **14** And when the Ammonites saw that the Syrians fled, they likewise fled before Abishai and entered the city. Then Joab returned from fighting against the Ammonites and came to Jerusalem.

David's army is victorious over Ammon's allies again
2 Sam. 10:15-19 [1 Chron. 19:16-19]

15 But when the Syrians saw that they had been defeated by Israel, they gathered themselves together. **16** And Hadadezer sent and brought out the Syrians who were beyond the Euphrates. They came to Helam, with <Shobach> [Shophach] the commander of the army of Hadadezer at their head. **17** And when it was told David, he gathered all Israel together and crossed the Jordan <and came to Helam> [and came to them and drew up his forces against them]. The Syrians arrayed themselves against David and fought with him. **18** And the Syrians fled before Israel, and

David killed of the Syrians the men of <700> [7,000] chariots, and 40,000 horsemen, and <wounded Shobach> [put to death Shophach] the commander of their army, so that he died there. [19] And when all the kings who were servants of Hadadezer saw that they had been defeated by Israel, they made peace with Israel and became subject to them. So the Syrians were afraid to save the Ammonites anymore.

David conquers Zobah and Damascus
2 Sam. 8:3-8 [1 Chron. 18:3-8] cf. 1 Kings 11:23-24

[3] David also defeated Hadadezer the son of Rehob, king of <Zobah> [Zobah-Hamath], <as he went to restore his power at the river Euphrates> [as he went to set up his monument at the river Euphrates]. [4] And David took from him <1,700 horsemen> [1,000 chariots, 7,000 horsemen], and 20,000 foot soldiers. And David hamstrung all the chariot horses but left enough for 100 chariots. [5] And when the Syrians of Damascus came to help Hadadezer king of Zobah, David struck down 22,000 men of the Syrians. [6] Then David put garrisons in Aram of Damascus, and the Syrians became servants to David and brought tribute. And the LORD gave victory to David wherever he went. [7] And David took the shields of gold that were carried by the servants of Hadadezer and brought them to Jerusalem. [8] And <from Betah and from Berothai> [from Tibhath and from Cun], cities of Hadadezer, King David took very much bronze. [+ With it Solomon made the bronze sea and the pillars and the vessels of bronze.]

David dedicates gifts and plunder to the Lord
2 Sam. 8:9-12 [1 Chron. 18:9-11]

[9] When Toi king of Hamath heard that David had defeated the whole army of Hadadezer, [+ king of Zobah] [10] Toi sent his son <Joram> [Hadoram] to King David, to ask about his health and to bless him because he had fought against Hadadezer and defeated him, for Hadadezer had often been at war with Toi. And Joram brought with him articles of silver, of gold, and of bronze. [11] These also King David dedicated to the LORD, together with the silver and gold that he <dedicated> [had carried off] from all the nations he subdued, [12] from Edom, Moab, the Ammonites, the Philistines, Amalek, and from the spoil of Hadadezer the son of Rehob, king of Zobah.

David conquers the Edomites
2 Sam. 8:13-14 [1 Chron. 18:12-13]
cf. 1 Kings 11:15-18; title of Psalm 60

13 <And David made a name for himself when he returned from striking down> [And Abishai, the son of Zeruiah, killed] 18,000 Edomites in the Valley of Salt. **14** Then he put garrisons in Edom; throughout all Edom he put garrisons, and all the Edomites became David's servants. And the LORD gave victory to David wherever he went.

The giant killers
2 Sam. 21:15-22 [1 Chron. 20:4-8]

15 <There was war again between the Philistines and Israel, and David went down together with his servants, and they fought against the Philistines. And David grew weary. **16** And Ishbi-benob, one of the descendants of the giants, whose spear weighed three hundred shekels of bronze, and who was armed with a new sword, thought to kill David. **17** But Abishai the son of Zeruiah came to his aid and attacked the Philistine and killed him. Then David's men swore to him, "You shall no longer go out with us to battle, lest you quench the lamp of Israel."> [0]

18 After this there was again war with the Philistines at <Gob> [Gezer]. Then Sibbecai the Hushathite struck down <Saph> [Sappai], who was one of the descendants of the giants [+ and the Philistines were subdued].

19 And there was again war with the Philistines <at Gob> [0], and Elhanan the son of <Jaare-oregim, the Bethlehemite> [Jair], struck down [+ Lahmi the brother of] Goliath the Gittite, the shaft of whose spear was like a weaver's beam.

20 And there was again war at Gath, where there was a man of great stature, who had six fingers on each hand, and six toes on each foot, twenty-four in number, and he also was descended from the giants. **21** And when he taunted Israel, Jonathan the son of <Shimei> [Shimea], David's brother, struck him down. **22** These <four> [0] were descended from the giants in Gath, and they fell by the hand of David and by the hand of his servants.

Three mighty men
2 Sam. 23:8-17 [1 Chron. 11:10-19]

8 These are <the names of the mighty men whom David had> [the chiefs of David's mighty men, who gave him strong support in his kingdom, together with all Israel, to make him king, according to the word of the LORD concerning Israel]: <Josheb-basshebeth a Tahchemonite; he> [Jashobeam, a Hachmonite] was chief of the three. He wielded his spear against <eight hundred> [300] whom he killed at one time.

9 And next to him among the three mighty men was Eleazar the son of Dodo, son of Ahohi. He was with David [+ at Pas-dammim] when they defied the Philistines who were gathered there for battle, <and the men of Israel withdrew. **10** He rose and struck down the Philistines until his hand was weary, and his hand clung to the sword. And the LORD brought about a great victory that day, and the men returned after him only to strip the slain.

11 And next to him was Shammah, the son of Agee the Hararite. The Philistines gathered together at Lehi, where> [0] there was a plot of ground full of <lentils> [barley], and the men fled from the Philistines. **12** But he took his stand in the midst of the plot and defended it and struck down the Philistines, and the LORD <worked> [saved them by] a great victory.

13 And three of the thirty chief men went down <and came about harvest time> [to the rock] to David at the cave of Adullam, when a band of Philistines was encamped in the Valley of Rephaim. **14** David was then in the stronghold, and the garrison of the Philistines was then at Bethlehem. **15** And David said longingly, "Oh, that someone would give me water to drink from the well of Bethlehem that is by the gate!" **16** Then the three mighty men broke through the camp of the Philistines and drew water out of the well of Bethlehem that was by the gate and carried and brought it to David. But he would not drink of it. He poured it out to the LORD **17** and said, "Far be it from me, O LORD, that I should do this. <Shall I drink the blood of the men who went at the risk of their lives?> [Shall I drink the lifeblood of these men? For at the risk of their lives they brought it.]" Therefore he would not drink it. These things the three mighty men did.

Abishai and Benaiah
2 Sam. 23:18-23 [1 Chron. 11:20-25]

[18] Now Abishai, the brother of Joab, the son of Zeruiah, was chief of the thirty. And he wielded his spear against three hundred men and killed them and won a name beside the three. [19] He was the most renowned of the thirty and became their commander, but he did not attain to the three.

[20] And Benaiah the son of Jehoiada was a valiant man of Kabzeel, a doer of great deeds. He struck down two <ariels> [heroes] of Moab. He also went down and struck down a lion in a pit on a day when snow had fallen. [21] And he struck down an Egyptian, <a handsome man> [a man of great stature, five cubits tall]. The Egyptian had a spear <in his hand> [like a weaver's beam], but Benaiah went down to him with a staff and snatched the spear out of the Egyptian's hand and killed him with his own spear. [22] These things did Benaiah the son of Jehoiada, and won a name beside the three mighty men. [23] He was renowned among the thirty, but he did not attain to the three. And David set him over his bodyguard.

Thirty mighty men
2 Sam. 23:24-39 [1 Chron. 11:26-47]

[24] Asahel the brother of Joab was one of the thirty; Elhanan the son of Dodo of Bethlehem, [25] <Shammah> [Shammoth] of Harod, <Elika of Harod,> [0] [26] Helez the <Paltite> [Pelonite], Ira the son of Ikkesh of Tekoa, [27] Abiezer of Anathoth, <Mebunnai> [Sibbecai] the Hushathite, [28] <Zalmon> [Ilai] the Ahohite, Maharai of Netophah, [29] <Heleb> [Heled] the son of Baanah of Netophah, Ittai the son of Ribai of Gibeah of the people of Benjamin, [30] Benaiah of Pirathon, Hiddai of the brooks of Gaash, [31] <Abi-albon> [Abiel] the Arbathite, Azmaveth of <Bahurim> [Baharum], [32] Eliahba the Shaalbonite, <the sons of Jashen> [Hashem the Gizonite], <Jonathan, [33] Shammah the Hararite> [Jonathan the son of Shagee the Hararite], Ahiam the son of <Sharar> [Sachar] the Hararite, [34] <Eliphelet the son of Ahasbai of Maacah> [Eliphal the son of Ur], <Eliam the son of Ahithophel of Gilo> [0] [+ Hepher the Mecherathite, Ahijah the Pelonite,] [35] Hezro of Carmel, <Paarai the Arbite, [36] Igal the son of Nathan of Zobah, Bani the Gadite> [0], [+Naarai the son of Ezbai, [38] Joel the brother of Nathan, Mibhar the son of Hagri,] [37] Zelek the Ammonite, Naharai of Beeroth, the armor-bearer of Joab the son of Zeruiah, [38] Ira the Ithrite, Gareb the Ithrite, [39] Uriah the Hittite [+ Zabad the son of Ahlai, [42] Adina the son of Shiza the

Reubenite, a leader of the Reubenites, and thirty with him, [43] Hanan the son of Maacah, and Joshaphat the Mithnite, [44] Uzzia the Ashterathite, Shama and Jeiel the sons of Hotham the Aroerite, [45] Jediael the son of Shimri, and Joha his brother, the Tizite, [46] Eliel the Mahavite, and Jeribai, and Joshaviah, the sons of Elnaam, and Ithmah the Moabite, [47] Eliel, and Obed, and Jaasiel the Mezobaite.]: thirty-seven in all.

Part Seven: Favor and Forgiveness

992-990 B.C.; age 47-50; regnal years 17-20

David desires to build a temple for God
2 Sam. 7:1-17 [1 Chron. 17:1-15]

7 Now when the king lived in his house <and the LORD had given him rest from all his surrounding enemies,> [0] **2** the king said to Nathan the prophet, "See now, I dwell in a house of cedar, but the ark of God dwells in a tent." **3** And Nathan said to the king, "Go, do all that is in your heart, for the LORD is with you."

4 But that same night the word of the LORD came to Nathan, **5** "Go and tell my servant David, 'Thus says the LORD: Would you build me a house to dwell in? **6** I have not lived in a house since the day I brought up the people of Israel from Egypt to this day, but I have been moving about in a tent for my dwelling. **7** In all places where I have moved with all the people of Israel, did I speak a word with any of the judges of Israel, whom I commanded to shepherd my people Israel, saying, "Why have you not built me a house of cedar?" ' **8** Now, therefore, thus you shall say to my servant David, 'Thus says the LORD of hosts, I took you from the pasture, from following the sheep, that you should be prince over my people Israel. **9** And I have been with you wherever you went and have cut off all your enemies from before you. And I will make for you a great name, like the name of the great ones of the earth. **10** And I will appoint a place for my people Israel and will plant them, so that they may dwell in their own place and be disturbed no more. And violent men shall afflict them no more, as formerly, **11** from the time that I appointed judges over my people Israel. And I will give you rest from all your enemies. Moreover, the LORD declares to you that the LORD will make you a house. **12** When your days are fulfilled <and you lie down with your fathers> [to walk with your fathers], I will raise up your offspring after you, <who shall come from your body> [one of your own sons], and I will establish his kingdom. **13** He shall build a house for my name, and I will establish the throne of his kingdom forever. **14** I will be to him a father, and he shall be to me a son. When he commits iniquity, I will discipline him with the rod of men, with the stripes of the sons of men, **15** but my steadfast love will not depart from him, as I took it from <Saul, whom I put away from before you> [him who was before you]. **16** <And your house and your kingdom shall be made sure forever before me> [but

I will confirm him in my house and in my kingdom forever]. <Your> [and his] throne shall be established forever.' " **17** In accordance with all these words, and in accordance with all this vision, Nathan spoke to David.

David gives thanks to God
2 Sam. 7:18-29 [1 Chron. 17:16-27]

18 Then King David went in and sat before the LORD and said, "Who am I, O Lord GOD, and what is my house, that you have brought me thus far? **19** And yet this was a small thing in your eyes, O Lord GOD. You have spoken also of your servant's house for a great while to come, <and this is instruction for mankind> [and have shown me future generations], O Lord GOD! **20** And what more can David say to you [+ for honoring your servant]? For you know your servant, O Lord GOD! **21** <Because of your promise> [For your servant's sake, O LORD], and according to your own heart, you have brought about all this greatness, to make your servant know it. **22** Therefore you are great, O LORD God. For there is none like you, and there is no God besides you, according to all that we have heard with our ears. **23** And who is like your people Israel, the one nation on earth whom God went to redeem to be his people, making himself a name and doing for them great and awesome things by driving out before your people, whom you redeemed for yourself from Egypt, a nation and its gods? **24** And you established for yourself your people Israel to be your people forever. And you, O LORD, became their God. **25** And now, O LORD God, confirm forever the word that you have spoken concerning your servant and concerning his house, and do as you have spoken. **26** And your name will be [+ established and] magnified forever, saying, 'The LORD of hosts is God over Israel,' and the house of your servant David will be established before you. **27** For you, O LORD of hosts, the God of Israel, have made this revelation to your servant, saying, 'I will build you a house.' Therefore your servant has found courage to pray this prayer to you. **28** And now, O Lord GOD, you are God, and your words are true, and you have promised this good thing to your servant. **29** Now therefore <may it please you> [you have been pleased] to bless the house of your servant, so that it may continue forever before you. For you, O Lord GOD, have spoken, and with your blessing shall the house of your servant be blessed forever."

Joab lays siege to Rabbah
2 Sam. 11:1 [1 Chron. 20:1a]

11 In the spring of the year, the time when kings go out to battle, <David sent Joab, and his servants with him, and all Israel. And they> [Joab led out the army and] ravaged the Ammonites and besieged Rabbah. But David remained at Jerusalem.

David commits adultery
Samuel 11:2-5

2 It happened, late one afternoon, when David arose from his couch and was walking on the roof of the king's house, that he saw from the roof a woman bathing; and the woman was very beautiful. **3** And David sent and inquired about the woman. And one said, "Is not this Bathsheba, the daughter of Eliam, the wife of Uriah the Hittite?" **4** So David sent messengers and took her, and she came to him, and he lay with her. (Now she had been purifying herself from her uncleanness.) Then she returned to her house. **5** And the woman conceived, and she sent and told David, "I am pregnant."

David tries to hide his sin
Samuel 11:6-13

6 So David sent word to Joab, "Send me Uriah the Hittite." And Joab sent Uriah to David. **7** When Uriah came to him, David asked how Joab was doing and how the people were doing and how the war was going. **8** Then David said to Uriah, "Go down to your house and wash your feet." And Uriah went out of the king's house, and there followed him a present from the king. **9** But Uriah slept at the door of the king's house with all the servants of his lord, and did not go down to his house. **10** When they told David, "Uriah did not go down to his house," David said to Uriah, "Have you not come from a journey? Why did you not go down to your house?" **11** Uriah said to David, "The ark and Israel and Judah dwell in booths, and my lord Joab and the servants of my lord are camping in the open field. Shall I then go to my house, to eat and to drink and to lie with my wife? As you live, and as your soul lives, I will not do this thing." **12** Then David said to Uriah, "Remain here today also, and tomorrow I will send you back." So Uriah remained in Jerusalem that day and the next. **13** And David invited him, and he ate in his presence and drank, so that he made him drunk. And in the evening he went out to lie on his couch with the servants of his lord, but he did not go down to his house.

David has Uriah killed
2 Sam. 11:14-26

14 In the morning David wrote a letter to Joab and sent it by the hand of Uriah. **15** In the letter he wrote, "Set Uriah in the forefront of the hardest fighting, and then draw back from him, that he may be struck down, and die." **16** And as Joab was besieging the city, he assigned Uriah to the place where he knew there were valiant men. **17** And the men of the city came out and fought with Joab, and some of the servants of David among the people fell. Uriah the Hittite also died. **18** Then Joab sent and told David all the news about the fighting. **19** And he instructed the messenger, "When you have finished telling all the news about the fighting to the king, **20** then, if the king's anger rises, and if he says to you, 'Why did you go so near the city to fight? Did you not know that they would shoot from the wall? **21** Who killed Abimelech the son of Jerubbesheth? Did not a woman cast an upper millstone on him from the wall, so that he died at Thebez? Why did you go so near the wall?' then you shall say, 'Your servant Uriah the Hittite is dead also.' "

22 So the messenger went and came and told David all that Joab had sent him to tell. **23** The messenger said to David, "The men gained an advantage over us and came out against us in the field, but we drove them back to the entrance of the gate. **24** Then the archers shot at your servants from the wall. Some of the king's servants are dead, and your servant Uriah the Hittite is dead also." **25** David said to the messenger, "Thus shall you say to Joab, 'Do not let this matter displease you, for the sword devours now one and now another. Strengthen your attack against the city and overthrow it.' And encourage him."

26 When the wife of Uriah heard that Uriah her husband was dead, she lamented over her husband.

Nathan rebukes David
2 Sam. 12:1-12

12 And the LORD sent Nathan to David. He came to him and said to him, "There were two men in a certain city, the one rich and the other poor. **2** The rich man had very many flocks and herds, **3** but the poor man had nothing but one little ewe lamb, which he had bought. And he brought it up, and it grew up with him and with his children. It used to eat of his morsel and drink from his cup and lie in his arms, and it was like a daughter to him. **4** Now there came a traveler to the rich man, and he was unwilling to take one of his own flock or herd to prepare for the guest who had come to him, but he took the poor man's lamb and prepared it for the man who had come to him." **5** Then David's anger was greatly kindled against the man, and he said to Nathan, "As the LORD lives, the man who has done this deserves to die, **6** and he shall restore the lamb fourfold, because he did this thing, and because he had no pity."

7 Nathan said to David, "You are the man! Thus says the LORD, the God of Israel, 'I anointed you king over Israel, and I delivered you out of the hand of Saul. **8** And I gave you your master's house and your master's wives into your arms and gave you the house of Israel and of Judah. And if this were too little, I would add to you as much more. **9** Why have you despised the word of the LORD, to do what is evil in his sight? You have struck down Uriah the Hittite with the sword and have taken his wife to be your wife and have killed him with the sword of the Ammonites. **10** Now therefore the sword shall never depart from your house, because you have despised me and have taken the wife of Uriah the Hittite to be your wife.' **11** Thus says the LORD, 'Behold, I will raise up evil against you out of your own house. And I will take your wives before your eyes and give them to your neighbor, and he shall lie with your wives in the sight of this sun. **12** For you did it secretly, but I will do this thing before all Israel and before the sun.' "

David repents and is restored
2 Sam. 12:13-23

13 David said to Nathan, "I have sinned against the LORD." And Nathan said to David, "The LORD also has put away your sin; you shall not die. **14** Nevertheless, because by this deed you have utterly scorned the LORD, the child who is born to you shall die." **15** Then Nathan went to his house.

And the LORD afflicted the child that Uriah's wife bore to David, and he became sick. **16** David therefore sought God on behalf of the child. And David fasted and went in and lay all night on the ground. **17** And the elders of his house stood beside him, to raise him from the ground, but he would not, nor did he eat food with them. **18** On the seventh day the child died. And the servants of David were afraid to tell him that the child was dead, for they said, "Behold, while the child was yet alive, we spoke to him, and he did not listen to us. How then can we say to him the child is dead? He may do himself some harm." **19** But when David saw that his servants were whispering together, David understood that the child was dead. And David said to his servants, "Is the child dead?" They said, "He is dead." **20** Then David arose from the earth and washed and anointed himself and changed his clothes. And he went into the house of the LORD and worshiped. He then went to his own house. And when he asked, they set food before him, and he ate. **21** Then his servants said to him, "What is this thing that you have done? You fasted and wept for the child while he was alive; but when the child died, you arose and ate food." **22** He said, "While the child was still alive, I fasted and wept, for I said, 'Who knows whether the LORD will be gracious to me, that the child may live?' **23** But now he is dead. Why should I fast? Can I bring him back again? I shall go to him, but he will not return to me."

David takes Rabbah of the Ammonites
2 Sam. 12:26-31 [1 Chron. 20:1b-3]

26 Now Joab <fought against Rabbah of the Ammonites and took the royal city> [struck down Rabbah and overthrew it]. <**27** And Joab sent messengers to David and said, "I have fought against Rabbah; moreover, I have taken the city of waters. **28** Now then gather the rest of the people together and encamp against the city and take it, lest I take the city and it be called by my name." **29** So David gathered all the people together and went to Rabbah and fought against it and took it.> [0] **30** And <he> [David] took the crown of their king from his head. The weight of it was a talent of gold, and in it was a precious stone, and it was placed on David's head. And he brought out the spoil of the city, a very great amount. **31** And he brought out the people who were in it and set them to labor with saws and iron picks and iron axes <and made them toil at the brick kilns> [0]. And thus he did to all the cities of the Ammonites. Then David and all the people returned to Jerusalem.

Solomon is born
2 Sam. 12:24-25

24 Then David comforted his wife, Bathsheba, and went in to her and lay with her, and she bore a son, and he called his name Solomon. And the LORD loved him **25** and sent a message by Nathan the prophet. So he called his name Jedidiah, because of the LORD.

Part Eight: Family Trouble

989-977 B.C.; age 51-63; regnal years 21-33

Amnon rapes Tamar
2 Sam. 13:1-22

13 Now Absalom, David's son, had a beautiful sister, whose name was Tamar. And after a time Amnon, David's son, loved her. **²** And Amnon was so tormented that he made himself ill because of his sister Tamar, for she was a virgin, and it seemed impossible to Amnon to do anything to her. **³** But Amnon had a friend, whose name was Jonadab, the son of Shimeah, David's brother. And Jonadab was a very crafty man. **⁴** And he said to him, "O son of the king, why are you so haggard morning after morning? Will you not tell me?" Amnon said to him, "I love Tamar, my brother Absalom's sister." **⁵** Jonadab said to him, "Lie down on your bed and pretend to be ill. And when your father comes to see you, say to him, 'Let my sister Tamar come and give me bread to eat, and prepare the food in my sight, that I may see it and eat it from her hand.' " **⁶** So Amnon lay down and pretended to be ill. And when the king came to see him, Amnon said to the king, "Please let my sister Tamar come and make a couple of cakes in my sight, that I may eat from her hand."

⁷ Then David sent home to Tamar, saying, "Go to your brother Amnon's house and prepare food for him." **⁸** So Tamar went to her brother Amnon's house, where he was lying down. And she took dough and kneaded it and made cakes in his sight and baked the cakes. **⁹** And she took the pan and emptied it out before him, but he refused to eat. And Amnon said, "Send out everyone from me." So everyone went out from him. **¹⁰** Then Amnon said to Tamar, "Bring the food into the chamber, that I may eat from your hand." And Tamar took the cakes she had made and brought them into the chamber to Amnon her brother. **¹¹** But when she brought them near him to eat, he took hold of her and said to her, "Come, lie with me, my sister." **¹²** She answered him, "No, my brother, do not violate me, for such a thing is not done in Israel; do not do this outrageous thing. **¹³** As for me, where could I carry my shame? And as for you, you would be as one of the outrageous fools in Israel. Now therefore, please speak to the king, for he will not withhold me from you." **¹⁴** But he would not listen to her, and being stronger than she, he violated her and lay with her.

15 Then Amnon hated her with very great hatred, so that the hatred with which he hated her was greater than the love with which he had loved her. And Amnon said to her, "Get up! Go!" **16** But she said to him, "No, my brother, for this wrong in sending me away is greater than the other that you did to me." But he would not listen to her. **17** He called the young man who served him and said, "Put this woman out of my presence and bolt the door after her." **18** Now she was wearing a long robe with sleeves, for thus were the virgin daughters of the king dressed. So his servant put her out and bolted the door after her. **19** And Tamar put ashes on her head and tore the long robe that she wore. And she laid her hand on her head and went away, crying aloud as she went.

20 And her brother Absalom said to her, "Has Amnon your brother been with you? Now hold your peace, my sister. He is your brother; do not take this to heart." So Tamar lived, a desolate woman, in her brother Absalom's house. **21** When King David heard of all these things, he was very angry. **22** But Absalom spoke to Amnon neither good nor bad, for Absalom hated Amnon, because he had violated his sister Tamar.

Absalom kills Amnon
2 Sam. 13:23-39

23 After two full years Absalom had sheepshearers at Baal-hazor, which is near Ephraim, and Absalom invited all the king's sons. **24** And Absalom came to the king and said, "Behold, your servant has sheepshearers. Please let the king and his servants go with your servant." **25** But the king said to Absalom, "No, my son, let us not all go, lest we be burdensome to you." He pressed him, but he would not go but gave him his blessing. **26** Then Absalom said, "If not, please let my brother Amnon go with us." And the king said to him, "Why should he go with you?" **27** But Absalom pressed him until he let Amnon and all the king's sons go with him. **28** Then Absalom commanded his servants, "Mark when Amnon's heart is merry with wine, and when I say to you, 'Strike Amnon,' then kill him. Do not fear; have I not commanded you? Be courageous and be valiant." **29** So the servants of Absalom did to Amnon as Absalom had commanded. Then all the king's sons arose, and each mounted his mule and fled.

30 While they were on the way, news came to David, "Absalom has struck down all the king's sons, and not one of them is left." **31** Then the king arose and tore his garments and lay on the earth. And all his servants who were standing by tore their garments. ³² But Jonadab the son of Shimeah, David's brother, said, "Let not my lord suppose that they have killed all the young men, the king's sons, for Amnon alone is dead. For by the command of Absalom this has been determined from the day he violated his sister Tamar. ³³ Now therefore let not my lord the king so take it to heart as to suppose that all the king's sons are dead, for Amnon alone is dead."

³⁴ But Absalom fled. And the young man who kept the watch lifted up his eyes and looked, and behold, many people were coming from the road behind him by the side of the mountain. ³⁵ And Jonadab said to the king, "Behold, the king's sons have come; as your servant said, so it has come about." ³⁶ And as soon as he had finished speaking, behold, the king's sons came and lifted up their voice and wept. And the king also and all his servants wept very bitterly.

³⁷ But Absalom fled and went to Talmai the son of Ammihud, king of Geshur. And David mourned for his son day after day. ³⁸ So Absalom fled and went to Geshur, and was there three years. ³⁹ And the spirit of the king longed to go out to Absalom, because he was comforted about Amnon, since he was dead.

Absalom recalled to Jerusalem
2 Sam. 14:1-24

14 Now Joab the son of Zeruiah knew that the king's heart went out to Absalom. ² And Joab sent to Tekoa and brought from there a wise woman and said to her, "Pretend to be a mourner and put on mourning garments. Do not anoint yourself with oil, but behave like a woman who has been mourning many days for the dead. ³ Go to the king and speak thus to him." So Joab put the words in her mouth.

⁴ When the woman of Tekoa came to the king, she fell on her face to the ground and paid homage and said, "Save me, O king." ⁵ And the king said to her, "What is your trouble?" She answered, "Alas, I am a widow; my husband is dead. ⁶ And your servant had two sons, and they quarreled with one another in the field. There was no one to separate them, and one struck the other and killed him. ⁷ And now the whole clan has risen against your servant, and they say, 'Give up the man who struck his brother, that we may put him to death for the life of his brother whom he killed.' And so they would destroy the heir also. Thus they would quench

my coal that is left and leave to my husband neither name nor remnant on the face of the earth.”

⁸ Then the king said to the woman, “Go to your house, and I will give orders concerning you.” ⁹ And the woman of Tekoa said to the king, “On me be the guilt, my lord the king, and on my father’s house; let the king and his throne be guiltless.” ¹⁰ The king said, “If anyone says anything to you, bring him to me, and he shall never touch you again.” ¹¹ Then she said, “Please let the king invoke the LORD your God, that the avenger of blood kill no more, and my son be not destroyed.” He said, “As the LORD lives, not one hair of your son shall fall to the ground.”

¹² Then the woman said, “Please let your servant speak a word to my lord the king.” He said, “Speak.” ¹³ And the woman said, “Why then have you planned such a thing against the people of God? For in giving this decision the king convicts himself, inasmuch as the king does not bring his banished one home again. ¹⁴ We must all die; we are like water spilled on the ground, which cannot be gathered up again. But God will not take away life, and he devises means so that the banished one will not remain an outcast. ¹⁵ Now I have come to say this to my lord the king because the people have made me afraid, and your servant thought, ‘I will speak to the king; it may be that the king will perform the request of his servant. ¹⁶ For the king will hear and deliver his servant from the hand of the man who would destroy me and my son together from the heritage of God.’ ¹⁷ And your servant thought, ‘The word of my lord the king will set me at rest,’ for my lord the king is like the angel of God to discern good and evil. The LORD your God be with you!”

¹⁸ Then the king answered the woman, “Do not hide from me anything I ask you.” And the woman said, “Let my lord the king speak.” ¹⁹ The king said, “Is the hand of Joab with you in all this?” The woman answered and said, “As surely as you live, my lord the king, one cannot turn to the right hand or to the left from anything that my lord the king has said. It was your servant Joab who commanded me; it was he who put all these words in the mouth of your servant. ²⁰ In order to change the course of things your servant Joab did this. But my lord has wisdom like the wisdom of the angel of God to know all things that are on the earth.”

²¹ Then the king said to Joab, “Behold now, I grant this; go, bring back the young man Absalom.” ²² And Joab fell on his face to the ground and paid homage and blessed the king. And Joab said, “Today your servant knows that I have found favor in your sight, my lord the king, in that the

king has granted the request of his servant." ²³ So Joab arose and went to Geshur and brought Absalom to Jerusalem. ²⁴ And the king said, "Let him dwell apart in his own house; he is not to come into my presence." So Absalom lived apart in his own house and did not come into the king's presence.

David forgives Absalom
2 Sam. 14:25-33

²⁵ Now in all Israel there was no one so much to be praised for his handsome appearance as Absalom. From the sole of his foot to the crown of his head there was no blemish in him. ²⁶ And when he cut the hair of his head (for at the end of every year he used to cut it; when it was heavy on him, he cut it), he weighed the hair of his head, two hundred shekels by the king's weight. ²⁷ There were born to Absalom three sons, and one daughter whose name was Tamar. She was a beautiful woman.

²⁸ So Absalom lived two full years in Jerusalem, without coming into the king's presence. ²⁹ Then Absalom sent for Joab, to send him to the king, but Joab would not come to him. And he sent a second time, but Joab would not come. ³⁰ Then he said to his servants, "See, Joab's field is next to mine, and he has barley there; go and set it on fire." So Absalom's servants set the field on fire. ³¹ Then Joab arose and went to Absalom at his house and said to him, "Why have your servants set my field on fire?" ³² Absalom answered Joab, "Behold, I sent word to you, 'Come here, that I may send you to the king, to ask, "Why have I come from Geshur? It would be better for me to be there still." Now therefore let me go into the presence of the king, and if there is guilt in me, let him put me to death.' " ³³ Then Joab went to the king and told him, and he summoned Absalom. So he came to the king and bowed himself on his face to the ground before the king, and the king kissed Absalom.

Absalom wins the favor of the people
2 Sam. 15:1-6

15 After this Absalom got himself a chariot and horses, and fifty men to run before him. ² And Absalom used to rise early and stand beside the way of the gate. And when any man had a dispute to come before the king for judgment, Absalom would call to him and say, "From what city are you?" And when he said, "Your servant is of such and such a tribe in Israel," ³ Absalom would say to him, "See, your claims are good and right, but there is no man designated by the king to hear you." **4** Then Absalom would say, "Oh that I were judge in the land! Then every man with a dispute or cause might come to me, and I would give him justice." **5** And whenever a man came near to pay homage to him, he would put out his hand and take hold of him and kiss him. **6** Thus Absalom did to all of Israel who came to the king for judgment. So Absalom stole the hearts of the men of Israel.

Absalom proclaims himself king in Hebron
2 Sam. 15:7-12

7 And at the end of four years Absalom said to the king, "Please let me go and pay my vow, which I have vowed to the LORD, in Hebron. **8** For your servant vowed a vow while I lived at Geshur in Aram, saying, 'If the LORD will indeed bring me back to Jerusalem, then I will offer worship to the LORD.' " **9** The king said to him, "Go in peace." So he arose and went to Hebron. **10** But Absalom sent secret messengers throughout all the tribes of Israel, saying, "As soon as you hear the sound of the trumpet, then say, 'Absalom is king at Hebron!' " **11** With Absalom went two hundred men from Jerusalem who were invited guests, and they went in their innocence and knew nothing. **12** And while Absalom was offering the sacrifices, he sent for Ahithophel the Gilonite, David's counselor, from his city Giloh. And the conspiracy grew strong, and the people with Absalom kept increasing.

David flees Jerusalem
2 Sam. 15:13-23

13 And a messenger came to David, saying, "The hearts of the men of Israel have gone after Absalom." **14** Then David said to all his servants who were with him at Jerusalem, "Arise, and let us flee, or else there will be no escape for us from Absalom. Go quickly, lest he overtake us quickly and bring down ruin on us and strike the city with the edge of the sword." **15** And the king's servants said to the king, "Behold, your servants are ready to do whatever my lord the king decides." **16** So the king went out, and all his household after him. And the king left ten concubines to keep the house. **17** And the king went out, and all the people after him. And they halted at the last house.

18 And all his servants passed by him, and all the Cherethites, and all the Pelethites, and all the six hundred Gittites who had followed him from

Gath, passed on before the king. [19] Then the king said to Ittai the Gittite, "Why do you also go with us? Go back and stay with the king, for you are a foreigner and also an exile from your home. [20] You came only yesterday, and shall I today make you wander about with us, since I go I know not where? Go back and take your brothers with you, and may the LORD show steadfast love and faithfulness to you." [21] But Ittai answered the king, "As the LORD lives, and as my lord the king lives, wherever my lord the king shall be, whether for death or for life, there also will your servant be." [22] And David said to Ittai, "Go then, pass on." So Ittai the Gittite passed on with all his men and all the little ones who were with him. [23] And all the land wept aloud as all the people passed by, and the king crossed the brook Kidron, and all the people passed on toward the wilderness.

David leaves agents inside Jerusalem
2 Sam. 15:24-37

[24] And Abiathar came up, and behold, Zadok came also with all the Levites, bearing the ark of the covenant of God. And they set down the ark of God until the people had all passed out of the city. [25] Then the king said to Zadok, "Carry the ark of God back into the city. If I find favor in the eyes of the LORD, he will bring me back and let me see both it and his dwelling place. [26] But if he says, 'I have no pleasure in you,' behold, here I am, let him do to me what seems good to him." [27] The king also said to Zadok the priest, "Are you not a seer? Go back to the city in peace, with your two sons, Ahimaaz your son, and Jonathan the son of Abiathar. [28] See, I will wait at the fords of the wilderness until word comes from you to inform me." [29] So Zadok and Abiathar carried the ark of God back to Jerusalem, and they remained there.

[30] But David went up the ascent of the Mount of Olives, weeping as he went, barefoot and with his head covered. And all the people who were with him covered their heads, and they went up, weeping as they went. [31] And it was told David, "Ahithophel is among the conspirators with Absalom." And David said, "O LORD, please turn the counsel of Ahithophel into foolishness."

[32] While David was coming to the summit, where God was worshiped, behold, Hushai the Archite came to meet him with his coat torn and dirt on his head. [33] David said to him, "If you go on with me, you will be a burden to me. [34] But if you return to the city and say to Absalom, 'I will be your servant, O king; as I have been your father's servant in time past,

so now I will be your servant,' then you will defeat for me the counsel of Ahithophel. **35** Are not Zadok and Abiathar the priests with you there? So whatever you hear from the king's house, tell it to Zadok and Abiathar the priests. **36** Behold, their two sons are with them there, Ahimaaz, Zadok's son, and Jonathan, Abiathar's son, and by them you shall send to me everything you hear." **37** So Hushai, David's friend, came into the city, just as Absalom was entering Jerusalem.

Ziba slanders Mephibosheth
2 Sam. 16:1-4

16 When David had passed a little beyond the summit, Ziba the servant of Mephibosheth met him, with a couple of donkeys saddled, bearing two hundred loaves of bread, a hundred bunches of raisins, a hundred of summer fruits, and a skin of wine. **2** And the king said to Ziba, "Why have you brought these?" Ziba answered, "The donkeys are for the king's household to ride on, the bread and summer fruit for the young men to eat, and the wine for those who faint in the wilderness to drink." **3** And the king said, "And where is your master's son?" Ziba said to the king, "Behold, he remains in Jerusalem, for he said, 'Today the house of Israel will give me back the kingdom of my father.' " **4** Then the king said to Ziba, "Behold, all that belonged to Mephibosheth is now yours." And Ziba said, "I pay homage; let me ever find favor in your sight, my lord the king."

Shimei curses David
2 Sam. 16:5-14

5 When King David came to Bahurim, there came out a man of the family of the house of Saul, whose name was Shimei, the son of Gera, and as he came he cursed continually. **6** And he threw stones at David and at all the servants of King David, and all the people and all the mighty men were on his right hand and on his left. **7** And Shimei said as he cursed, "Get out, get out, you man of blood, you worthless man! **8** The LORD has avenged on you all the blood of the house of Saul, in whose place you have reigned, and the LORD has given the kingdom into the hand of your son Absalom. See, your evil is on you, for you are a man of blood."

9 Then Abishai the son of Zeruiah said to the king, "Why should this dead dog curse my lord the king? Let me go over and take off his head." **10** But the king said, "What have I to do with you, you sons of Zeruiah? If he is cursing because the LORD has said to him, 'Curse David,' who then shall say, 'Why have you done so?' " **11** And David said to Abishai and to all his servants, "Behold, my own son seeks my life; how much more now may this Benjaminite! Leave him alone, and let him curse, for the LORD has told him to. **12** It may be that the LORD will look on the wrong done to me, and that the LORD will repay me with good for his cursing today." **13** So David and his men went on the road, while Shimei went along on the hillside opposite him and cursed as he went and threw stones at him and flung dust. **14** And the king, and all the people who were with him, arrived weary at the Jordan. And there he refreshed himself.

Hushai infiltrates Absalom's inner council
2 Sam. 16:15-19

15 Now Absalom and all the people, the men of Israel, came to Jerusalem, and Ahithophel with him. **16** And when Hushai the Archite, David's friend, came to Absalom, Hushai said to Absalom, "Long live the king! Long live the king!" **17** And Absalom said to Hushai, "Is this your loyalty to your friend? Why did you not go with your friend?" **18** And Hushai said to Absalom, "No, for whom the LORD and this people and all the men of Israel have chosen, his I will be, and with him I will remain. **19** And again, whom should I serve? Should it not be his son? As I have served your father, so I will serve you."

Absalom disgraces David's concubines
2 Sam. 16:20-23

20 Then Absalom said to Ahithophel, "Give your counsel. What shall we do?" **21** Ahithophel said to Absalom, "Go in to your father's concubines, whom he has left to keep the house, and all Israel will hear that you have made yourself a stench to your father, and the hands of all who are with you will be strengthened." **22** So they pitched a tent for Absalom on the roof. And Absalom went in to his father's concubines in the sight of all Israel. **23** Now in those days the counsel that Ahithophel gave was as if one consulted the word of God; so was all the counsel of Ahithophel esteemed, both by David and by Absalom.

Hushai opposes Ahithophel's advice
2 Sam. 17:1-14

17 Moreover, Ahithophel said to Absalom, "Let me choose twelve thousand men, and I will arise and pursue David tonight. **2** I will come upon him while he is weary and discouraged and throw him into a panic, and all the people who are with him will flee. I will strike down only the king, **3** and I will bring all the people back to you as a bride comes home to her husband. You seek the life of only one man, and all the people will be at peace." **4** And the advice seemed right in the eyes of Absalom and all the elders of Israel.

5 Then Absalom said, "Call Hushai the Archite also, and let us hear what he has to say." **6** And when Hushai came to Absalom, Absalom said to him, "Thus has Ahithophel spoken; shall we do as he says? If not, you speak." **7** Then Hushai said to Absalom, "This time the counsel that Ahithophel has given is not good." **8** Hushai said, "You know that your father and his men are mighty men, and that they are enraged, like a bear robbed of her cubs in the field. Besides, your father is expert in war; he will not spend the night with the people. **9** Behold, even now he has hidden himself in one of the pits or in some other place. And as soon as some of the people fall at the first attack, whoever hears it will say, 'There has been a slaughter among the people who follow Absalom.' **10** Then even the valiant man, whose heart is like the heart of a lion, will utterly melt with fear, for all Israel knows that your father is a mighty man, and that those who are with him are valiant men. **11** But my counsel is that all Israel be gathered to you, from Dan to Beersheba, as the sand by the sea for multitude, and that you go to battle in person. **12** So we shall come upon him in some place where he is to be found, and we shall light upon him as the dew falls on the ground, and of him and all the men with him not one will be left. **13** If he withdraws into a city, then all Israel will bring ropes to that city, and we shall drag it into the valley, until not even a pebble is to be found there." **14** And Absalom and all the men of Israel said, "The counsel of Hushai the Archite is better than the counsel of Ahithophel." For the LORD had ordained to defeat the good counsel of Ahithophel, so that the LORD might bring harm upon Absalom.

Hushai sends a secret message to David
2 Sam. 17:15-23

[15] Then Hushai said to Zadok and Abiathar the priests, "Thus and so did Ahithophel counsel Absalom and the elders of Israel, and thus and so have I counseled. [16] Now therefore send quickly and tell David, 'Do not stay tonight at the fords of the wilderness, but by all means pass over, lest the king and all the people who are with him be swallowed up.'" [17] Now Jonathan and Ahimaaz were waiting at En-rogel. A female servant was to go and tell them, and they were to go and tell King David, for they were not to be seen entering the city. [18] But a young man saw them and told Absalom. So both of them went away quickly and came to the house of a man at Bahurim, who had a well in his courtyard. And they went down into it. [19] And the woman took and spread a covering over the well's mouth and scattered grain on it, and nothing was known of it. [20] When Absalom's servants came to the woman at the house, they said, "Where are Ahimaaz and Jonathan?" And the woman said to them, "They have gone over the brook of water." And when they had sought and could not find them, they returned to Jerusalem.

[21] After they had gone, the men came up out of the well, and went and told King David. They said to David, "Arise, and go quickly over the water, for thus and so has Ahithophel counseled against you." [22] Then David arose, and all the people who were with him, and they crossed the Jordan. By daybreak not one was left who had not crossed the Jordan.

[23] When Ahithophel saw that his counsel was not followed, he saddled his donkey and went off home to his own city. He set his house in order and hanged himself, and he died and was buried in the tomb of his father.

David finds refuge in Mahanaim
2 Sam. 17:24-29

[24] Then David came to Mahanaim. And Absalom crossed the Jordan with all the men of Israel. [25] Now Absalom had set Amasa over the army instead of Joab. Amasa was the son of a man named Ithra the Ishmaelite, who had married Abigal the daughter of Nahash, sister of Zeruiah, Joab's mother. [26] And Israel and Absalom encamped in the land of Gilead.

[27] When David came to Mahanaim, Shobi the son of Nahash from Rabbah of the Ammonites, and Machir the son of Ammiel from Lo-

debar, and Barzillai the Gileadite from Rogelim, **28** brought beds, basins, and earthen vessels, wheat, barley, flour, parched grain, beans and lentils, **29** honey and curds and sheep and cheese from the herd, for David and the people with him to eat, for they said, "The people are hungry and weary and thirsty in the wilderness."

Joab defeats and kills Absalom
2 Sam. 18:1-18

18 Then David mustered the men who were with him and set over them commanders of thousands and commanders of hundreds. **2** And David sent out the army, one third under the command of Joab, one third under the command of Abishai the son of Zeruiah, Joab's brother, and one third under the command of Ittai the Gittite. And the king said to the men, "I myself will also go out with you." **3** But the men said, "You shall not go out. For if we flee, they will not care about us. If half of us die, they will not care about us. But you are worth ten thousand of us. Therefore it is better that you send us help from the city." **4** The king said to them, "Whatever seems best to you I will do." So the king stood at the side of the gate, while all the army marched out by hundreds and by thousands. **5** And the king ordered Joab and Abishai and Ittai, "Deal gently for my sake with the young man Absalom." And all the people heard when the king gave orders to all the commanders about Absalom.

6 So the army went out into the field against Israel, and the battle was fought in the forest of Ephraim. **7** And the men of Israel were defeated there by the servants of David, and the loss there was great on that day, twenty thousand men. **8** The battle spread over the face of all the country, and the forest devoured more people that day than the sword.

9 And Absalom happened to meet the servants of David. Absalom was riding on his mule, and the mule went under the thick branches of a great oak, and his head caught fast in the oak, and he was suspended between heaven and earth, while the mule that was under him went on. **10** And a certain man saw it and told Joab, "Behold, I saw Absalom hanging in an oak." **11** Joab said to the man who told him, "What, you saw him! Why then did you not strike him there to the ground? I would have been glad to give you ten pieces of silver and a belt." **12** But the man said to Joab, "Even if I felt in my hand the weight of a thousand pieces of silver, I would not reach out my hand against the king's son, for in our hearing the king commanded you and Abishai and Ittai, 'For my sake protect the young man Absalom.' ¹³ On the other hand, if I had dealt treacherously against his life (and there is nothing hidden from the king), then you yourself would have stood aloof." ¹⁴ Joab said, "I will not waste time like this with you." And he took three javelins in his hand and thrust them into the heart of Absalom while he was still alive in the oak. ¹⁵ And ten young men, Joab's armor-bearers, surrounded Absalom and struck him and killed him.

¹⁶ Then Joab blew the trumpet, and the troops came back from pursuing Israel, for Joab restrained them. ¹⁷ And they took Absalom and threw him into a great pit in the forest and raised over him a very great heap of stones. And all Israel fled every one to his own home. ¹⁸ Now Absalom in his lifetime had taken and set up for himself the pillar that is in the King's Valley, for he said, "I have no son to keep my name in remembrance." He called the pillar after his own name, and it is called Absalom's monument to this day.

David mourns for Absalom
2 Sam. 18:19-33

¹⁹ Then Ahimaaz the son of Zadok said, "Let me run and carry news to the king that the LORD has delivered him from the hand of his enemies." ²⁰ And Joab said to him, "You are not to carry news today. You may carry news another day, but today you shall carry no news, because the king's son is dead." ²¹ Then Joab said to the Cushite, "Go, tell the king what you have seen." The Cushite bowed before Joab, and ran. ²² Then Ahimaaz the son of Zadok said again to Joab, "Come what may, let me also run after the Cushite." And Joab said, "Why will you run, my son, seeing that you will have no reward for the news?" ²³ "Come what may," he said, "I will run." So he said to him, "Run." Then Ahimaaz ran by the way of the plain, and outran the Cushite.

²⁴ Now David was sitting between the two gates, and the watchman went up to the roof of the gate by the wall, and when he lifted up his eyes and looked, he saw a man running alone. ²⁵ The watchman called out and told the king. And the king said, "If he is alone, there is news in his mouth." And he drew nearer and nearer. ²⁶ The watchman saw another man running. And the watchman called to the gate and said, "See, another man running alone!" The king said, "He also brings news." ²⁷ The watchman said, "I think the running of the first is like the running of Ahimaaz the son of Zadok." And the king said, "He is a good man and comes with good news."

28 Then Ahimaaz cried out to the king, "All is well." And he bowed before the king with his face to the earth and said, "Blessed be the LORD your God, who has delivered up the men who raised their hand against my lord the king." **29** And the king said, "Is it well with the young man Absalom?" Ahimaaz answered, "When Joab sent the king's servant, your servant, I saw a great commotion, but I do not know what it was." **30** And the king said, "Turn aside and stand here." So he turned aside and stood still.

31 And behold, the Cushite came, and the Cushite said, "Good news for my lord the king! For the LORD has delivered you this day from the hand of all who rose up against you." **32** The king said to the Cushite, "Is it well with the young man Absalom?" And the Cushite answered, "May the enemies of my lord the king and all who rise up against you for evil be like that young man." **33** And the king was deeply moved and went up to the chamber over the gate and wept. And as he went, he said, "O my son Absalom, my son, my son Absalom! Would I had died instead of you, O Absalom, my son, my son!"

Joab rebukes David
2 Sam. 19:1-8

19 It was told Joab, "Behold, the king is weeping and mourning for Absalom." **2** So the victory that day was turned into mourning for all the people, for the people heard that day, "The king is grieving for his son." **3** And the people stole into the city that day as people steal in who are ashamed when they flee in battle. **4** The king covered his face, and the king cried with a loud voice, "O my son Absalom, O Absalom, my son, my son!" **5** Then Joab came into the house to the king and said, "You have today covered with shame the faces of all your servants, who have this day saved your life and the lives of your sons and your daughters and the lives of your wives and your concubines, **6** because you love those who hate you and hate those who love you. For you have made it clear today that commanders and servants are nothing to you, for today I know that if Absalom were alive and all of us were dead today, then you would be pleased. **7** Now therefore arise, go out and speak kindly to your servants, for I swear by the LORD, if you do not go, not a man will stay with you this night, and this will be worse for you than all the evil that has come upon you from your youth until now." **8** Then the king arose and took his seat in the gate. And the people were all told, "Behold, the king is sitting in the gate." And all the people came before the king.

Now Israel had fled every man to his own home.

Israel and Judah recall David
2 Sam. 19:9-15

[9] And all the people were arguing throughout all the tribes of Israel, saying, "The king delivered us from the hand of our enemies and saved us from the hand of the Philistines, and now he has fled out of the land from Absalom. [10] But Absalom, whom we anointed over us, is dead in battle. Now therefore why do you say nothing about bringing the king back?"

[11] And King David sent this message to Zadok and Abiathar the priests: "Say to the elders of Judah, 'Why should you be the last to bring the king back to his house, when the word of all Israel has come to the king? [12] You are my brothers; you are my bone and my flesh. Why then should you be the last to bring back the king?' [13] And say to Amasa, 'Are you not my bone and my flesh? God do so to me and more also, if you are not commander of my army from now on in place of Joab.' " [14] And he swayed the heart of all the men of Judah as one man, so that they sent word to the king, "Return, both you and all your servants." [15] So the king came back to the Jordan, and Judah came to Gilgal to meet the king and to bring the king over the Jordan.

Shimei meets David at the Jordan
2 Sam. 19:16-23

[16] And Shimei the son of Gera, the Benjaminite, from Bahurim, hurried to come down with the men of Judah to meet King David. [17] And with him were a thousand men from Benjamin. And Ziba the servant of the house of Saul, with his fifteen sons and his twenty servants, rushed down to the Jordan before the king, [18] and they crossed the ford to bring over the king's household and to do his pleasure. And Shimei the son of Gera fell down before the king, as he was about to cross the Jordan, [19] and said to the king, "Let not my lord hold me guilty or remember how your servant did wrong on the day my lord the king left Jerusalem. Do not let the king take it to heart. [20] For your servant knows that I have sinned. Therefore, behold, I have come this day, the first of all the house of Joseph to come down to meet my lord the king." [21] Abishai the son of Zeruiah answered, "Shall not Shimei be put to death for this, because he cursed the LORD's anointed?" [22] But David said, "What have I to do with you, you sons of Zeruiah, that you should this day be as an adversary to me? Shall anyone be put to death in Israel this day? For do I not know that I am this day

king over Israel?" **23** And the king said to Shimei, "You shall not die." And the king gave him his oath.

Mephibosheth meets David at the Jordan
2 Sam. 19:24-30

24 And Mephibosheth the son of Saul came down to meet the king. He had neither taken care of his feet nor trimmed his beard nor washed his clothes, from the day the king departed until the day he came back in safety. **25** And when he came to Jerusalem to meet the king, the king said to him, "Why did you not go with me, Mephibosheth?" **26** He answered, "My lord, O king, my servant deceived me, for your servant said to him, 'I will saddle a donkey for myself, that I may ride on it and go with the king.' For your servant is lame. **27** He has slandered your servant to my lord the king. But my lord the king is like the angel of God; do therefore what seems good to you. **28** For all my father's house were but men doomed to death before my lord the king, but you set your servant among those who eat at your table. What further right have I, then, to cry to the king?" **29** And the king said to him, "Why speak any more of your affairs? I have decided: you and Ziba shall divide the land." **30** And Mephibosheth said to the king, "Oh, let him take it all, since my lord the king has come safely home."

David parts from Barzillai
2 Sam. 19:31-40

31 Now Barzillai the Gileadite had come down from Rogelim, and he went on with the king to the Jordan, to escort him over the Jordan. **32** Barzillai was a very aged man, eighty years old. He had provided the king with food while he stayed at Mahanaim, for he was a very wealthy man. **33** And the king said to Barzillai, "Come over with me, and I will provide for you with me in Jerusalem." **34** But Barzillai said to the king, "How many years have I still to live, that I should go up with the king to Jerusalem? **35** I am this day eighty years old. Can I discern what is pleasant and what is not? Can your servant taste what he eats or what he drinks? Can I still listen to the voice of singing men and singing women? Why then should your servant be an added burden to my lord the king? **36** Your servant will go a little way over the Jordan with the king. Why should the king repay me with such a reward? **37** Please let your servant return, that I may die in my own city near the grave of my father and my mother. But here is your servant Chimham. Let him go over with my lord the king, and do for him whatever seems good to you." **38** And the king answered, "Chimham shall go over with me, and I will do for him whatever seems good to you, and all that you desire of me I will do for you." **39** Then all the people went over the Jordan, and the king went over. And the king kissed Barzillai and blessed him, and he returned to his own home. **40** The king went on to Gilgal, and Chimham went on with him. All the people of Judah, and also half the people of Israel, brought the king on his way.

Part Nine: National Problems

976-973 B.C.; age 64-67; regnal years 34-37

Conflict arises between Judah and Israel
2 Sam. 19:41 - 20:2

41 Then all the men of Israel came to the king and said to the king, "Why have our brothers the men of Judah stolen you away and brought the king and his household over the Jordan, and all David's men with him?" **42** All the men of Judah answered the men of Israel, "Because the king is our close relative. Why then are you angry over this matter? Have we eaten at all at the king's expense? Or has he given us any gift?" **43** And the men of Israel answered the men of Judah, "We have ten shares in the king, and in David also we have more than you. Why then did you despise us? Were we not the first to speak of bringing back our king?" But the words of the men of Judah were fiercer than the words of the men of Israel.

20 Now there happened to be there a worthless man, whose name was Sheba, the son of Bichri, a Benjaminite. And he blew the trumpet and said,

> "We have no portion in David,
> and we have no inheritance in the son of Jesse;
> every man to his tents, O Israel!"

2 So all the men of Israel withdrew from David and followed Sheba the son of Bichri. But the men of Judah followed their king steadfastly from the Jordan to Jerusalem.

Joab murders Amasa
2 Sam. 20:3-13

3 And David came to his house at Jerusalem. And the king took the ten concubines whom he had left to care for the house and put them in a house under guard and provided for them, but did not go in to them. So they were shut up until the day of their death, living as if in widowhood.

4 Then the king said to Amasa, "Call the men of Judah together to me within three days, and be here yourself." **5** So Amasa went to summon Judah, but he delayed beyond the set time that had been appointed him.

[6] And David said to Abishai, "Now Sheba the son of Bichri will do us more harm than Absalom. Take your lord's servants and pursue him, lest he get himself to fortified cities and escape from us." [7] And there went out after him Joab's men and the Cherethites and the Pelethites, and all the mighty men. They went out from Jerusalem to pursue Sheba the son of Bichri. [8] When they were at the great stone that is in Gibeon, Amasa came to meet them. Now Joab was wearing a soldier's garment, and over it was a belt with a sword in its sheath fastened on his thigh, and as he went forward it fell out. [9] And Joab said to Amasa, "Is it well with you, my brother?" And Joab took Amasa by the beard with his right hand to kiss him. [10] But Amasa did not observe the sword that was in Joab's hand. So Joab struck him with it in the stomach and spilled his entrails to the ground without striking a second blow, and he died.

Then Joab and Abishai his brother pursued Sheba the son of Bichri. [11] And one of Joab's young men took his stand by Amasa and said, "Whoever favors Joab, and whoever is for David, let him follow Joab." [12] And Amasa lay wallowing in his blood in the highway. And anyone who came by, seeing him, stopped. And when the man saw that all the people stopped, he carried Amasa out of the highway into the field and threw a garment over him. [13] When he was taken out of the highway, all the people went on after Joab to pursue Sheba the son of Bichri.

Sheba executed at Abel of Beth-maacah
2 Sam. 20:14-22

[14] And Sheba passed through all the tribes of Israel to Abel of Beth-maacah, and all the Bichrites assembled and followed him in. [15] And all the men who were with Joab came and besieged him in Abel of Beth-maacah. They cast up a mound against the city, and it stood against the rampart, and they were battering the wall to throw it down. [16] Then a wise woman called from the city, "Listen! Listen! Tell Joab, 'Come here, that I may speak to you.'" [17] And he came near her, and the woman said, "Are you Joab?" He answered, "I am." Then she said to him, "Listen to the words of your servant." And he answered, "I am listening." [18] Then she said, "They used to say in former times, 'Let them but ask counsel at Abel,' and so they settled a matter. [19] I am one of those who are peaceable and faithful in Israel. You seek to destroy a city that is a mother in Israel. Why will you swallow up the heritage of the LORD?" [20] Joab answered, "Far be it from me, far be it, that I should swallow up or destroy! [21] That is not true. But a man of the hill country of Ephraim, called Sheba the son of Bichri, has lifted up his hand against King David. Give up him alone,

and I will withdraw from the city." And the woman said to Joab, "Behold, his head shall be thrown to you over the wall." **22** Then the woman went to all the people in her wisdom. And they cut off the head of Sheba the son of Bichri and threw it out to Joab. So he blew the trumpet, and they dispersed from the city, every man to his home. And Joab returned to Jerusalem to the king.

David's advisors
2 Sam. 20:23-26

23 Now Joab was in command of all the army of Israel; and Benaiah the son of Jehoiada was in command of the Cherethites and the Pelethites; **24** and Adoram was in charge of the forced labor; and Jehoshaphat the son of Ahilud was the recorder; **25** and Sheva was secretary; and Zadok and Abiathar were priests; **26** and Ira the Jairite was also David's priest.

David takes a census
2 Sam. 24:1-10 [1 Chron. 21:1-8]
[[1 Chron. 27:23-24]]

24 <Again the anger of the LORD was kindled against Israel, and he> [Then Satan stood against Israel and] incited David <against them, saying, "Go, number Israel and Judah.">[to number Israel.] **2** So the king said to Joab, <the commander> [and the commanders] of the army, who was with him, "Go through all the tribes of Israel, from Dan to Beersheba, and number the people, that I may know the number of the people." **3** But Joab said to the king, "May the LORD your God add to the people a hundred times as many as they are , while the eyes of my lord the king still see it, but why does my lord the king delight in this thing? [+ Are they not, my lord the king, all of them my lord's servants? Why then should my lord require this? Why should it be a cause of guilt for Israel?]" **4** But the king's word prevailed against Joab and the commanders of the army. So Joab <and the commanders of the army went out from the presence of the king to number the people of Israel. **5** They crossed the Jordan and began from Aroer, and from the city that is in the middle of the valley, toward Gad and on to Jazer. **6** Then they came to Gilead, and to Kadesh in the land of the Hittites; and they came to Dan, and from Dan they went around to Sidon, **7** and came to the fortress of Tyre and to all the cities of the Hivites and Canaanites; and they went out to the Negeb of Judah at Beersheba. **8** So when they had gone through all the land, they came to Jerusalem at the end of nine months and twenty days> [departed and went throughout all Israel and came back to Jerusalem]. ⁹ And Joab gave the sum of the numbering of the people to the king: in Israel there were <800,000 valiant> [1,100,000] men who drew the sword, and the men of Judah were <500,000> [470,000 who drew the sword. But he did not include Levi and Benjamin in the numbering, for the king's command was abhorrent to Joab]. [[+ David did not count those below twenty years of age, for the LORD had promised to make Israel as many as the stars of heaven. ²⁴ Joab the son of Zeruiah began to count, but did not finish. Yet wrath came upon Israel for this, and the number was not entered in the chronicles of King David.]]

<¹⁰ But David's heart struck him after he had numbered the people> [But God was displeased with this thing, and he struck Israel]. And David said to the LORD, "I have sinned greatly in what I have done. But now, O LORD, please take away the iniquity of your servant, for I have done very foolishly."

God sends a plague
2 Sam. 24:11-17 [1 Chron. 21:9-17]

¹¹ And when David arose in the morning, the word of the LORD came to the prophet Gad, David's seer, saying, ¹² "Go and say to David, 'Thus says the LORD, Three things I offer you. Choose one of them, that I may do it to you.'" ¹³ So Gad came to David and told him, and said to him, "Shall three years of famine come to you in your land? Or will you flee three months before your foes while they pursue you? Or shall there be three days' pestilence in your land? Now consider, and decide what answer I shall return to him who sent me." ¹⁴ Then David said to Gad, "I am in great distress. Let us fall into the hand of the LORD, for his mercy is great; but let me not fall into the hand of man."

¹⁵ So the LORD sent a pestilence on Israel from the morning until the appointed time. And there died of the people from Dan to Beersheba 70,000 men. ¹⁶ And <when the angel stretched out his hand toward> [God sent the angel to] Jerusalem to destroy it, the LORD relented from the calamity and said to the angel who was working destruction among the people, "It is enough; now stay your hand." And the angel of the LORD was [+ standing] by the threshing floor of <Araunah> [Ornan] the Jebusite. [+ And David lifted his eyes and saw the angel of the LORD standing between earth and heaven, and in his hand a drawn sword stretched out over Jerusalem. Then David and the elders, clothed in sackcloth, fell upon their faces.] ¹⁷ Then David spoke to the LORD when

he saw the angel who was striking the people, and said, "[+ Was it not I who gave command to number the people?] Behold, I have sinned, and I have done wickedly. But these sheep, what have they done? Please let your hand be against me and against my father's house. [+But do not let the plague be on your people.]"

David builds an altar
2 Sam. 24:18-25 [1 Chron. 21:18-27]

18 <And Gad came that day to David and said to him, "Go up, raise an altar to the LORD on the threshing floor of Araunah the Jebusite."> [Now the angel of the LORD had commanded Gad to say to David that David should go up and raise an altar to the LORD on the threshing floor of Ornan the Jebusite.] **19** So David went up at Gad's word, as the LORD commanded. [+ Now Ornan was threshing wheat. He turned and saw the angel, and his four sons who were with him hid themselves. **21** As David came to Ornan,] **20** And when <Araunah> [Ornan] looked down, he saw the king and his servants coming on toward him. And Araunah went out and paid homage to the king with his face to the ground. **21** And Araunah said, "Why has my lord the king come to his servant?" David said [+ to Ornan], "To buy the threshing floor from you [+ at its full price], in order to build an altar to the LORD, that the plague may be averted from the people." **22** Then <Araunah> [Ornan] said to David, "<Let my lord the king take and offer up what seems good to him> [Take it, and let my lord the king do what seems good to him]. Here are the oxen for the burnt offering and the threshing sledges and the yokes of the oxen for the wood [+ and the wheat for a grain offering]. **23** All this, O king, Araunah gives to the king." <And Araunah said to the king, "May the LORD your God accept you."> [0] **24** But the king said to <Araunah> [Ornan], "No, but I will buy <it from you for a price> [them for the full price]. I will not [+ take for the LORD what is yours, nor] offer burnt offerings to the LORD my God that cost me nothing." <So David bought the threshing floor and the oxen for fifty shekels of silver.> [So David paid Ornan 600 shekels of gold by weight for the site.] **25** And David built there an altar to the LORD and offered burnt offerings and peace offerings [+ and called on the LORD, and the LORD answered him with fire from heaven upon the altar of burnt offering]. <So the LORD responded to the plea for the land, and the plague was averted from Israel.> [Then the LORD commanded the angel, and he put his sword back into its sheath.]

David dedicates land for the house of the Lord
1 Chron. 21:28 - 22:1

[28] At that time, when David saw that the LORD had answered him at the threshing floor of Ornan the Jebusite, he sacrificed there. [29] For the tabernacle of the LORD, which Moses had made in the wilderness, and the altar of burnt offering were at that time in the high place at Gibeon, [30] but David could not go before it to inquire of God, for he was afraid of the sword of the angel of the LORD.

22 Then David said, "Here shall be the house of the LORD God and here the altar of burnt offering for Israel."

Part Ten: Transfer of Power

972-970 B.C.; age 68-70; regnal years 38-40

David's health declines
1 Kings 1:1-4

1 Now King David was old and advanced in years. And although they covered him with clothes, he could not get warm. **2** Therefore his servants said to him, "Let a young woman be sought for my lord the king, and let her wait on the king and be in his service. Let her lie in your arms, that my lord the king may be warm." **3** So they sought for a beautiful young woman throughout all the territory of Israel, and found Abishag the Shunammite, and brought her to the king. **4** The young woman was very beautiful, and she was of service to the king and attended to him, but the king knew her not.

Adonijah proclaims himself king
1 Kings 1:5-10

5 Now Adonijah the son of Haggith exalted himself, saying, "I will be king." And he prepared for himself chariots and horsemen, and fifty men to run before him. **6** His father had never at any time displeased him by asking, "Why have you done thus and so?" He was also a very handsome man, and he was born next after Absalom. **7** He conferred with Joab the son of Zeruiah and with Abiathar the priest. And they followed Adonijah and helped him. **8** But Zadok the priest and Benaiah the son of Jehoiada and Nathan the prophet and Shimei and Rei and David's mighty men were not with Adonijah.

9 Adonijah sacrificed sheep, oxen, and fattened cattle by the Serpent's Stone, which is beside En-rogel, and he invited all his brothers, the king's sons, and all the royal officials of Judah, **10** but he did not invite Nathan the prophet or Benaiah or the mighty men or Solomon his brother.

Bathsheba and Nathan appeal to David
1 Kings 1:11-27

11 Then Nathan said to Bathsheba the mother of Solomon, "Have you not heard that Adonijah the son of Haggith has become king and David our lord does not know it? **12** Now therefore come, let me give you advice, that you may save your own life and the life of your son Solomon. **13** Go in at once to King David, and say to him, 'Did you not, my lord the king, swear to your servant, saying, "Solomon your son shall reign after me, and he shall sit on my throne"? Why then is Adonijah king?' **14** Then while you are still speaking with the king, I also will come in after you and confirm your words."

15 So Bathsheba went to the king in his chamber (now the king was very old, and Abishag the Shunammite was attending to the king). **16** Bathsheba bowed and paid homage to the king, and the king said, "What do you desire?" **17** She said to him, "My lord, you swore to your servant by the LORD your God, saying, 'Solomon your son shall reign after me, and he shall sit on my throne.' **18** And now, behold, Adonijah is king, although you, my lord the king, do not know it. **19** He has sacrificed oxen, fattened cattle, and sheep in abundance, and has invited all the sons of the king, Abiathar the priest, and Joab the commander of the army, but Solomon your servant he has not invited. **20** And now, my lord the king, the eyes of all Israel are on you, to tell them who shall sit on the throne of my lord the king after him. **21** Otherwise it will come to pass, when my lord the king sleeps with his fathers, that I and my son Solomon will be counted offenders."

22 While she was still speaking with the king, Nathan the prophet came in. **23** And they told the king, "Here is Nathan the prophet." And when he came in before the king, he bowed before the king, with his face to the ground. **24** And Nathan said, "My lord the king, have you said, 'Adonijah shall reign after me, and he shall sit on my throne'? **25** For he has gone down this day and has sacrificed oxen, fattened cattle, and sheep in abundance, and has invited all the king's sons, the commanders of the army, and Abiathar the priest. And behold, they are eating and drinking before him, and saying, 'Long live King Adonijah!' **26** But me, your servant, and Zadok the priest, and Benaiah the son of Jehoiada, and your servant Solomon he has not invited. **27** Has this thing been brought about by my lord the king and you have not told your servants who should sit on the throne of my lord the king after him?"

David has Solomon proclaimed king the first time
1 Kings 1:28-40

28 Then King David answered, "Call Bathsheba to me." So she came into the king's presence and stood before the king. **29** And the king swore, saying, "As the LORD lives, who has redeemed my soul out of every adversity, **30** as I swore to you by the LORD, the God of Israel, saying, 'Solomon your son shall reign after me, and he shall sit on my throne in my place,' even so will I do this day." **31** Then Bathsheba bowed with her face to the ground and paid homage to the king and said, "May my lord King David live forever!"

32 King David said, "Call to me Zadok the priest, Nathan the prophet, and Benaiah the son of Jehoiada." So they came before the king. **33** And the king said to them, "Take with you the servants of your lord and have Solomon my son ride on my own mule, and bring him down to Gihon. **34** And let Zadok the priest and Nathan the prophet there anoint him king over Israel. Then blow the trumpet and say, 'Long live King Solomon!' **35** You shall then come up after him, and he shall come and sit on my throne, for he shall be king in my place. And I have appointed him to be ruler over Israel and over Judah." **36** And Benaiah the son of Jehoiada answered the king, "Amen! May the LORD, the God of my lord the king, say so. **37** As the LORD has been with my lord the king, even so may he be with Solomon, and make his throne greater than the throne of my lord King David."

38 So Zadok the priest, Nathan the prophet, and Benaiah the son of Jehoiada, and the Cherethites and the Pelethites went down and had Solomon ride on King David's mule and brought him to Gihon. **39** There Zadok the priest took the horn of oil from the tent and anointed Solomon. Then they blew the trumpet, and all the people said, "Long live King Solomon!" **40** And all the people went up after him, playing on pipes, and rejoicing with great joy, so that the earth was split by their noise.

Adonijah obtains clemency
1 Kings 1:41-53

41 Adonijah and all the guests who were with him heard it as they finished feasting. And when Joab heard the sound of the trumpet, he said, "What does this uproar in the city mean?" **42** While he was still speaking, behold, Jonathan the son of Abiathar the priest came. And Adonijah said, "Come in, for you are a worthy man and bring good news." **43** Jonathan answered Adonijah, "No, for our lord King David has made Solomon king, **44** and the king has sent with him Zadok the priest, Nathan the prophet, and Benaiah the son of Jehoiada, and the Cherethites and the Pelethites. And they had him ride on the king's mule. **45** And Zadok the priest and Nathan the prophet have anointed him king at Gihon, and they have gone up from there rejoicing, so that the city is in an uproar. This is the noise that you have heard. **46** Solomon sits on the royal throne. **47** Moreover, the king's servants came to congratulate our lord King David, saying, 'May your God make the name of Solomon more famous than yours, and make his throne greater than your throne.' And the king bowed himself on the bed. **48** And the king also said, 'Blessed be the LORD, the God of Israel, who has granted someone to sit on my throne this day, my own eyes seeing it.' "

49 Then all the guests of Adonijah trembled and rose, and each went his own way. **50** And Adonijah feared Solomon. So he arose and went and took hold of the horns of the altar. **51** Then it was told Solomon, "Behold, Adonijah fears King Solomon, for behold, he has laid hold of the horns of the altar, saying, 'Let King Solomon swear to me first that he will not put his servant to death with the sword.' " **52** And Solomon said, "If he will show himself a worthy man, not one of his hairs shall fall to the earth, but if wickedness is found in him, he shall die." **53** So King Solomon sent, and they brought him down from the altar. And he came and paid homage to King Solomon, and Solomon said to him, "Go to your house."

David makes plans for building the temple
1 Chron. 22:2-5

2 David commanded to gather together the resident aliens who were in the land of Israel, and he set stonecutters to prepare dressed stones for building the house of God. **3** David also provided great quantities of iron for nails for the doors of the gates and for clamps, as well as bronze in quantities beyond weighing, **4** and cedar timbers without number, for the Sidonians and Tyrians brought great quantities of cedar to David. **5** For David said, "Solomon my son is young and inexperienced, and the house that is to be built for the LORD must be exceedingly magnificent, of fame and glory throughout all lands. I will therefore make preparation for it." So David provided materials in great quantity before his death.

David reveals his plans to Solomon
1 Chron. 22:6-19

[6] Then he called for Solomon his son and charged him to build a house for the LORD, the God of Israel. [7] David said to Solomon, "My son, I had it in my heart to build a house to the name of the LORD my God. [8] But the word of the LORD came to me, saying, 'You have shed much blood and have waged great wars. You shall not build a house to my name, because you have shed so much blood before me on the earth. [9] Behold, a son shall be born to you who shall be a man of rest. I will give him rest from all his surrounding enemies. For his name shall be Solomon, and I will give peace and quiet to Israel in his days. [10] He shall build a house for my name. He shall be my son, and I will be his father, and I will establish his royal throne in Israel forever.'

[11] "Now, my son, the LORD be with you, so that you may succeed in building the house of the LORD your God, as he has spoken concerning you. [12] Only, may the LORD grant you discretion and understanding, that when he gives you charge over Israel you may keep the law of the LORD your God. [13] Then you will prosper if you are careful to observe the statutes and the rules that the LORD commanded Moses for Israel. Be strong and courageous. Fear not; do not be dismayed. [14] With great pains I have provided for the house of the LORD 100,000 talents of gold, a million talents of silver, and bronze and iron beyond weighing, for there is so much of it; timber and stone, too, I have provided. To these you must add. [15] You have an abundance of workmen: stonecutters, masons, carpenters, and all kinds of craftsmen without number, skilled in working [16] gold, silver, bronze, and iron. Arise and work! The LORD be with you!"

[17] David also commanded all the leaders of Israel to help Solomon his son, saying, [18] "Is not the LORD your God with you? And has he not given you peace on every side? For he has delivered the inhabitants of the land into my hand, and the land is subdued before the LORD and his people. [19] Now set your mind and heart to seek the LORD your God. Arise and build the sanctuary of the LORD God, so that the ark of the covenant of the LORD and the holy vessels of God may be brought into a house built for the name of the LORD."

David organizes temple service under Solomon
1 Chron. 23:1 - 26:32

The Levites

23 When David was old and full of days, he made Solomon his son king over Israel.

² David assembled all the leaders of Israel and the priests and the Levites. ³ The Levites, thirty years old and upward, were numbered, and the total was 38,000 men. ⁴ "Twenty-four thousand of these," David said, "shall have charge of the work in the house of the LORD, 6,000 shall be officers and judges, ⁵ 4,000 gatekeepers, and 4,000 shall offer praises to the LORD with the instruments that I have made for praise." ⁶ And David organized them in divisions corresponding to the sons of Levi: Gershon, Kohath, and Merari.

⁷ The sons of Gershon were Ladan and Shimei. ⁸ The sons of Ladan: Jehiel the chief, and Zetham, and Joel, three. ⁹ The sons of Shimei: Shelomoth, Haziel, and Haran, three. These were the heads of the fathers' houses of Ladan. ¹⁰ And the sons of Shimei: Jahath, Zina, and Jeush and Beriah. These four were the sons of Shimei. ¹¹ Jahath was the chief, and Zizah the second; but Jeush and Beriah did not have many sons, therefore they became counted as a single father's house.

¹² The sons of Kohath: Amram, Izhar, Hebron, and Uzziel, four. ¹³ The sons of Amram: Aaron and Moses. Aaron was set apart to dedicate the most holy things, that he and his sons forever should make offerings before the LORD and minister to him and pronounce blessings in his name forever. ¹⁴ But the sons of Moses the man of God were named among the tribe of Levi. ¹⁵ The sons of Moses: Gershom and Eliezer. ¹⁶ The sons of Gershom: Shebuel the chief. ¹⁷ The sons of Eliezer: Rehabiah the chief. Eliezer had no other sons, but the sons of Rehabiah were very many. ¹⁸ The sons of Izhar: Shelomith the chief. ¹⁹ The sons of Hebron: Jeriah the chief, Amariah the second, Jahaziel the third, and Jekameam the fourth. ²⁰ The sons of Uzziel: Micah the chief and Isshiah the second.

²¹ The sons of Merari: Mahli and Mushi. The sons of Mahli: Eleazar and Kish. ²² Eleazar died having no sons, but only daughters; their kinsmen,

the sons of Kish, married them. [23] The sons of Mushi: Mahli, Eder, and Jeremoth, three.

[24] These were the sons of Levi by their fathers' houses, the heads of fathers' houses as they were listed according to the number of the names of the individuals from twenty years old and upward who were to do the work for the service of the house of the LORD. [25] For David said, "The LORD, the God of Israel, has given rest to his people, and he dwells in Jerusalem forever. [26] And so the Levites no longer need to carry the tabernacle or any of the things for its service." [27] For by the last words of David the sons of Levi were numbered from twenty years old and upward. [28] For their duty was to assist the sons of Aaron for the service of the house of the LORD, having the care of the courts and the chambers, the cleansing of all that is holy, and any work for the service of the house of God. [29] Their duty was also to assist with the showbread, the flour for the grain offering, the wafers of unleavened bread, the baked offering, the offering mixed with oil, and all measures of quantity or size. [30] And they were to stand every morning, thanking and praising the LORD, and likewise at evening, [31] and whenever burnt offerings were offered to the LORD on Sabbaths, new moons, and feast days, according to the number required of them, regularly before the LORD. [32] Thus they were to keep charge of the tent of meeting and the sanctuary, and to attend the sons of Aaron, their brothers, for the service of the house of the LORD.

The Priests

24 The divisions of the sons of Aaron were these. The sons of Aaron: Nadab, Abihu, Eleazar, and Ithamar. [2] But Nadab and Abihu died before their father and had no children, so Eleazar and Ithamar became the priests. [3] With the help of Zadok of the sons of Eleazar, and Ahimelech of the sons of Ithamar, David organized them according to the appointed duties in their service. [4] Since more chief men were found among the sons of Eleazar than among the sons of Ithamar, they organized them under sixteen heads of fathers' houses of the sons of Eleazar, and eight of the sons of Ithamar. [5] They divided them by lot, all alike, for there were sacred officers and officers of God among both the sons of Eleazar and the sons of Ithamar. [6] And the scribe Shemaiah, the son of Nethanel, a Levite, recorded them in the presence of the king and the princes and Zadok the priest and Ahimelech the son of Abiathar and the heads of the fathers' houses of the priests and of the Levites, one father's house being chosen for Eleazar and one chosen for Ithamar.

[7] The first lot fell to Jehoiarib, the second to Jedaiah, [8] the third to Harim, the fourth to Seorim, [9] the fifth to Malchijah, the sixth to Mijamin, [10] the seventh to Hakkoz, the eighth to Abijah, [11] the ninth to Jeshua, the tenth to Shecaniah, [12] the eleventh to Eliashib, the twelfth to Jakim, [13] the thirteenth to Huppah, the fourteenth to Jeshebeab, [14] the fifteenth to Bilgah, the sixteenth to Immer, [15] the seventeenth to Hezir, the eighteenth to Happizzez, [16] the nineteenth to Pethahiah, the twentieth to Jehezkel, [17] the twenty-first to Jachin, the twenty-second to Gamul, [18] the twenty-third to Delaiah, the twenty-fourth to Maaziah. [19] These had as their appointed duty in their service to come into the house of the LORD according to the procedure established for them by Aaron their father, as the LORD God of Israel had commanded him.

[20] And of the rest of the sons of Levi: of the sons of Amram, Shubael; of the sons of Shubael, Jehdeiah. [21] Of Rehabiah: of the sons of Rehabiah, Isshiah the chief. [22] Of the Izharites, Shelomoth; of the sons of Shelomoth, Jahath. [23] The sons of Hebron: Jeriah the chief, Amariah the second, Jahaziel the third, Jekameam the fourth. [24] The sons of Uzziel, Micah; of the sons of Micah, Shamir. [25] The brother of Micah, Isshiah; of the sons of Isshiah, Zechariah. [26] The sons of Merari: Mahli and Mushi. The sons of Jaaziah: Beno. [27] The sons of Merari: of Jaaziah, Beno, Shoham, Zaccur, and Ibri. [28] Of Mahli: Eleazar, who had no sons. [29] Of Kish, the sons of Kish: Jerahmeel. [30] The sons of Mushi: Mahli, Eder, and Jerimoth. These were the sons of the Levites according to their fathers' houses. [31] These also, the head of each father's house and his younger brother alike, cast lots, just as their brothers the sons of Aaron, in the presence of King David, Zadok, Ahimelech, and the heads of fathers' houses of the priests and of the Levites.

The Musicians

25 David and the chiefs of the service also set apart for the service the sons of Asaph, and of Heman, and of Jeduthun, who prophesied with lyres, with harps, and with cymbals. The list of those who did the work and of their duties was: [2] Of the sons of Asaph: Zaccur, Joseph, Nethaniah, and Asharelah, sons of Asaph, under the direction of Asaph, who prophesied under the direction of the king. [3] Of Jeduthun, the sons of Jeduthun: Gedaliah, Zeri, Jeshaiah, Shimei, Hashabiah, and Mattithiah, six, under the direction of their father Jeduthun, who prophesied with the lyre in thanksgiving and praise to the LORD. [4] Of Heman, the sons of Heman: Bukkiah, Mattaniah, Uzziel, Shebuel and Jerimoth, Hananiah,

Hanani, Eliathah, Giddalti, and Romamti-ezer, Joshbekashah, Mallothi, Hothir, Mahazioth. [5] All these were the sons of Heman the king's seer, according to the promise of God to exalt him, for God had given Heman fourteen sons and three daughters. [6] They were all under the direction of their father in the music in the house of the LORD with cymbals, harps, and lyres for the service of the house of God. Asaph, Jeduthun, and Heman were under the order of the king. [7] The number of them along with their brothers, who were trained in singing to the LORD, all who were skillful, was 288. [8] And they cast lots for their duties, small and great, teacher and pupil alike.

[9] The first lot fell for Asaph to Joseph; the second to Gedaliah, to him and his brothers and his sons, twelve; [10] the third to Zaccur, his sons and his brothers, twelve; [11] the fourth to Izri, his sons and his brothers, twelve; [12] the fifth to Nethaniah, his sons and his brothers, twelve; [13] the sixth to Bukkiah, his sons and his brothers, twelve; [14] the seventh to Jesharelah, his sons and his brothers, twelve; [15] the eighth to Jeshaiah, his sons and his brothers, twelve; [16] the ninth to Mattaniah, his sons and his brothers, twelve; [17] the tenth to Shimei, his sons and his brothers, twelve; [18] the eleventh to Azarel, his sons and his brothers, twelve; [19] the twelfth to Hashabiah, his sons and his brothers, twelve; [20] to the thirteenth, Shubael, his sons and his brothers, twelve; [21] to the fourteenth, Mattithiah, his sons and his brothers, twelve; [22] to the fifteenth, to Jeremoth, his sons and his brothers, twelve; [23] to the sixteenth, to Hananiah, his sons and his brothers, twelve; [24] to the seventeenth, to Joshbekashah, his sons and his brothers, twelve; [25] to the eighteenth, to Hanani, his sons and his brothers, twelve; [26] to the nineteenth, to Mallothi, his sons and his brothers, twelve; [27] to the twentieth, to Eliathah, his sons and his brothers, twelve; [28] to the twenty-first, to Hothir, his sons and his brothers, twelve; [29] to the twenty-second, to Giddalti, his sons and his brothers, twelve; [30] to the twenty-third, to Mahazioth, his sons and his brothers, twelve; [31] to the twenty-fourth, to Romamti-ezer, his sons and his brothers, twelve.

The Gatekeepers

26 As for the divisions of the gatekeepers: of the Korahites, Meshelemiah the son of Kore, of the sons of Asaph. [2] And Meshelemiah had sons: Zechariah the firstborn, Jediael the second, Zebadiah the third, Jathniel the fourth, [3] Elam the fifth, Jehohanan the sixth, Eliehoenai the seventh. ⁴ And Obed-edom had sons: Shemaiah the firstborn, Jehozabad the second, Joah the third, Sachar the fourth, Nethanel the fifth, ⁵ Ammiel the sixth, Issachar the seventh, Peullethai the eighth, for God blessed him. ⁶ Also to his son Shemaiah were sons born who were rulers in their fathers' houses, for they were men of great ability. ⁷ The sons of Shemaiah: Othni, Rephael, Obed and Elzabad, whose brothers were able men, Elihu and Semachiah. ⁸ All these were of the sons of Obed-edom with their sons and brothers, able men qualified for the service; sixty-two of Obed-edom. ⁹ And Meshelemiah had sons and brothers, able men, eighteen. ¹⁰ And Hosah, of the sons of Merari, had sons: Shimri the chief (for though he was not the firstborn, his father made him chief), ¹¹ Hilkiah the second, Tebaliah the third, Zechariah the fourth: all the sons and brothers of Hosah were thirteen.

¹² These divisions of the gatekeepers, corresponding to their chief men, had duties, just as their brothers did, ministering in the house of the LORD. ¹³ And they cast lots by fathers' houses, small and great alike, for their gates. ¹⁴ The lot for the east fell to Shelemiah. They cast lots also for his son Zechariah, a shrewd counselor, and his lot came out for the north. ¹⁵ Obed-edom's came out for the south, and to his sons was allotted the gatehouse. ¹⁶ For Shuppim and Hosah it came out for the west, at the gate of Shallecheth on the road that goes up. Watch corresponded to watch. ¹⁷ On the east there were six each day, on the north four each day, on the south four each day, as well as two and two at the gatehouse. ¹⁸ And for the colonnade on the west there were four at the road and two at the colonnade. ¹⁹ These were the divisions of the gatekeepers among the Korahites and the sons of Merari.

Treasurers

²⁰ And of the Levites, Ahijah had charge of the treasuries of the house of God and the treasuries of the dedicated gifts. ²¹ The sons of Ladan, the sons of the Gershonites belonging to Ladan, the heads of the fathers' houses belonging to Ladan the Gershonite: Jehieli.

²² The sons of Jehieli, Zetham, and Joel his brother, were in charge of the treasuries of the house of the LORD. ²³ Of the Amramites, the Izharites, the Hebronites, and the Uzzielites— ²⁴ and Shebuel the son of Gershom, son of Moses, was chief officer in charge of the treasuries. ²⁵ His brothers: from Eliezer were his son Rehabiah, and his son Jeshaiah, and his son Joram, and his son Zichri, and his son Shelomoth. ²⁶ This Shelomoth and

his brothers were in charge of all the treasuries of the dedicated gifts that David the king and the heads of the fathers' houses and the officers of the thousands and the hundreds and the commanders of the army had dedicated. ²⁷ From spoil won in battles they dedicated gifts for the maintenance of the house of the LORD. ²⁸ Also all that Samuel the seer and Saul the son of Kish and Abner the son of Ner and Joab the son of Zeruiah had dedicated—all dedicated gifts were in the care of Shelomoth and his brothers.

Other Officials

²⁹ Of the Izharites, Chenaniah and his sons were appointed to external duties for Israel, as officers and judges. ³⁰ Of the Hebronites, Hashabiah and his brothers, 1,700 men of ability, had the oversight of Israel westward of the Jordan for all the work of the LORD and for the service of the king. ³¹ Of the Hebronites, Jerijah was chief of the Hebronites of whatever genealogy or fathers' houses. (In the fortieth year of David's reign search was made and men of great ability among them were found at Jazer in Gilead.) ³² King David appointed him and his brothers, 2,700 men of ability, heads of fathers' houses, to have the oversight of the Reubenites, the Gadites and the half-tribe of the Manassites for everything pertaining to God and for the affairs of the king.

David transfers the army, government, and royal property to Solomon
1 Chron. 27:1-34

Military Divisions

27 This is the number of the people of Israel, the heads of fathers' houses, the commanders of thousands and hundreds, and their officers who served the king in all matters concerning the divisions that came and went, month after month throughout the year, each division numbering 24,000:

² Jashobeam the son of Zabdiel was in charge of the first division in the first month; in his division were 24,000. ³ He was a descendant of Perez and was chief of all the commanders. He served for the first month. ⁴ Dodai the Ahohite was in charge of the division of the second month; in his division were 24,000. ⁵ The third commander, for the third month, was Benaiah, the son of Jehoiada the chief priest; in his division were 24,000.

[6] This is the Benaiah who was a mighty man of the thirty and in command of the thirty; Ammizabad his son was in charge of his division. [7] Asahel the brother of Joab was fourth, for the fourth month, and his son Zebadiah after him; in his division were 24,000. [8] The fifth commander, for the fifth month, was Shamhuth the Izrahite; in his division were 24,000. [9] Sixth, for the sixth month, was Ira, the son of Ikkesh the Tekoite; in his division were 24,000. [10] Seventh, for the seventh month, was Helez the Pelonite, of the sons of Ephraim; in his division were 24,000. [11] Eighth, for the eighth month, was Sibbecai the Hushathite, of the Zerahites; in his division were 24,000. [12] Ninth, for the ninth month, was Abiezer of Anathoth, a Benjaminite; in his division were 24,000. [13] Tenth, for the tenth month, was Maharai of Netophah, of the Zerahites; in his division were 24,000. [14] Eleventh, for the eleventh month, was Benaiah of Pirathon, of the sons of Ephraim; in his division were 24,000. [15] Twelfth, for the twelfth month, was Heldai the Netophathite, of Othniel; in his division were 24,000.

Leaders of Tribes

[16] Over the tribes of Israel, for the Reubenites, Eliezer the son of Zichri was chief officer; for the Simeonites, Shephatiah the son of Maacah; [17] for Levi, Hashabiah the son of Kemuel; for Aaron, Zadok; [18] for Judah, Elihu, one of David's brothers; for Issachar, Omri the son of Michael; [19] for Zebulun, Ishmaiah the son of Obadiah; for Naphtali, Jeremoth the son of Azriel; [20] for the Ephraimites, Hoshea the son of Azaziah; for the half-tribe of Manasseh, Joel the son of Pedaiah; [21] for the half-tribe of Manasseh in Gilead, Iddo the son of Zechariah; for Benjamin, Jaasiel the son of Abner; [22] for Dan, Azarel the son of Jeroham. These were the leaders of the tribes of Israel. [23] David did not count those below twenty years of age, for the LORD had promised to make Israel as many as the stars of heaven. [24] Joab the son of Zeruiah began to count, but did not finish. Yet wrath came upon Israel for this, and the number was not entered in the chronicles of King David.

[25] Over the king's treasuries was Azmaveth the son of Adiel; and over the treasuries in the country, in the cities, in the villages, and in the towers, was Jonathan the son of Uzziah; [26] and over those who did the work of the field for tilling the soil was Ezri the son of Chelub; [27] and over the vineyards was Shimei the Ramathite; and over the produce of the vineyards for the wine cellars was Zabdi the Shiphmite. [28] Over the olive and sycamore trees in the Shephelah was Baal-hanan the Gederite; and

over the stores of oil was Joash. [29] Over the herds that pastured in Sharon was Shitrai the Sharonite; over the herds in the valleys was Shaphat the son of Adlai. [30] Over the camels was Obil the Ishmaelite; and over the donkeys was Jehdeiah the Meronothite. Over the flocks was Jaziz the Hagrite. [31] All these were stewards of King David's property.

[32] Jonathan, David's uncle, was a counselor, being a man of understanding and a scribe. He and Jehiel the son of Hachmoni attended the king's sons. [33] Ahithophel was the king's counselor, and Hushai the Archite was the king's friend. [34] Ahithophel was succeeded by Jehoiada the son of Benaiah, and Abiathar. Joab was commander of the king's army.

David commits the plans for the temple to Israel and Solomon
1 Chron. 28:1-21

28 David assembled at Jerusalem all the officials of Israel, the officials of the tribes, the officers of the divisions that served the king, the commanders of thousands, the commanders of hundreds, the stewards of all the property and livestock of the king and his sons, together with the palace officials, the mighty men and all the seasoned warriors. [2] Then King David rose to his feet and said: "Hear me, my brothers and my people. I had it in my heart to build a house of rest for the ark of the covenant of the LORD and for the footstool of our God, and I made preparations for building. [3] But God said to me, 'You may not build a house for my name, for you are a man of war and have shed blood.' [4] Yet the LORD God of Israel chose me from all my father's house to be king over Israel forever. For he chose Judah as leader, and in the house of Judah my father's house, and among my father's sons he took pleasure in me to make me king over all Israel. [5] And of all my sons (for the LORD has given me many sons) he has chosen Solomon my son to sit on the throne of the kingdom of the LORD over Israel. [6] He said to me, 'It is Solomon your son who shall build my house and my courts, for I have chosen him to be my son, and I will be his father. [7] I will establish his kingdom forever if he continues strong in keeping my commandments and my rules, as he is today.' [8] Now therefore in the sight of all Israel, the assembly of the LORD, and in the hearing of our God, observe and seek out all the commandments of the LORD your God, that you may possess this good land and leave it for an inheritance to your children after you forever.

[9] "And you, Solomon my son, know the God of your father and serve him with a whole heart and with a willing mind, for the LORD searches all hearts and understands every plan and thought. If you seek him, he will be found by you, but if you forsake him, he will cast you off forever. [10] Be careful now, for the LORD has chosen you to build a house for the sanctuary; be strong and do it."

[11] Then David gave Solomon his son the plan of the vestibule of the temple, and of its houses, its treasuries, its upper rooms, and its inner chambers, and of the room for the mercy seat; [12] and the plan of all that he had in mind for the courts of the house of the LORD, all the surrounding chambers, the treasuries of the house of God, and the treasuries for dedicated gifts; [13] for the divisions of the priests and of the Levites, and all the work of the service in the house of the LORD; for all the vessels for the service in the house of the LORD, [14] the weight of gold for all golden vessels for each service, the weight of silver vessels for each service, [15] the weight of the golden lampstands and their lamps, the weight of gold for each lampstand and its lamps, the weight of silver for a lampstand and its lamps, according to the use of each lampstand in the service, [16] the weight of gold for each table for the showbread, the silver for the silver tables, [17] and pure gold for the forks, the basins and the cups; for the golden bowls and the weight of each; for the silver bowls and the weight of each; [18] for the altar of incense made of refined gold, and its weight; also his plan for the golden chariot of the cherubim that spread their wings and covered the ark of the covenant of the LORD. [19] "All this he made clear to me in writing from the hand of the LORD, all the work to be done according to the plan."

[20] Then David said to Solomon his son, "Be strong and courageous and do it. Do not be afraid and do not be dismayed, for the LORD God, even my God, is with you. He will not leave you or forsake you, until all the work for the service of the house of the LORD is finished. [21] And behold the divisions of the priests and the Levites for all the service of the house of God; and with you in all the work will be every willing man who has skill for any kind of service; also the officers and all the people will be wholly at your command."

David collects and dedicates gifts for the temple
1 Chron. 29:1-20

29 And David the king said to all the assembly, "Solomon my son, whom alone God has chosen, is young and inexperienced, and the work is great, for the palace will not be for man but for the LORD God. **²** So I have provided for the house of my God, so far as I was able, the gold for the things of gold, the silver for the things of silver, and the bronze for the things of bronze, the iron for the things of iron, and wood for the things of wood, besides great quantities of onyx and stones for setting, antimony, colored stones, all sorts of precious stones and marble. **³** Moreover, in addition to all that I have provided for the holy house, I have a treasure of my own of gold and silver, and because of my devotion to the house of my God I give it to the house of my God: **⁴** 3,000 talents of gold, of the gold of Ophir, and 7,000 talents of refined silver, for overlaying the walls of the house, **⁵** and for all the work to be done by craftsmen, gold for the things of gold and silver for the things of silver. Who then will offer willingly, consecrating himself today to the LORD?"

⁶ Then the leaders of fathers' houses made their freewill offerings, as did also the leaders of the tribes, the commanders of thousands and of hundreds, and the officers over the king's work. **⁷** They gave for the service of the house of God 5,000 talents and 10,000 darics of gold, 10,000 talents of silver, 18,000 talents of bronze and 100,000 talents of iron. **⁸** And whoever had precious stones gave them to the treasury of the house of the LORD, in the care of Jehiel the Gershonite. **⁹** Then the people rejoiced because they had given willingly, for with a whole heart they had offered freely to the LORD. David the king also rejoiced greatly.

¹⁰ Therefore David blessed the LORD in the presence of all the assembly. And David said: "Blessed are you, O LORD, the God of Israel our father, forever and ever. **¹¹** Yours, O LORD, is the greatness and the power and the glory and the victory and the majesty, for all that is in the heavens and in the earth is yours. Yours is the kingdom, O LORD, and you are exalted as head above all. **¹²** Both riches and honor come from you, and you rule over all. In your hand are power and might, and in your hand it is to make great and to give strength to all. **¹³** And now we thank you, our God, and praise your glorious name.

¹⁴ "But who am I, and what is my people, that we should be able thus to offer willingly? For all things come from you, and of your own have we given you. **15** For we are strangers before you and sojourners, as all our fathers were. Our days on the earth are like a shadow, and there is no abiding. **16** O LORD our God, all this abundance that we have provided for building you a house for your holy name comes from your hand and is all your own. **17** I know, my God, that you test the heart and have pleasure in uprightness. In the uprightness of my heart I have freely offered all these things, and now I have seen your people, who are present here, offering freely and joyously to you. **18** O LORD, the God of Abraham, Isaac, and Israel, our fathers, keep forever such purposes and thoughts in the hearts of your people, and direct their hearts toward you. **19** Grant to Solomon my son a whole heart that he may keep your commandments, your testimonies, and your statutes, performing all, and that he may build the palace for which I have made provision."

20 Then David said to all the assembly, "Bless the LORD your God." And all the assembly blessed the LORD, the God of their fathers, and bowed their heads and paid homage to the LORD and to the king.

David has Solomon proclaimed king a second time
1 Chron. 29:21-25

21 And they offered sacrifices to the LORD, and on the next day offered burnt offerings to the LORD, 1,000 bulls, 1,000 rams, and 1,000 lambs, with their drink offerings, and sacrifices in abundance for all Israel. **22** And they ate and drank before the LORD on that day with great gladness.

And they made Solomon the son of David king the second time, and they anointed him as prince for the LORD, and Zadok as priest.

23 Then Solomon sat on the throne of the LORD as king in place of David his father. And he prospered, and all Israel obeyed him. **24** All the leaders and the mighty men, and also all the sons of King David, pledged their allegiance to King Solomon. **25** And the LORD made Solomon very great in the sight of all Israel and bestowed on him such royal majesty as had not been on any king before him in Israel.

David advises Solomon privately
1 Kings 2:1-9

2 When David's time to die drew near, he commanded Solomon his son, saying, **2** "I am about to go the way of all the earth. Be strong, and show yourself a man, ³ and keep the charge of the LORD your God, walking in his ways and keeping his statutes, his commandments, his rules, and his testimonies, as it is written in the Law of Moses, that you may prosper in all that you do and wherever you turn, ⁴ that the LORD may establish his word that he spoke concerning me, saying, 'If your sons pay close attention to their way, to walk before me in faithfulness with all their heart and with all their soul, you shall not lack a man on the throne of Israel.'

⁵ "Moreover, you also know what Joab the son of Zeruiah did to me, how he dealt with the two commanders of the armies of Israel, Abner the son of Ner, and Amasa the son of Jether, whom he killed, avenging in time of peace for blood that had been shed in war, and putting the blood of war on the belt around his waist and on the sandals on his feet. ⁶ Act therefore according to your wisdom, but do not let his gray head go down to Sheol in peace. ⁷ But deal loyally with the sons of Barzillai the Gileadite, and let them be among those who eat at your table, for with such loyalty they met me when I fled from Absalom your brother. ⁸ And there is also with you Shimei the son of Gera, the Benjaminite from Bahurim, who cursed me with a grievous curse on the day when I went to Mahanaim. But when he came down to meet me at the Jordan, I swore to him by the LORD, saying, 'I will not put you to death with the sword.' ⁹ Now therefore do not hold him guiltless, for you are a wise man. You will know what you ought to do to him, and you shall bring his gray head down with blood to Sheol."

David dies
1 Kings 2:10-12 [1 Chron. 29:26-30]

¹⁰ <Then David slept with his fathers and was buried in the city of David> [²⁶ Thus David the son of Jesse reigned over all Israel]. ¹¹ And the time that David reigned over Israel was forty years. He reigned seven years in Hebron and thirty-three years in Jerusalem. [+ ²⁸ Then he died at a good age, full of days, riches, and honor.] ¹² <So Solomon sat on the throne of David his father> [And Solomon his son reigned in his place], and his kingdom was firmly established. [+ ²⁹ Now the acts of King David, from first to last, are written in the Chronicles of Samuel the seer, and in the Chronicles of Nathan the prophet, and in the Chronicles of Gad the seer, ³⁰ with accounts of all his rule and his might and of the circumstances that came upon him and upon Israel and upon all the kingdoms of the countries.]

The last words of David
2 Sam. 23:1-7

23 Now these are the last words of David:

> The oracle of David, the son of Jesse,
>> the oracle of the man who was raised on high,
> the anointed of the God of Jacob,
>> the sweet psalmist of Israel:
> 2 "The Spirit of the LORD speaks by me;
>> his word is on my tongue.
> 3 The God of Israel has spoken;
>> the Rock of Israel has said to me:
> When one rules justly over men,
>> ruling in the fear of God,
> 4 he dawns on them like the morning light,
>> like the sun shining forth on a cloudless morning,
>> like rain that makes grass to sprout from the earth.
> 5 "For does not my house stand so with God?
>> For he has made with me an everlasting covenant,
>> ordered in all things and secure.
> For will he not cause to prosper
>> all my help and my desire?
> 6 But worthless men are all like thorns that are thrown
>>> away,
>> for they cannot be taken with the hand;
> 7 but the man who touches them
>> arms himself with iron and the shaft of a spear,
>> and they are utterly consumed with fire."

Reflections

Part One: Saul's Court

1023–1016 B.C.; age 17-24

Samuel anoints David to replace Saul
1 Sam. 16:1-13

APPEARANCES

Have you ever seen something and immediately known that you had to have it? Of course you have, but there is a problem with that. Appearances can be deceiving. Or as the old proverb says, "You can't judge a book by its cover."

God is different than us. He can see what is inside the book. The difference between how we see and how God sees is emphasized in this story about the anointing of David.

NEW KING WANTED. Saul looked like a king. He stood a head taller than his fellow Israelites. The Israelites were looking for a king like the kings of other nations, and when they saw him, they were impressed (1 Sam. 10:23-24). They shouted, "Long live the king!" Sometime later, however, God became dissatisfied with Saul because he did not have an obedient heart. Accordingly, the Lord "sought out a man after his own heart" to be ruler of God's people (1 Sam. 13:14). He tore the kingdom from Saul and gave it to a neighbor better than him (1 Sam. 15:28). Thus, the story of David begins with God sending Samuel to anoint a man whose heart was more pleasing to him than Saul's heart.

APPEARANCE MISLEADING. When Samuel saw Eliab, Jesse's oldest son, he was impressed with what he saw, but God had rejected Eliab because He could see his heart as well as his physical appearance. In fact, God had not chosen any of the seven sons of Jesse at the sacrifice. When Samuel asked if there was another son, Jesse replied that there remained one, the youngest, who was tending his sheep while the rest of the family attended the feast. The word "youngest" might also mean "smallest" or "least important" (BDB, qāṭōn, pp. 881-882). So unlike Saul or even Eliab,

David did not appear kingly or important. But God, who sees the heart, had chosen him.

INNER BEAUTY. At Samuel's request, Jesse sent for David. Soon David arrived at the feast, but though God had chosen David because of what He saw in David's heart, David is introduced to us with a description of his appearance: "He was ruddy and had beautiful eyes and was handsome" (v. 12). The NKJV translates "handsome" as "good looking." Somehow we are pleased that David was good looking. Appearance is not everything, but it is important, especially that appearance which comes from a beautiful heart and godly character. The beauty of Jesus, the one man fully after God's own heart, came from the heart rather than from His physical appearance. Isa. 53:2 says,

> He had no form or majesty that we should look at him,
> and no beauty that we should desire him.

ANOINTED. God chose this handsome shepherd whose heart was also tender toward God, and commanded Samuel to anoint him king with the sacred oil from the Tent of Meeting. Psalm 89:20 records the event from God's viewpoint:

> I have found David, my servant;
> with my holy oil I have anointed him.

God originally limited the use of the holy oil to the anointing of priests and furnishings in the Tent of Meeting. This anointing signified not only selection but also consecration to serving the Lord (Ex. 30:22-33). However, in the days of Eli, the priests had made a mockery of their consecration to the Lord and failed to lead Israel properly.

Because the priests failed in their duty to God, God decided to assign a part of their role to another whom He would also anoint (1 Sam. 2:35; see Briggs, 1886, pp. 122-23). Thus, it happened that kings as well as priests were anointed and consecrated to serving God. God selected David to be king because He saw that David wished to serve Him with his whole heart. Centuries later, God would anoint David's Son, whose heart was perfect before Him, as both priest and king.

CHOSEN AND ANOINTED. Like David, Christians are also chosen of God. After he cleansed our hearts, he consecrated us to his work. When people see us, they may not be impressed with our physical appearance, but they should see an inner beauty that makes our face shine with God's love, joy, and peace.

Goliath insults the Israelite army
1 Sam. 17:1-11

THE BULLY

Brats annoy us, but bullies intimidate us with their greater size and superior strength.

THE BULLY. Goliath was a bully. He stood more than nine feet tall. His reputation as a champion was intimidating. He wore bronze armor weighing 125 pounds and carried the heaviest weapons the Israelites had ever seen. He stood daily between the Philistine and Israelite armies in the Valley of Elah, about 15 miles west of Bethlehem, where he confronted the Israelites and insulted them. Saul and the Israelites were intimidated.

A SHADOW OF HIS FORMER SELF. At an earlier time, Saul would not have been intimidated. At the beginning of his reign, Nahash, the Ammonite king, determined to insult the Israelites of Jabesh Gilead by gouging out their right eyes. When Saul heard it, God's Spirit had come mightily upon him. He called Israel to battle and led them in a stirring surprise attack on the Ammonites (1 Sam. 11:1-11). But now God's Spirit had departed from Saul. Though he was a head taller than the other Israelite soldiers, he did not accept Goliath's challenge. He was as intimidated as his soldiers.

NEED FOR A LEADER. Saul's leadership abilities had forsaken him. The Israelites were leaderless; they were like sheep without a shepherd. Little did they know that their shepherd was about to appear. The shepherd God had chosen would lead his people; they would hear his voice and follow him (2 Sam. 5:2). Similarly, when God's people were leaderless in the first century and scattered like sheep without a shepherd (Matt. 9:36), the Good Shepherd appeared. Even today, his sheep know his voice and follow him (John 10:4).

David enters the Israelite camp
1 Sam. 17:12-31

BIG BROTHER

Big brothers often despise little brothers and accuse them of neglecting their insignificant responsibilities, especially if they aspire to something that encroaches on the older brother's territory. God is not like a big brother. He operates on the principle that if a person is faithful in little things, he will be faithful in bigger things (see the parable of the talents in Matt. 25:21).

RESPONSIBLE. Actually David was a faithful servant in ordinary, even lowly, duties. He shepherded his father's sheep responsibly, leaving them in the care of another shepherd when called to run an errand for Jesse. Furthermore, he dutifully delivered the food to the quartermaster before entering the camp to find his brothers.

BUT DESPISED. Despite David's responsible behavior, his oldest brother, Eliab, thought he was irresponsible. He said, "Why have you come down? And with whom have you left those few sheep in the wilderness? I know your presumption and the evil of your heart, for you have come down to see the battle" (1 Sam. 17:28). Obviously, he thought David had been irresponsible in a trivial duty so that he could be an idle spectator of real men engaged in the grave responsibilities of war.

THE SHEPHERD OF ISRAEL. Eliab's reaction to David reminds us that the brothers of Jesus did not believe in Him when he began his ministry (John 7:5). They could not comprehend that He was actually obeying His Father just as David had obeyed Jesse. And like the brothers of Jesus, Eliab's perception was quite short-sighted. He failed to recognize that those who are faithful in little things will be faithful in big things (Luke 16:10). Qualities that make one capable of fulfilling small responsibilities are the very same qualities needed to fulfill big responsibilities. But God knew that a good shepherd like David would also make a good king. Notice the words of Psalm 78:70-72.

> He chose David his servant
>   and took him from the sheepfolds;
> from following the nursing ewes he brought him
>   to shepherd Jacob his people,
>   Israel his inheritance.

With upright heart he shepherded them
and guided them with his skillful hand.

A FAITHFUL KING.   As a faithful king, David prefigured his descendant, the Messiah, who was faithful in all things. Isaiah describes the Messiah as one who wore faithfulness as a belt (Isa. 11:5), and John says that his name is "Faithful and True" (Rev. 19:11). We who follow him must also be faithful (1 Cor. 4:2) and keep his words to the end. Then he will give us authority over the nations just as he received authority from his Father (Rev. 2:26-27), and he will permit us to sit with him on his throne just as he sat on his Father's throne (Rev. 3:21-22).

David prepares for battle
1 Sam. 17:32-40

THE EMPEROR'S CLOTHES

Mark Twain once said, "Clothes make the man." Certainly, a man dressed in a three-piece suit will act differently than one dressed like a clown. On the other hand, dressing a drunken bum in a three-piece suit does not make him a businessman any more than a lion's body made the lion a courageous beast in The Wizard of Oz.

ARMOR WITHOUT BRAVERY. Saul's royal armor did not give him a kingly heart. David could see, as everyone could, that he was as terrified of Goliath as any of his soldiers. But David wisely did not mention Saul's fear when he spoke to him saying, "Let no man's heart fail because of him. Your servant will go and fight with this Philistine" (1 Sam. 17:32).

BRAVERY WITHOUT ARMOR. Although impressed with David's bravery, Saul obviously thought David was too young. Saul reminded David that he was merely a youth (probably younger than 20 years; see Num. 1:3; 26:2) and that he was not experienced in the ways of war. Ignoring the statement about his youth, David argued that as a shepherd he was experienced in battle having fought with vicious lions and bears while protecting his father's flocks.   Still, Saul appeared to be unconvinced. When Saul said nothing in response to his exploits against the wild beasts, David delivered the final thrust of his argument: God had delivered him from the mouths of the lion and the bear, and He would deliver him from Goliath, too.

ARMOR OFFERED. Saul could not argue with David without appearing impious, but he still thought that David was poorly armed for the battle. In his own heart he still relied more on the "arm of flesh" than on the "arm of the Lord," so he clothed David in his own armor. After doing so, Saul demonstrated how much he had become a king like the kings of the nations. All those kings relied on superior armor and weapons. Likewise, Saul naively thought that armor and weapons would make a victorious soldier, but he was wrong. God did not want a person who relied on them to be the king.

ARMOR REJECTED. When David rejected Saul's armor, he was not naïve. He simply knew that the armor and sword did not suit his skills or experience. The armor would limit his ability to use the weapon God had trained him to use, the shepherd's sling. He undoubtedly knew that in skilled hands the sling could be an effective weapon (see Judges 20:16) even if it was outdated and unconventional. But more importantly, David was not going to be a king who relied on the "arm of flesh" or on armor, weapons, numbers, and physical strength. By rejecting Saul's armor, he rejected the kind of king Saul had become (Bergen, 1996, p. 194). Unlike Saul, he would rely on the God in whom he had placed his faith. He understood that if God fought for Israel, Israel had no need to become like the nations. Accordingly, he removed Saul's armor, chose five stones for his sling, and went out to meet the blasphemous giant as he carried his shepherd's staff and the invisible shield of faith.

David kills Goliath
1 Sam. 17:41-54

TRASH TALK

On Sunday, in the final seconds of the first game of the 1997 NBA Finals, Karl "The Mailman" Malone was shooting free throws at the line with the game tied. Scotty Pippin taunted him, "The mailman don't deliver on Sundays." Of course, Pippin was trying to rattle Malone so he would miss. Malone did miss both free throws, and the Bulls won the game.

INSULT FOR INSULT. Similarly, the fight between David and Goliath began with psychological sparring. Goliath thought that Israel was insulting him by sending a mere youth to fight against him. He said (v. 43), "Am I a dog, that you come to me with sticks?" Goliath's reference to "sticks" may show that he saw the shepherd's staff David carried but failed to see the sling (see v. 40). Then after cursing David by his gods, he tried to intimidate David by promising to leave his flesh on the field of battle for the vultures and animals that feed on carrion. David's reply was, in part, similar: "I will strike you down and cut off your head. And I will give the dead bodies of the host of the Philistines this day to the birds of the air and to the wild beasts of the earth…" (1 Sam. 17:46).

DAVID'S FAITH. Although David's words surely baited Goliath and were perhaps similar to the "trash talking" that occurs between athletes today, there was also a difference. Unlike Goliath who cursed David by his gods, David simply said that he came in the name of the LORD Almighty whom Goliath had defied. The battle then became not one between Goliath and David but between the gods of the Philistines and the God of the armies of Israel.

GOLIATH'S ARROGANCE. While Goliath tried to intimidate David, he himself approached the fight with overconfidence. He considered himself a seasoned warrior facing an inexperienced youth. He carried a sword, a spear, and a javelin, and he wore protective armor while his opponent was dressed in a shepherd's garment and carried a staff. Perhaps his confidence caused him to overlook the sling that David carried in his other hand. If so, pride led to his defeat. Prov. 16:18 says, "Pride goes before destruction, and a haughty spirit before a fall." Instead of mocking David, he would have done well to heed Ahab's advice to Ben-Hadad: "Let not him who straps on his armor boast himself as he who takes it off" (1 Kings 20:11).

GOD EXALTED. David's son Solomon later observed that "the race is not to the swift, nor the battle to the strong, nor bread to the wise, nor riches to the intelligent, nor favor to those with knowledge, but time and chance happen to them all" (Ecc. 9:11). Solomon was right in that David's victory over Goliath was not due to strength, wisdom, or ingenuity of any kind. On the other hand, because Solomon limited himself to what he could observe under the sun, he attributed the victory to "time and chance" rather than God as David did. "God opposes the proud, but gives grace to the humble" (James 4:6). Isaiah says, "The haughty looks of man shall be brought low, and the lofty pride of men shall be humbled, and the Lord alone will be exalted in that day" (Isa. 2:11).

IDOLS DETHRONED. David did not allow Goliath to intimidate him. He had faith that God would exalt His name so that "all the earth may know that there is a God in Israel." Just as God had thrown down and decapitated the idol of Dagon in the presence of the Ark of the Covenant years earlier, so God threw Goliath face down and decapitated him in the presence of one coming in the name of the Lord (Youngblood, 1992, pp. 701-02).

Saul inquires about David
1 Sam. 17:55-18:1

CURIOUS KING

Saul asked the same question of two different people at two different times. First, he asked Abner while watching David going out to meet Goliath, "Whose son is this youth?" Second, he asked David when he returned from striking down the Philistine, "Whose son are you, young man?" He may not have been asking for the same reason each time.

FOOLISH. The first time, he may have been thinking, "This is crazy. He's only a kid, and he's going to get slaughtered by that veteran Philistine (see 17:33). I'm going to have to notify his dad that he got killed." Then he turned and asked, "Abner, whose kid is this?"

NAÏVE. Or he may have been thinking something like this the first time. "This kid is naïve, but I like his pluck. If he harasses the Philistine and somehow survives to grow into a suit of armor and to learn to wield a sword, he'd make a good recruit" (see 17:38-39). Turning to Abner, he asked, "Whose kid is this?"

VALIANT. The second time Saul asked the question, David was returning with Goliath's head in his hand. Then Saul may have been thinking, "He isn't just plucky. He's valiant and lucky too. I'm going to have to make his dad's family free from taxation" (see 17:24). Then Saul said to David, "Young man, whose son are you?"

What kind of faith do people see in you? Do they think it nothing more than foolish talk? Do they think that you are merely naïve and that experience of real life will destroy your idealism? Or do they see that you live your faith even in difficult circumstances and that you come through those trials even stronger in faith?

(In this chronology, the killing of Goliath is placed before David is introduced to Saul as a "man of valor, a man of war" (1 Sam. 16:18), before Saul sent to Jesse to ask that he be relieved of his duties with the sheep and be sent to him (1 Sam. 16:19-20), and before he had become familiar with armor and weapons as Saul's armor-bearer (1 Sam. 16:21). For the reasons for arranging the chronology in this way, see the Note on Part One Chronology.)

David arouses Saul's jealousy
1 Sam. 18:6-9

UNLIKELY HERO

When I was young, a small university was playing in a national championship game. With only a few seconds left on the clock, one of their players fouled out of the game, and the opposing team hit free throws giving them a one-point lead. The coach was just about out of players. Reluctantly, he put his own son in the game. Although his son was a senior, he had played in only a few games. After the team inbounded the ball and called a time out, the coach drew up a play to get the ball to their best shooter on the court. When the team tried to inbound the ball again with only a couple of seconds left, no one could get open except the coach's son near midcourt. He put up a desperate shot which hit the back of the rim and popped high above the basket as time ran off the clock. After what seemed an eternity, the ball came back down through the basket for the winning score, the only basket scored all year by the coach's son. All season, others had carried the team. Others had put the team in the championship game, but on this night, a benchwarmer came into the game, shot the winning basket, and became the player of the game!

MIGHTY WARRIOR. Saul was a mighty warrior who had led Israel to many victories. When Nahash the Ammonite had threatened to gouge out the right eyes of all the people in Jabesh Gilead, Saul had immediately gathered a force and marched to Jabesh where he routed the Ammonite army and saved the city. He had fought "valiantly" on many occasions and delivered Israel "out of the hands of those who plundered them." Among the armies he had defeated were the Moabites, the Edomites, the kings of Zobah, the Philistines, and the Amalekites (1 Sam. 14:47-48). Undoubtedly, his name had been sung on many occasions when his victorious army returned home.

PLAYER OF THE GAME. On this occasion, however, David was the "player of the game." He had killed Goliath and inspired the army. As the victorious army returned home, the women sang, "Saul has struck down his thousands, and David his tens thousands" (1 Sam. 18:7).

Knowing that Samuel had told him that God was going to take the kingdom from him and give it to another, Saul felt insecure when he heard the song which credited David with slaying more enemies than he had. Although Saul had won more battles and killed more enemies, he feared his grasp on the kingdom was slipping. Consequently, he "eyed" David from that day on (1 Sam. 18:9). The word "eye" in Hebrew sounds like the word that means "transgress," and suggests that Saul was watching David for an opportunity to harm him from this day on (Bergen, 1996, p. 201).

Saul sends for David
1 Sam. 16:14-23 [1 Sam. 18:2]

THE POWER OF MUSIC

Lucas Foss, a composer who had Parkinson's disease, found it difficult to walk to his piano, often freezing and then taking hurried, uncontrolled steps. Likewise, he had difficulty moving his arms in a controlled manner, but when he started playing a nocturne by Chopin, he played with nearly perfect timing and control. As soon as the music stopped, he again had difficulty controlling his movements (Oliver Sacks, **Brain**, 2006, 129, p. 2528). Music can have a profound effect on people even if that effect is temporary.

MUSIC THERAPY. After God rejected the rebellious king, he sent a "harmful spirit" which tormented Saul. This harmful spirit may refer to an evil disposition which overwhelmed the king because he was resisting God like a stubborn animal kicks against a prod or goad. During one of these fits of despondency, an attendant suggested that someone be found to play a lyre for the king so he would feel better. Saul issued the order to find such a man, and a servant suggested that they bring David, who was known to play skillfully on the lyre.

TEMPORARY RELIEF. Music apparently had a powerful effect on Saul, calming his evil disposition. David would play the lyre, and Saul would be relieved and feel better. The music that David played changed Saul's feelings at the moment (1 Sam. 16:23), but it did not change the underlying cause, which was his habitual self-centeredness and rebellion against God. Those habitual thinking patterns continued, he was reminded again of his alienation from God, and the same foul mood would overwhelm him. So David was called repeatedly to calm the distraught king, but the music was not a cure.

MORE THAN MUSIC. David also experienced problems, and music also benefited him. However, music had a more permanent influence on David than it did on Saul. None of David's music has survived to this day, but his lyrics have survived in many of the Psalms. In the lyrics, we find the secret to the power of David's music. Whatever the state of David's feelings or emotions, he directed his thoughts expressed in words toward God. Then, the music combined with the words made a profound change in his heart, and that in turn helped steer his will toward righteous deeds. For example, Psalm 43 reveals his despondency when not only Saul but many of his own countrymen were pursuing him, but then he remembered the light and joy in God's truth which irresistibly drew him into God's presence with gratitude and praise. He was so overwhelmed with God's loving kindness that he wondered why he had been discouraged. Ps. 43:5 summarizes this drawing near to God:

> Why are you cast down, O my soul,
> and why are you in turmoil within me?
> Hope in God; for I shall again praise him,
> my salvation and my God.

Those memories of God's loving kindness and faithfulness were then reinforced every time David took up his lyre. Music combined with words contributed to a transformed heart which enabled David to show kindness even to his enemies.

A BIG DIFFERENCE. In Saul's case, the sounds of the lyre soothed his nerves. The music helped Saul forget temporarily his alienation from God. The lyrics were insignificant, if any were sung. In David's case, the words were significant, and reinforced by the music of the lyre, they reminded David of God's lovingkindness. The music and words not only calmed his nerves, they transformed his life.

So then, we should not merely enjoy music that temporarily changes our moods. We should also employ that music which directs our thoughts toward God and his ways, and we should reinforce godly and righteous thoughts by repeating such music, so that godly thoughts and feelings might strengthen our wills to do His good pleasure.

Jonathan makes a covenant with David
1 Sam. 18:3-5

BEST FRIENDS

"There is a friend who sticks closer than a brother" (Prov. 18:24). A man with such a friend is more fortunate than a man with "many companions." In difficult times, companions may abandon you, but your friend who is "closer than a brother" will always stand at your side. Jonathan, King Saul's son, proved to be such a friend to David.

SHARED FAITH. Although Jonathan was a member of the royal family and older than David, he was much like David. Both had great faith in God when faced with powerful enemies. David said, "The Lord who delivered me from the paw of the lion and from the paw of the bear will deliver me from the hand of this Philistine" (1 Sam. 17:37), and Jonathan had said, "Nothing can hinder the Lord from saving by many or by few" (1 Sam. 14:6). Not only did both have faith, but that faith gave them both courage to act when the king was paralyzed with fear. David faced Goliath while Saul watched from the safety of the Israelite camp (1 Sam. 17:40), and Jonathan had attacked a garrison of the Philistines while Saul fretted at home (1 Sam. 14:1-3). The actions of both men had given courage to soldiers who were faint in heart and roused them to action and victory (1 Sam. 17:52; 1 Sam. 14:20-22).

KINDRED SPIRIT. Jonathan found in David a kindred spirit, and "was knit to the soul of David" (1 Sam. 18:1). This reminds us of a similar phrase in Gen. 44:30 which describes Jacob's love for his son Benjamin. Jacob was very reluctant to allow Benjamin to leave home, and here Saul and Jonathan did not allow David to leave their home to return to Bethlehem (1 Sam. 18:2).

FAMILY LOVE. Furthermore, Jonathan loved David "as his own soul" (1 Sam. 18:1). This phrase is used in Deut. 13:6 to refer to a friend who is as close to a person as a family member, and it should be understood in that light here because, as noted above, David was being drawn into Saul's household. In Middle Eastern families, and especially a royal family, there would have been stronger friendship ties among males than between males and females. Relationships between males and females were almost non-existent except for marital relationships, but even in the marital relationship, male and female worlds were so different that strong friendships often existed only between members of the same sex. For that reason, David could say that Jonathan's love surpassed "the love of women" (2 Sam. 1:26) without implying a homosexual relationship (Cabal, et al., 2007, p. 435). Furthermore, this Hebrew word for "love" often describes love within a family: Abraham loved his son Isaac; Jacob loved his son Joseph; Ruth loved her mother-in-law Naomi; Elkanah loved his wife Hannah, and Rebekah loved her son Jacob (TWOT, #29). It is never used in the Old Testament "to express homosexual desire or activity," for which the OT uses a different word (Youngblood, 1992, p. 706). As David was being brought into the royal family, both Saul (1 Sam. 16:21) and Jonathan were said to love David. Jonathan, David, and Saul all were, or would be, married and have many children.

A COVENANT. Jonathan's attraction for David was not merely based their shared activities as soldiers, or even their shared courage. Instead, it was based primarily on their shared faith, and for that reason it was sealed with a covenant made before God (cf. 1 Sam. 20:8). Then in a symbolic gesture, perhaps anticipating Jonathan's recognition that David would be the next king, the heir apparent gave David his own robe and armor, in effect making David the heir to the throne (Youngblood, 1992, p. 707). (The garment/kingdom theme is also found in 1 Sam. 15:27-28; 24:4, 11, 20.) Because both were committed to God in heart and life, Jonathan would later go to David, who was in great despair at the time because his own people had abandoned him, and "strengthened his hand in God" (1 Sam 23:16).

David eludes Saul and becomes successful
1 Sam. 18:10-16

GREEN WITH ENVY

The ancient Greek playwright Aeschylus said, "It is in the character of very few men to honor without envy a friend who has prospered." King Saul was not one of those few men. Even though the song the women sang as the army returned from the killing of Goliath had disturbed Saul, he loved David greatly, made him is personal armor bearer (1 Sam. 16:21), and finally made him a commander in his army (1 Sam. 18:5). However, when David prospered, Saul became insanely envious because he remained self-centered and rebellious in heart.

FAILURE. While Saul was in an evil mood and "prophesying," David was playing the lyre with his hand (the ESV omits the words "with his hand" found in the KJV and Hebrew text). Saul, however, was sitting in his own house with a spear "in his hand" and suddenly attempted to pin his imagined rival to the wall with it. The lyre and spear in their hands contrast the peaceful intentions of David with the malicious intentions of Saul (Youngblood, 1992, p. 709). When Saul failed two times, he knew that God was with David. He became more envious and fearful because he failed while David enjoyed God's favor.

MISCALCULATION. Finally, Saul was so tormented by the sight of David that he sent him out on military campaigns. David enjoyed such great success that "all Israel and Judah loved David" (v. 16). Saul's torments only increased. He had put David in the public eye, and David's popularity grew with every successful campaign. Saul found himself watching the kingdom being torn from him and given to another. Saul was proving Baltasar Gracian's statement true: "The envious die not once, but as oft' as the envied win applause."

David marries Michal
1 Sam. 18:17-30

FIRST LOVE

> Love and marriage, love and marriage,
> Go together like horse and carriage.
> This I tell ya, brother,
> You can't have one without the other.

Frank Sinatra's song suggests that love is the most important factor in marriage, but is it? What about money? Social status? Intrigue? David's first marriage may have included them all.

BROKEN PROMISE. Saul had made a promise to give his daughter in marriage to the man who would kill Goliath. This, of course, offered common soldiers the chance to move up in social status by marrying into the royal family. And with that new status also came an exemption from taxes (1 Sam. 17:25). Saul, however, did not immediately keep his promise because he was controlled by jealousy and malice. Wishing to destroy David, he required that David fight more battles against the Philistines. Because of his inferior social position, David accepted the additional requirement without complaining (v. 18): "Who am I, and who are my relatives, my father's clan in Israel, that I should be son-in-law to the king?" Saul, fully expecting David to be killed, promised his daughter Merab to another man. When the time for the wedding arrived and David had not been killed as he expected, Saul saw giving Merab to the man from Meholah in the prosperous Jordan Valley as a way to humiliate a poor soldier whose popularity made him jealous.

BRUTAL BRIDE PRICE. But humiliating David did not satisfy Saul. He wanted to destroy him, so he was pleased to hear that his daughter Michal loved David. A second opportunity for David to marry a daughter of Saul was also a second opportunity to have David killed by the Philistines. Saul sent a private offer to make David his son-in-law. When David responded to Saul, he had to be careful. He could not reject the offer without insulting the king, and he could not accept the offer eagerly without appearing presumptuous. Accordingly, he replied (v. 23), "Does it seem to you a little thing to become the king's son-in-law, since I am a poor man and have no reputation?" David did what was socially appropriate – he recognized the social distance between himself and the king and left the initiative with the socially superior king (compare with Alter, 1981, p. 119). Saul did take the initiative and named the bride price as a hundred foreskins of the Philistines. (Saul's use of this barbaric practice showed how much he had become a king like the kings of other nations.) But just as Saul failed twice to pin David to the wall with his javelin, so he failed a second time to kill David by the hands of the Philistines. Furthermore, David paid double the bride price, and became the king's son-in-law.

TRUE LOVE. After the marriage, Saul found it disturbing that his daughter, Michal, loved David. Surprisingly, this is the only time (outside the Song of Solomon) a Bible writer records that a woman loved a man (Alter, 1981, p. 118). Undoubtedly, Michal had heard reports of David's bravery, overheard him singing to her father, and caught glimpses of his handsome features when in her father's court. She loved David with the idealistic first love of youth. The writer also tells us that David was pleased to become the king's son-in-law, but he does not tell us whether David loved Michal. According to the customs of the day, David probably had had few opportunities to be with Michal though he may have seen her on occasion when in attendance to her father.

David's marriage to Michal was the first of three marriages (to Michal, Abigail, and Bathsheba) which are reported in some detail. This first marriage stands in contrast to the way David obtained Bathsheba. In order to marry the first time, David was sent into battle to be killed, but survived and won a bride who loved him. In order to marry the last time, David sent another into battle to be killed and then took that man's wife for himself. In this way, the writer shows both the greatness of David, and the greatness of the sin into which he fell.

Jonathan intercedes for David
1 Sam. 19:1-7

INTENTIONS OF HEART AND MIND

Knowledge and feelings are both powerful influences on behavior. When a person's rational thoughts and feelings are not the same, he is double-minded, and his behavior becomes unstable and unpredictable. Saul's heart and his mind did not always work together. He was a double-minded man.

INTENTION OF THE HEART. When King Saul saw that David was successful and his name highly esteemed, his jealousy and defensive intuitions took over. His feelings said that he had to defend his throne. Accordingly, he told his son Jonathan and all his officers to look for an opportunity to kill David, perhaps making it look like an accident. Although many of Saul's officers might have been reluctant to obey his command, one would eventually have an opportunity and a reason to desire the king's gratitude.

INTENTION OF THE MIND. After Jonathan warned David that Saul was looking for a chance to kill him, he personally confronted his father with the truth: David had been of great service to Saul and had done nothing against him. Further, Saul himself had rejoiced when David slew the Philistine giant. King Saul listened to reason, and he knew that Jonathan was right. He promised with an oath not to kill David. Jonathan then brought David out of hiding and into Saul's presence as he had been before.

Sadly, Saul's oath not to kill David was the determination of his mind but not his heart. In his heart, he still resented that God was going to take the throne from him and give it to another. In his heart, he was convinced that God was unfair. In his heart, he was still fighting to preserve his throne. In his heart, he could not tolerate rivals. He was double-minded and unstable. He was bound to fail in his rational intention not to seek David's life.

DESPERATE HOUSEWIFE

Michal was a desperate housewife trying to save her beloved husband
from her insanely jealous father, King Saul. After Saul tried to kill David
with his spear, David fled to his own house where Michal discovered that
the door was being watched by Saul's men. She urged David to leave and
helped him escape through a window. Then in order to buy time for
David, she used a household idol to make it look like someone was in bed
and told Saul's officers that David was ill. When Saul discovered her
deception, Michal lied again telling Saul that she only let David leave
because he had threatened to kill her.

MOTIVES. Michal's lies differ significantly from Saul's lie about wanting
David to be his son-in-law. When Saul lied, he masked an evil motive and
tried to put David in a situation where he would be killed. When Michal
lied the first time, she was trying to save David's life. When she lied the
second time, she was merely trying to escape her father's insane anger.

JUSTIFIABLE? It is easy to excuse Michal's lies while condemning Saul's
because she had "justifiable" motives. Some would go so far as to say
that when she lied the first time, she did not break the spirit of the Law
because she did not testify "against" her neighbor. She was trying to help
her neighbor, and it is hard to imagine what else Michal could have done
but lie to buy more time for David to escape. Some would say she was
justified in lying to an insanely angry person when she accused David of
threatening to kill her. Indeed, a short time later he did try to kill
Jonathan for excusing David from the new moon feast at Saul's house (1
Sam. 20:33). Although she slandered David, she was not lying in a
courtroom before impartial judges trying to pervert justice. She was trying
to escape unjust anger.

PRIORITIES. Both lies showed Michal's priorities. Her first lie show
that she placed David before her father, but the second lie also showed
that she placed herself before David because she was willing to slander
him to save herself. Her slander brought into question the love Michal
and David had for each other, and Saul eventually gave her to another
man (see 1 Sam. 25:44). Furthermore, the item she used to deceive Saul's
soldiers revealed something of her broader priorities. Just as Rachel had
brought a household idol into Jacob's tent (Gen. 31:30-35), so Michal had

brought a household idol into David's house. She turned to this lifeless idol for help when Saul's soldiers came to the house, but she lost the husband she loved. On the other hand, David trusted God, and God enabled him to escape.

David finds refuge with Samuel
1 Sam. 19:18-24

THE RESCUE MISSION

Where would a homeless, broke, hungry, cold, and depressed man go for help? David had just escaped Saul's attempt to kill him and fled his own home because Saul's men were waiting to ambush him. He had no food, money, or extra clothes. He could trust no one. There were no rescue missions in that day, but he did find refuge with Samuel and a group of prophets in Ramah about 5 miles away from Saul's home in Gibeah. The events that transpired while David was there were a public demonstration that God would protect David from Saul, and that God had stripped the kingdom from Saul.

SAUL STYMIED. God's protection of David was demonstrated when He sent His Spirit to frustrate Saul's intention to arrest David in Ramah. Three times God put His Spirit on Saul's men, and each time they failed to arrest David because they prophesied with the prophets. Finally, when Saul himself went to find David, God put His Spirit on him also. Instead of harming David, he prophesied until he was exhausted. Just as God put His Spirit in Balaam so that he could not curse Jacob, so He put His Spirit in Saul and his men so that they could not harm David. In one of David's darkest hours, God assured David that Saul would never harm him.

SAUL STRIPPED. Saul's public behavior in Ramah also demonstrated that God had stripped the kingdom from Saul. While prophesying in Samuel's presence, Saul stripped off his royal apparel in a symbolic portrayal of the last words he had heard Samuel say: "The Lord has torn the kingdom of Israel from you this day and has given it to a neighbor of yours, who is better than you" (1 Sam. 15:28). Though Saul continued to resist God's will, God assured David that Saul would not remain king for long.

David received much more than food and clothing while with Samuel and the prophets. He also received God's assurances that God would protect him from Saul and deliver the kingdom to him. God knew David needed this encouragement as he entered a frustrating period of his life that nevertheless prepared him to lead Israel.

Part Two: An Outcast in Judah

1016–1012 B.C.; age 24-28

David fails to renew Saul's favor
1 Sam. 20:1-42

A FRIEND IN NEED

Saul's erratic and deceptive behavior was a more pervasive test of David's faith and character than the Philistine giant Goliath, who had openly challenged David to physical combat. Saul, a fellow Israelite, did not confront David openly as an enemy, but engulfed him in an atmosphere of intrigue and deception. He made David one of his armor bearers, but then tried to pin him to the wall with a spear while in fit of "depression." He promoted David in the army, but insulted his most successful commander by giving his daughter Merab to another man. Then he flattered David by offering him his younger daughter Michal in marriage, but even this offer was a scheme to kill him. Saul tested David's wits and emotions so severely that David was not sure whom he could trust. He wasn't even sure he was safe among the prophets after Saul found out he was hiding there. In this situation, David found support from his friend Jonathan.

ADVERSITY. Jonathan was a friend indeed because he could be trusted in time of adversity. Prov. 17:17 says, "A friend loves at all times, and a brother is born for adversity." David didn't know whom he could trust. It seemed that many around him were conspiring against him when he wrote Psalm 59:3-4.

> For behold, they lie in wait for my life;
>   fierce men stir up strife against me.
> For no transgression or sin of mine, O LORD,
>   for no fault of mine, they run and make ready.
> Awake, come to meet me, and see!

In spite of the atmosphere of intrigue and deception, David was confident that he could trust Saul's son Jonathan. Accordingly, he went to Jonathan to ask a favor of him.

ASSISTANCE. Jonathan was also a friend in deed because he did what David asked of him. David was sure that Saul was hiding his evil intentions toward him from Jonathan. For that reason, David asked Jonathan to test his father by relaying a request to be excused from the royal family for the new moon festival (see Num. 10:10) in order to visit his father's family in Bethlehem. (A trip to his father's family was improbable though possible because Bethlehem was only 10 miles away.) The plot worked as anticipated. When Jonathan told King Saul that David requested permission to be with his father's family, the king insulted Jonathan for failing to fulfill his role as heir apparent:

> Then Saul's anger was kindled against Jonathan, and he said to him, "You son of a perverse, rebellious woman, do I not know that you have chosen the son of Jesse to your own shame, and to the shame of your mother's nakedness?
> -- 1 Sam. 20:30

Then King Saul heaped shame on David by accusing him of plotting to overthrow the royal family (vv. 31, 34b). Finally, Saul revealed full extent of his wrath by hurling a spear at Jonathan. Jonathan knew with certainty that Saul was determined to kill David.

OTHERS BEFORE SELF. Jonathan proved himself to be a true friend because he put David's interests above his own. He was confident that David would never raise his hand against King Saul or his family, but he also knew that one day God would subdue David's enemies (v. 15) and that he himself would be subject to David. Jonathan was content to see the kingdom slip from his own grasp and to see David rise to the role God had given him (1 Sam. 23:17). King Saul was incapable of understanding this attitude, which the Apostle Paul describes in Phil. 2:3-4 where he writes, "Do nothing from selfish ambition or conceit, but in humility count others more significant than yourselves. Let each of you look not only to his own interests, but also to the interests of others."

GREAT LOVE. Jonathan also showed the measure of his love for David by risking his life for him. Jesus said, "Greater love has no one than this, that someone lay down his life for his friends" (John 15:13). Although Jonathan did not actually lay down his life for David, he nevertheless is an example of the strength of the bond of friendship.

The friendship between David and Jonathan was a beautiful relationship. As far as we know, Jonathan saw David only once after this. When David was later living as an outcast in the Desert of Ziph, Jonathan sought out David and "strengthened his hand in God" (1 Sam. 23:16).

David obtains supplies from priests at Nob
1 Sam. 21:1-9

NEVER RIGHT TO DO WRONG

When I was a child, I remember vainly trying to explain to Dad why I had done something he had forbidden. No matter how I justified what I had done, my fate was always sealed by his concluding statement, "It is never right to do wrong."

DAVID'S UNLAWFUL ACT. On this occasion, David had been fleeing from Saul and was hungry. He asked Ahimelech the priest for some food, but the priest had only the consecrated bread which had just been replaced in the tabernacle (cf. Lev. 24:8-9). The priests ate this bread, but people outside of the priest's family, including guests, were forbidden to eat it (Lev. 22:10-16). Nevertheless, after some hesitation, the priest gave some of this bread to David and his companions to eat. When Jesus referred to this incident (Matt. 12:4), He said that David "ate the bread of the Presence, which it was not lawful for him to eat nor for those who were with him, but only for the priests."

THE UNLAWFUL ACT NOT CONDEMNED. Jesus was defending his apostles against the charge of breaking the Sabbath when he cited David's act. His point was that though David did what was unlawful, he was innocent just as the priests who desecrated the Sabbath by working in the temple on that day were innocent. He concluded his defense of the apostles with these words: "If you had known what this means, 'I desire mercy, and not sacrifice,' you would not have condemned the guiltless" (Matt. 12:7). Even while asserting that what David did was "not lawful," Jesus pointed out that David remained guiltless.

TRUE TO THE LAW'S INTENT. So why was David considered innocent? The debate Jesus had with the Jewish leaders over the Sabbath provides an answer. The Sabbath rest was God's provision of mercy to his people, and they were to grant that same mercy to their servants and animals (Deut. 5:12-15). Accordingly, a man could rescue his sheep from a pit on the Sabbath, though he could not tend flocks on the Sabbath because by so doing he was showing mercy to his sheep (Matt. 12:11). Failure to rescue the sheep for fear of breaking the law would show a fundamental misunderstanding of the law. Similarly, the priests made intercession for the people on the Sabbath, and in so doing "profaned" the Sabbath, but they were considered guiltless (Matt. 12:5) because the

Sabbath law was never intended to interfere with the greater purpose of the Law, which was to reconcile people to God.

NEED FOR RIGHT JUDGMENT. Jesus cited another example: "Moses gave you circumcision (not that it is from Moses, but from the fathers), and you circumcise a man on the Sabbath. If on the Sabbath a man receives circumcision, so that the law of Moses may not be broken, are you angry with me because on the Sabbath I made a man's whole body well? Do not judge by appearances, but judge with right judgment" (John 7:22-24). Jesus affirmed that God does not condemn what appears "unlawful" when it is in obedience to the primary intent of the law as a whole. Thus, Jesus affirmed that it was lawful to do good on the Sabbath (Matt. 12:12). Strangely, the Jewish leaders forgot that the Sabbath law was inseparable from God's overall desire that compassion be shown to others (Mark 2:27; Deut. 5:12-15).

DANGERS OF IMPROPER JUDGMENT. Some will argue that to justify the "unlawful" opens the door to excuse all kinds of sin. Unfortunately, many have used such arguments to justify the selfish desires of their own deceitful hearts. Nevertheless, we must recognize that to ignore the teaching of Jesus promotes a sterile, Pharisaic, religion that closes our eyes to the problems of real people in a lost world. If a child is sick, we could insist that mothers leave the child at home alone so that she might not forsake the assembling of the saints, but better judgment would say that she should show compassion to the child. If there is an automobile accident, we could insist that a passing motorist continue his journey uninterrupted lest he miss the appointed time to meet at the Lord's Table, but better judgment would say that the motorist should assist the injured. In neither case does better judgment intend to avoid responsibilities toward God. Rather, it always acts with the intention to fulfilling those responsibilities. To make improper judgment and neglect the ill or injured would violate the law of God at a fundamental level.

THE CASE OF THE CONSECRATED BREAD. Now, back to Ahimelech and David. David had asked Ahimelech for food, but the only food the priest had was the consecrated bread reserved for priests. (Perhaps God's law was intended to guarantee support for the priests who had no inheritance in Israel.) So the question became, "Does the law concerning consecrated bread prevent a priest from showing mercy to the hungry?" Ahimelech evidently struggled with the question because he was concerned that the bread not be treated with contempt, but he decided in favor of showing mercy. Accordingly, neither Ahimelech nor David were condemned for this decision.

So, is it ever right to do wrong? No, it is never right to do wrong. Furthermore, it is never wrong to do right. Jesus said it this way before healing a man on the Sabbath: "It is lawful to do good on the Sabbath" (Matt. 12:12).

David flees to Gath temporarily
1 Sam. 21:10-15

EVICTED

David probably felt elated when Samuel anointed him to be the next king of Israel. For a time, he appeared to be making some progress toward that goal. He killed Goliath, was called to serve in Saul's court, was made a commander in the army, was given the king's daughter in marriage, and won the favor of the people. Then calamity struck. In a few short days, he was

- Evicted from Saul's court and from his military command at the point of a spear (1 Sam. 19:10)
- Evicted from his own home when he fled through a window to escape Saul's men (1 Sam. 19:12). His wife was given to another man, and he was separated from his best friend, Jonathan.
- Evicted from his homeland when he could find safety with neither the prophets at Ramah nor the priests at Nob (1 Sam. 19:18 ff.; 21:1 ff.).

He was a man without a country. He felt cut off from his family, friends, traditions, and even his God. Later when describing the condition Saul's allies had imposed on him, he said, "They have driven me out this day that I should have no share in the heritage of the Lord, saying, 'Go, serve other gods.'" (1 Sam. 26:19). David was desperate, and in his desperation, he fled to Gath, one of the chief cities of the Philistines located 20 or 30 miles southwest of Nob.

When the Philistine court attendants recognized David as Israel's champion, they told Achish the king and apparently closed the city gates to cut off his escape. David had no wife to watch for him, no friend to mediate, and no prophets or priests to encourage him. He was alone and surrounded by enemies. Knowing he was watched, David pretended to be insane. He drooled in his beard and scribbled on the doors of the gate. At the same time, he sought the Lord.

> I sought the LORD, and he answered me
> and delivered me from all my fears.
> Those who look to him are radiant,
> and their faces shall never be ashamed.
> This poor man cried, and the LORD heard him
> and saved him out of all his troubles.
> The angel of the LORD encamps
> around those who fear him, and delivers them.
> -- Psalm 34:4-7

When Achish learned that David was a "madman," he allowed David to escape. David learned that even when he was brokenhearted and desperate, God would never abandon him.

> When the righteous cry for help, the LORD hears
> and delivers them out of all their troubles.
> The LORD is near to the brokenhearted
> and saves the crushed in spirit.
> -- Psalm 34:17-18

David becomes a leader of the oppressed
1 Sam. 22:1-5

FRIEND OF DEBTORS

At Adullam David began to see God fulfill his promise to give him the kingdom. Despite killing Goliath and marrying Saul's daughter, David had secured neither social advancement nor the kingdom. Instead he had become an outcast who even had to pretend madness in Gath to save his life. After fleeing Gath, David hid in a cave near the town of Adullam in the western foothills (Josh. 15:33-36) about 13 miles SW of Bethlehem. The territory was near the valley of Elah where David had killed Goliath. While hiding there, those who were "in distress" or "in debt" or "bitter in soul" began to gather around him. They became the nucleus of his army.

DAVID SYMPATHIZED. Actually, David's experiences prepared him to sympathize with the unfortunate. His willingness to take up their cause demonstrated that he had the heart of God:

But the LORD sits enthroned forever;
    he has established his throne for justice,
and he judges the world with righteousness;
    he judges the peoples with uprightness.
The LORD is a stronghold for the oppressed,
    a stronghold in times of trouble.
And those who know your name put their trust in you,
    for you, O LORD, have not forsaken those who seek
you.
-- Psalm 9:7-10

DAVID SET AN IDEAL. His compassion for the poor and oppressed established an ideal for following kings (Psalm 72:1-19), but they never lived up to the expectations. Isaiah foresaw that ideal being fulfilled by the Messiah who would restore the kingdom:

There shall come forth a shoot from the stump of
    Jesse,
    and a branch from his roots shall bear fruit.
And the Spirit of the LORD shall rest upon him,
    the Spirit of wisdom and understanding,
    the Spirit of counsel and might,
    the Spirit of knowledge and the fear of the LORD.
And his delight shall be in the fear of the LORD.
He shall not judge by what his eyes see,
    or decide disputes by what his ears hear,
but with righteousness he shall judge the poor,
    and decide with equity for the meek of the earth;
and he shall strike the earth with the rod of his mouth,
    and with the breath of his lips he shall kill the
    wicked.
Righteousness shall be the belt of his waist,
    and faithfulness the belt of his loins.
-- Isa. 11:1-5

JESUS FULFILLED THE IDEAL. Jesus came up from the stump of Jesse. He fulfilled the prophetic ideal for a Davidic king. He rebuked the rich and influential religious leaders who put heavy loads on men's shoulders but were unwilling themselves to lift a finger to move them (Matt. 23:4). When they rejected his message, he told them, "Truly, I say to you, the tax collectors and the prostitutes go into the kingdom of God before you" (Matt. 21:31). As with David, the oppressed, the weary, and the discontented formed the nucleus of Christ's kingdom. They found refuge in Him. He said to them, "Come to me, all who labor and are heavy laden, and I will give you rest. Take my yoke upon you, and learn from me, for I am gentle and lowly in heart, and you will find rest for your souls. For my yoke is easy, and my burden is light" (Matt. 11:28-30).

David gathers soldiers
1 Chron. 12:8-18

FRIEND OR FOE?

David had become the leader of men in distress and debt. At first, they hid in the cave of Adullam, but then sought refuge in Moab. When they returned to Judah, they hid in the forest of Hereth. For the most part, David's men seem to have been motivated more by fear than bravery. About this time, a number of soldiers from the tribes of Gad, Benjamin, and Judah joined David's small band.

SKILLED. The Gadites who went over to David were not only swift, brave, and experienced warriors capable of using shield and spear, but they were also officers. Their courage was demonstrated when they crossed the Jordan River during flood stage in the spring of the year. Their prowess was shown in putting those who lived in the valleys on either side of the river to flight.

LOYAL. When some men from Benjamin and Judah came to David, he wished to verify that they had not come to betray him. They affirmed that they were loyal friends, and that their loyalty was grounded in their conviction that God was with David. They understood that military strength without God's favor was useless.

COMMISSIONED. David immediately put the soldiers who came to him to work. He made them officers in his little band of men. Their leadership helped David transform this band of debtors into an efficient military force. Amasai (v. 18) apparently served as commanding officer over the thirty for a while, though his name does not appear in any of the lists.

David did not merely want men who were skilled warriors and officers, but he wanted such men who were loyal and devoted to the Lord. He knew that swords and spears did not win battles. There would be times when weapons would be lacking and soldiers outnumbered, but victory would still be possible through the Lord, for the battle belongs to him (1

Sam. 17:47). He needed men who would remain brave and loyal at times when those without faith would falter.

David gives refuge to Abiathar the priest
1 Sam. 22:6-23

WITH MALICE TOWARD NONE

David and his men had been in Moab until Gad, a prophet, instructed David to return to Judah. It was God's will that David gain the kingdom by helping the oppressed and defending the weak rather than creating even greater hardships by raising an outside force and invading the land. David obeyed the Lord's instruction given by Gad and hid his men in the Forest of Hereth, which was probably near Adullam in Judah (See 1 Sam. 22:3-5).

SAUL'S SUSPICIONS. When Saul heard that David had returned to Israel with his men, he suspected that David was plotting to kill him (vv. 8,13). Saul's suspicions were heightened by Jonathan's covenant with David, and increased when his soldiers did not tell him of the covenant (v. 8). Furthermore, the desertion of some Benjamites to David (1 Chron. 12:16) would have raised further questions about the loyalty of his own soldiers. Finally, the growth of David's army may explain why Saul suspected Ahimelech the priest of treason and would not listen to him. Though there is no evidence that David ever plotted to take Saul's life, Saul suspected a conspiracy wherever he looked.

SAUL'S MALICE. In addition to raising suspicions, Saul's fear produced in him an irresistible desire to harm those he suspected of disloyalty. People feel a necessity to vent their rage when they no longer trust God to be their defender and refuge. When Saul abandoned God, and God turned away from him, Saul felt he had to avenge himself. Consequently he violated God's command in Lev. 19:18: "You shall not take vengeance or bear a grudge against the sons of your own people, but you shall love your neighbor as yourself: I am the LORD." Because Ahimelech had inquired of God for David and had given him food and a weapon, Saul ordered that the priest and his entire family be slaughtered. Not even his loyal soldiers could dissuade him. He found a willing executioner in Doeg, the Edomite.

A CONTRAST. Saul's wrath put him in unfavorable light compared to David who declared his hands to be free from violence (1 Chron. 12:17).

David did not avenge himself, but left it to God (Rom. 12:19), and sought to "overcome evil with good" (Rom. 12:21). Both Saul and David experienced the consequences of their actions. Saul's actions weakened his hold on the kingdom and strengthened the hand of David. Surely his accusations and his unreasonable order to massacre the priests weakened the loyalty of his own soldiers. The massacre of priests undoubtedly destroyed the loyalty of other priestly families, especially after Abiathar found refuge with David. Thus, Saul alienated himself from the priests as well as the prophets and was totally cut off from God. In contrast to Saul, David had become the champion of the oppressed (22:2), a friend of brave soldiers (1 Chron. 12:8-18), an adherent of prophets (1 Sam. 22:5), and a refuge for a prominent priest (1 Sam. 22:20-23). David enjoyed God's favor.

David saves Keilah
1 Sam. 23:1-13

BASIC TRAINING

David had been a military leader in Saul's army, and now he was the leader of a band of men who had been in distress or in debt (1 Sam. 22:2). This band now had officers, seasoned soldiers from the tribes of Gad, Benjamin, and Judah (1 Chron. 12:8-18). When David heard that the Philistines were harassing the people of Keilah, David began training his men to become the nucleus of the army that God would use to free the Israelites from their enemies.

DAVID'S TRUST. David's training was not merely in the use of weapons or in winning strategies. He also trained his men to follow the will of God whether it was to trust his command to attack a formidable enemy or to withdraw from a seemingly safe position. On this occasion, David inquired of the Lord, "Shall I go and attack these Philistines?" We don't know how David inquired of God, but perhaps he asked Gad, the seer who had recently advised him to return to Judah from Moab (1 Sam. 22:5). God answered, "Go and attack the Philistines and save Keilah." David's men were terrified. They said, "Behold, we are afraid here in Judah; how much more then if we go to Keilah against the armies of the Philistines?" When David heard this, he inquired of the Lord again, and God assured him of victory. David persuaded his men to trust God despite their fears, and God gave them victory. Instead of hiding in the wilderness, they now could live in the comfort and safety of a city.

SAUL'S WISHFUL THINKING. When Saul learned that David was residing more or less permanently in a walled city, he was ecstatic. He declared confidently, "God has given him into my hand." Why was he so confident? It was because it appeared to him that God was helping him because David had "shut himself in by entering a town that has gates and bars." Despite his own disobedience to God's commands, despite his massacre of priests, Saul still saw God "speaking to him" in the circumstances of life and giving him hope. Instead of listening to the very words of God, Saul gave more attention to a message he erroneously imagined to be from God. So, Saul prepared to attack David in Keilah.

DAVID'S OBEDIENCE. When David heard that Saul was preparing to attack him in Keilah, he again inquired of the Lord. Abiathar, a priest who had escaped Saul's wrath in Nob, had joined David in Keilah, and David asked him to bring the ephod, which contained the Urim and Thummim, devices by which priests could determine the will of God (Lev. 8:8; Num. 27:21). God revealed to David that Saul would indeed attack Keilah, and that the men of Keilah would surrender David to Saul. So David again taught his men an important lesson. Even when God had recently given them victory, and even though they were now enjoying the comforts of city life, they were to follow God's leading and return to hiding in the wilderness. They might never understand why God had them save a town only to abandon it, but they would learn that doing God's will would assure them of God's favor and blessing.

David avoids Saul
1 Sam. 23:14-29

PROVIDENCE, NOT CHANCE

God's purpose throughout this part of David's life was to preserve and prepare him to be the next king of Israel. But how does God, who "works all things according to the counsel of his will" (Eph. 1:11), accomplish his purpose without making robots of his creation? The story of David's escape in the wilderness shows how God can providentially accomplish his purpose even while allowing men to oppose it.

DIVINE RESOLUTION. First, this story demonstrates that the wishes of men do not force God to abandon his purpose. When the Ziphites offered to help Saul capture David, Saul called upon the Lord to bless the Ziphites for assisting him in his efforts to capture David and kill him, but God was not obligated to act inconsistently with His purpose at man's bidding. The only prayers God promises to answer are those made in accordance with His will (1 John 5:14).

DIVINE LIMITATION. Second, this story shows that God does not force humans to submit their wills to Him. Saul's will was to hate David, and God did not force Saul to love David. Though God thwarted Saul's attempts to harm David, He left Saul free to live consistently with his character. The will of the Ziphites was to give Saul intelligence about where David usually traveled, what people frequently saw him (and probably helped him or did business with him), and where he hid. God did not stop the Ziphites from providing this intelligence. Saul used it well, and trapped David between two divisions of his army.

DIVINE DISTRACTION. Finally, the story shows that God has many means to accomplish His purpose. In this case, God providentially sent idolatrous Philistines into Israel. Their threat to the kingdom was so great that Saul was forced to abandon his pursuit of David at the very moment victory seemed within his grasp. In this way, God preserved David's life so that He might eventually give him the throne of Israel.

David spares Saul's life near Engedi
1 Sam. 24:1-22

TEMPTATION OR OPPORTUNITY?

Saul immediately returned to his pursuit of David when he finished fighting the Philistines. By this time, David had moved about ten miles east of Ziph to Engedi, which was near the west shore of the Dead Sea. During the pursuit, David and his men hid in a cave. With Saul's army outside, they were in grave danger if Saul had known where they were. But Saul did not know, so he went into a cave to relieve himself (the literal "cover his feet" in the KJV is a euphemism — see the BDB, *sûk*, p. 696-97). Because Saul was alone, in the dark, and unprepared for defending himself, David's men saw this as an opportunity sent by God for David to kill the unsuspecting Saul. David snuck up on Saul, but instead of killing him, cut off the corner of his outer garment.

REMORSE. An interesting aspect of this story is that David felt remorse even for cutting off a corner of Saul's robe (v. 5). The reason David felt this remorse was because his action was disrespectful to the king. According to Num. 15:37-41, God instructed Israelites to wear blue tassels in the corner of their garments. These tassels, which were extensions of the embroidery in the hem, were a kind of identification. For instance, priests had quite elaborate hems according to Ex. 28:33. Undoubtedly, the tassel of a king was more elaborate than the tassel of a common man and identified him as royalty. Evidently, each person's tassel was unique since Mesopotamian texts indicate that they were impressed into clay as a kind of signature. Furthermore, removing the hem and its tassels symbolized a change in the identification of a person. For instance, when a man divorced his wife, he cut off the hem of her garment which identified her as his wife (see Jacob Milgrom, "Of Hems and Tassels," *Biblical Archaeology Review*, May/June 1983, p. 61 ff.). In this case, David removed that which in part identified Saul as king, and in doing so he insulted the ruler of God's people. Hence, David felt remorse for his deed.

PERSUASION. When David returned to his men, he had to justify his refusal to kill Saul. David did not merely defend himself. He "persuaded" them (v. 7). Saul was his master because he was the Lord's anointed. He would not lift his hand against the Lord's anointed. On this basis, David saw the situation as a temptation rather than a providential opportunity. David wanted his men to show the same respect to Saul as he did.

DILEMMA. So how does one distinguish a temptation from a providential opportunity? In the story about how Ahab spared the Aramean king, Ben-Hadad, after defeating him in battle, a prophet rebuked Ahab for not taking advantage of a providential opportunity (I Kings 20:42). Ahab erred in sparing an enemy who had engaged God's people in battle (Deut. 20:13). David's situation was different because Saul had been anointed by God to rule Israel and as such was David's master. It was not lawful even to speak against the ruler of God's people (Ex. 22:28). Accordingly, David correctly identified what his men thought to be an opportunity to be a temptation. No opportunity is ever providential if it requires one to break God's law; such opportunities are nothing more than temptations.

LOYALTY. After Saul left the cave, David also left the cave and addressed Saul. In David's longest recorded speech in 1 Samuel (Bergen, 1996, pp. 239-240), he made it clear that he remained loyal to Saul and would not lift his hand against his "lord, for he is the LORD's anointed" (v. 10). David called Saul "my father" (v. 11) as he raised a portion of Saul's garment to prove that he had chosen not to kill Saul when he had the opportunity. David was a man of more noble character than Saul. He would not wrest the kingdom from Saul; instead, he would call upon the Lord to vindicate him.

REALIZATION. Saul was deeply shaken. Not only did he respond by calling David "my son," but he also completely understood the significance of David's deed. When Saul saw the hem of his own robe *in David's hand* (see v. 11), he said, "I know that you shall surely be king, and that the kingdom of Israel shall be established *in your hand*" (v. 20, emphasis mine). And again alluding to David's act of *cutting off the corner of his robe*, he pled, "Swear to me therefore by the LORD that you *will not cut off my offspring* after me" (v. 21, emphasis mine). In this speech, which is also Saul's longest recorded speech (Bergen, 1996, pp. 239-240), Saul acknowledged that David would indeed become king of Israel.

**Samuel dies
1 Sam. 25:1**

**Nabal insults David
1 Sam. 25:1b-13**

CHECK MATE!

I was playing a game of chess with a young lawyer and thought I was doing quite well. In fact, he apparently thought so too. After studying the board for a long time, he said, "I resign." A grad student who was watching asked me, "Do you mind if I finish the game?" This grad student hadn't lost a game in several years, and he was often seen playing several games at once in the student union. I felt quite secure in my position, so I thought to myself, "Here's a chance to brag that I beat Tommy J." I should have known better. Solomon said, "Fools plunge ahead with reckless confidence" (Prov. 14:16 NLT), but in the end, they die "for lack of sense" (Prov. 10:21). Tommy saw a move both the young lawyer and I had overlooked. I knew I was in trouble as soon as he moved. Three plays later, he announced, "Check mate!" Like me, Nabal felt secure in his position, but he would die suddenly.

RICH AND CONNECTED. Nabal was a very rich Calebite (vv. 2-3). Like neighboring Calebites in Ziph, he was probably allied with Saul (see 1 Sam. 23:19), and he was shearing his sheep in Carmel, a village in Judah (see Josh. 15:55) where Saul had erected a monument to himself celebrating his defeat of the Amalekites (1 Sam. 15:12). As a rich man, he found it easy to despise a poor outcast like David, who had broken away from his master (v. 10).

ARROGANT AND HARSH. Nabal was also a harsh man who behaved badly (v. 3). He asked rhetorically, "Who is David? Who is the son of Jesse?" The questions implied that David and his father Jesse were nobodies, unknowns. Then he insinuated that David was no more than one of the many slaves who were breaking away from their masters (v. 10) and that David's messengers were nobodies from "I do not know where" (v. 11). In one sentence (v. 11), he even emphasized his arrogance using "I" or "my" seven times (Youngblood, 1992, p. 756).

FOOL. Nabal was a fool just as his name implied (1 Sam. 25:25). He considered himself a self-made man, a man who by his own ingenuity and effort had accumulated great riches. He refused to recognize the protection provided by David's men (1 Sam. 25:15), or listen to his own servants who labored for him (1 Sam. 25:17). Like the rich fool in the parable told by Jesus, he did not consider that his wealth would pass from him to another if he were to die (see Luke 12:16-21). Indeed, he did die (1 Sam. 25:38), and his wealth was passed to another.

May we not be like arrogant Nabal in laying up treasures for ourselves on earth. Instead, may we lay up treasures in heaven with God.

Abigail intercedes for Nabal
1 Sam. 25:14-35

THE FOOL'S MATE

Someone has said that opposites attract. Nabal and Abigail were certainly opposites. Nabal was "harsh and badly behaved," but Abigail was "discerning and beautiful" (1 Sam. 25:3). Nabal was a fool. Abigail, the fool's mate, was quite different.

ATTENTIVE. Unlike Nabal, who did not listen to his servants, Abigail listened to the servant who reported that David's men had been good to them and protected them. She listened when the servant warned that Nabal's insults might bring harm to Nabal and his family.

APPRECIATIVE. Unlike Nabal, Abigail appreciated the protection David had provided. David wasn't in a protection racket. He was "fighting the battles of the Lord" (v. 28) against the marauding bands that harassed the Lord's people. Accordingly, she prepared a generous gift for David and his men.

RESPONSIBLE AND RESPECTFUL. Abigail took responsibility for the insults David's men had received from her family saying, "On me alone, my lord, be the guilt" (v. 24). Furthermore, she constantly addressed David as "my lord" and spoke of herself as "your servant."

DISCERNING. While respectful, Abigail also saw that David was in danger of putting the blot of bloodguilt on his character by seeking revenge with his own hand (v. 26). She discerned that David was not conspiring against Saul, but waiting patiently on the Lord's time. She discerned that David was protecting Judah from the enemies of the Lord's people even more than Saul was. She discerned that God would make David "a sure house" (v. 28; cf. 2 Sam. 7:11), that God had appointed him "prince over Israel" (v. 30). She discerned that David had no need to act out of character by "shedding blood without cause" or "working salvation" for himself (v. 31). If he started destroying God's people when they did not appreciate the protection he had given them, his "services" would have become a protection racket. Her gift was the Lord's restraining hand on his actions (v. 26).

Abigail obtained a pardon for her husband and safety for her household (v. 35). Abigail was the exact opposite of her husband. While Nabal died for his lack of sense, she nourished many with her righteous words (Prov. 10:21).

David marries Abigail
1 Sam. 25:36-44

MISMATCHED MATES

Just as the boy wearing mismatched socks remarked that he had another pair just like them in his dresser at home, so also David had mismatched mates at home. David's marriage to Abigail stands in contrast to his marriage to Michal. Although Michal was the daughter of a king and Abigail was the wife of a rich man who feasted like a king, the similarities end there.

Michal loved David, but Abigail respected him. David won Michal by killing 200 men, but he won Abigail by sparing the lives of many men. Michal preserved David's life by lying while Abigail preserved David's integrity by keeping him from taking revenge. Michal brought an idol into his house (1 Sam. 19:13), but Abigail brought five handmaids. Michal would later resent David praising God with female servants (2 Sam. 6:20), but Abigail was willing to wash the feet of David's servants. Michal would call David a vulgar fellow (2 Sam. 6:20), but Abigail called him "lord" fourteen times (Bergen, 1996, p. 251).

Actually, the mismatched wives did not live together in the same home. When Saul was seeking David's life, Michal had helped him escape. Saul then gave her to another man, Palti, who was less of a threat to his throne. Abigail was not, however, the only wife in David's home. David had previously married a woman from Jezreel by the name of Ahinoam (NASB and NIV have "had also taken/married" for the Hebrew perfect tense). Jezreel was a settlement in the same area of Judah as Carmel (Josh. 15:55-56). It was not the village with the same name in Issachar (Josh. 19:18). Having two wives probably indicated that David had become a man of great importance though not yet recognized as king.

David spares Saul's life in the Desert of Ziph
1 Sam. 26:1-25

FORGIVENESS BEYOND THE CALL OF DUTY

> There is no love without forgiveness, and there is no
> forgiveness without love.
> -- Bryant McGill

MANY OFFENSES. This chapter records Saul's last attempt on David's life. The first attempts came shortly after the women praised David's heroism in battle against Goliath. Twice Saul tried to pin David to the wall with a spear (1 Sam. 18:10-11). Then Saul sent David into numerous battles with the Philistines hoping that they would kill him, but that strategy only made David more famous because he was successful (1 Sam. 18:17 ff.). Then Saul commanded his attendants to kill David, but Jonathan intervened (19:1 ff.). Then Saul tried to pin David to the wall with a spear a third time, but David escaped (19:10). Saul sent men to David's house, but David escaped to Samuel in Naioth (19:11 ff.). Then when his men failed in their mission, Saul pursued David to Naioth himself, but God protected David (19:18 ff.). Saul took an army and pursued David in the Desert of Maon (23: 24ff.) and in the Desert of Engedi (24:1 ff.). Even after David spared Saul's life near Engedi, and Saul admitted his sin, Saul again pursued David with his army in the region near the hill of Hachilah.

So how did David react to Saul's persistence in pursuing him? What did he do when he had opportunity to pin Saul to the ground with a spear when Saul had tried three times to pin him to the wall with a spear? David refused to avenge himself on the anointed king. In refusing to kill Saul, he is an example of both forgiving and forbearing.

FORGIVENESS. A willingness to forgive is a virtue every Christian should have. Jesus said that if a man repents after a rebuke, we are to forgive him even seven times in one day (Luke 17:3-4). Forgiveness is offered to all offenders and given to the penitent so that reconciliation can be achieved (see also Matt. 18:15). Consequently, to forgive means to release a person from a consequence or penalty for a moral failure (BDAG, ἀφίημι, p. 156). Both parties recognize the moral failure and forgiveness is both offered and given on the basis of repentance. Forgiveness loves the sinner but rejects the sin. When David spared Saul's life, his actions and words rebuked Saul, and Saul expressed repentance and requested David's mercy (1 Sam. 24:17-21; 26:21, 25). Considering all that Saul had done to David, it appears that David would have forgiven Saul seventy times seven times (cf. Matt. 18:22).

FORBEARANCE. Forbearance is another Christian virtue. Sometimes a person who has committed an offense is not moved to repent by the offer of forgiveness. The person who has been offended has two choices: 1) bring the matter to the church for judgment (Matt. 18:15-17), or 2) bear the wrong patiently (1 Cor. 6:5-7). Bearing the wrong patiently is called forbearance. Paul urged the Ephesians to live worthy of their calling "with all humility and gentleness, with patience, bearing with one another in love" (Eph. 4:2). We must not avenge ourselves, but with humility, patience, and love give God time to deal with the person so that reconciliation might be achieved. David did this. Even when Saul repeated his offenses, David continued to address Saul as "my lord" (repeatedly in v. 17 and following). Furthermore, he endured not merely out of a sense of duty to the Lord's anointed but also out of a sense of love. Recall that when David spared Saul's life the first time, he called Saul "my father" (1 Sam. 24:11), and when Saul was finally killed in a battle with the Philistines, David sang that Saul was loved and lovely (2 Sam. 1:23). Somehow, David continued to love Saul, and that helped him to bear patiently with Saul's insane jealousy and wrath rather than to seek revenge.

TOLERANCE. Tolerance differs from both forgiveness and forbearance. Forgiveness is the act of mercifully freeing a penitent person from the penalty for an acknowledged offense; it accepts the sinner but rejects the sin. Tolerance, on the other hand, hopes enmity will not escalate into something worse and allows a tolerable offense to continue; it accepts the sin but rejects the sinner. Forbearance, motivated by love, refuses to seek revenge against an obstinate offender but hopes that God will soften the heart and produce reconciliation before justice is executed. Tolerance, on the other hand, motivated by fear of making things worse, does not confront an offender but nevertheless hopes that the person will go away or get what they deserve.

David was not merely tolerant. Rather, he was both forgiving and forbearing. He was forbearing because Saul had too often forgotten his good intentions. Therefore, David could not return with Saul or even stay in Judah.

Part Three: Refuge in Philistia

1011–1010 B.C.; age 29-30

David flees to Philistia
1 Sam. 27:1-12

A COMPROMISING SITUATION

We often blame David's troubles on Saul, but if Saul was the only problem David had in Israel, he probably never would have felt compelled to flee Israel and seek refuge among the archenemies of Israel, the Philistines.

FRIENDS LIKE THESE. David's own kinsmen drove him into exile by constantly feeding Saul's suspicions. When David spared Saul's life in the cave, he said to Saul, "Why do you listen to the words of men who say, 'Behold, David seeks your harm'? …. See, my father, see the corner of your robe in my hand. For by the fact that I cut off the corner of your robe and did not kill you, you may know and see that there is no wrong or treason in my hands" (1 Sam. 24:9-11). When David spared Saul's life a second time, David again protested against those of his kinsmen who were slandering him to Saul, "Now therefore let my lord the king hear the words of his servant. If it is the LORD who has stirred you up against me, may he accept an offering, but if it is men, may they be cursed before the LORD, for they have driven me out this day that I should have no share in the heritage of the LORD, saying, 'Go, serve other gods'" (1 Sam. 26:19). With friends like these, David didn't need any enemies. It is a sad day when God's people drive out a brother by listening to and assisting those who falsely accuse that brother. Sadly, David felt that the only way he could escape Saul and his informers was to flee to Philistia.

DANGEROUS CONCESSIONS. Although we are not told, David apparently fled to Achish, king of Gath, without inquiring of Abiathar the priest or seeking the advice of Gad the prophet as he had done on previous occasions. By seeking refuge in Philistia, David put himself, his family, and his men in a compromising situation.

- David, his family, and his men left Israel and those who worshiped God.
- David, his men, and their families lived among people who worshiped idols and who would have a corrupting influence.

- David had to depend on an enemy of Israel for protection and pretend loyalty to them. David lived a lie.
- David had to pay tribute to an enemy of Israel.

ADVANTAGES. David was keenly aware of the dangers he faced and was, for the most part, able to neutralize them and even turn the situation to his advantage.

- David's kinsmen ceased to give intelligence to Saul, so Saul abandoned his pursuit of David.
- David asked for and received a city, Ziklag, for himself, his soldiers, and their families. Although Ziklag had been in the hands of the Philistines, God had assigned the town first to Judah (Josh. 15:31), and later to Simeon (Josh. 19:5). The move to Ziklag helped neutralize the influence of Philistine culture and enabled them to continue their devotion to God. From this time on, Ziklag remained under the control of Israel.
- David and his men secured the southern border of Judah. He did this without raising Achish's suspicions by telling him that he had attacked regions belonging to Judah when he really attacked the enemies of Judah who often wandered through those regions.
- David and his men made progress in blotting out the memory of the Amalekites as God intended (Deut. 25:17-19). God had rejected Saul as king because he had not completely destroyed them as he commanded (1 Sam. 15:1-3, 22-23).

Mighty men join David in Ziklag
1 Chron. 12:1-7

While David was in Ziklag, some more soldiers came from Benjamin from among Saul's kinsmen and joined David. The Gadites who joined David earlier were skilled with shield and spear, but these men of Benjamin were skilled in shooting arrows and slinging stones. Two of them, Jeziel and Pelet, were the sons of Azmaveth (v. 3), a Benjamite from Bahurim who was one of David's 30 mighty men (2 Sam. 23:31; 1 Chron. 11:33). Although not mentioned among the thirty, Ishmaiah would apparently become their leader for a time (v. 4). Jashobeam (v. 6), a Levite from the clan of Korah living in the territory of Benjamin, became one of David's three mighty men (1 Chron. 11:11; cf. 2 Sam. 23:8).

Achish conscripts David into the Philistine army
1 Sam. 28:1-2

Saul consults a witch at Endor
1 Sam. 28:3-14

BEWITCHED

The imminent battle that faced Saul was further north than most of the battles with the Philistines. Apparently they decided to try to take control of the major trade route from the east through the Valley of Jezreel (Josh. 17:16). The Philistines assembled at Shunem, a city allotted to Issachar (Josh. 19:18) near the southwest slope of the hill of Moreh, which divides the eastern end of the valley. Saul's troops were stationed seven or eight miles south across the valley on Mt. Gilboa. Saul was distressed by the looming battle and desired guidance from the Lord, but no guidance was available either by dream, Urim, or prophet (v. 6).

NO DREAM. There is no record of God communicating with Saul through dreams, but he may have heard about Gideon overhearing a dream in the Midianite army which was camped on the hill of Moreh (Judges 7:9-14), where his army was now camped. That dream and its interpretation greatly encouraged Gideon to attack. Saul, however, had no encouraging dream.

NO PRIEST. Furthermore, Saul could not go to the high priest, who could inquire of the Lord using the Urim and Thummim. At one time, Saul had inquired by Urim and Thummim (1 Sam. 14:37-43), but when the priests have food and a weapon to David, Saul commanded that all the priests be executed (1 Sam. 22). Abiathar, however, escaped and carried the ephod with the Urim and Thummim to David (1 Sam. 23:6-12). So in addition to having no dream from God, Saul could not inquire of the Lord through the priests.

NO PROPHET. Even early in his reign when Saul sought the Lord's favor, he had done so in an unlawful way by performing the priestly duties himself. At that time, the Lord warned Saul that the kingdom was not secure because of his foolish disobedience (1 Sam. 13:12-14). Saul, however, did not heed the Lord's warning. When he rejected the word of the Lord with regard to the Amalekites, Samuel informed him that the Lord had rejected him from being king over Israel (1 Sam. 15:26). From that day on, Saul was alienated from Samuel and the prophets. Samuel never saw Saul again (1 Sam. 15:35). Now, years later, he wanted to consult the Lord through the prophets, but the Lord was no longer to be found. Saul had not sought the Lord when he could be found (Isa. 55:6), and now he was facing the Philistines alone.

ONE WITCH. In his desperation, Saul asked for a medium whom he hoped could communicate with the prophet Samuel, and his men found one in En-dor, a town in the territory of Issachar inhabited by people of Manasseh on the northeast slope of the hill of Moreh (Josh. 17:11). Formerly, Saul had tried to eradicate the mediums from Israel because Moses had instructed the Israelites that they were not to consult mediums (Lev. 19:31) or permit them to remain in the land when they possessed it (Deut. 18:10-12). Now he wanted a medium to bring Samuel up from the dead. Previously, Samuel had told Saul that his rebellion against the Lord was as the sin of witchcraft (1 Sam. 15:23 KJV; divination in ESV). In his rebellion and alienation, Saul actually stooped to witchcraft. Witchcraft saved neither his kingdom nor his life.

Samuel's words fill Saul with fear
1 Sam. 28:15-25

SEEKING STRENGTH

Perhaps you have watched your favorite basketball team or football team being trounced by their opponent. Your team seems to have no energy, no strength. Then you notice their body language. The problem is not just that they are physically exhausted, but they are mentally exhausted as well. They are in despair in their mind and have ceased to believe in themselves. At that moment, something happens that changes everything. Someone steals the ball and breaks away for a dunk at the other end of the court, or someone recovers a fumble. Suddenly body language changes. Heads are lifted, shoulders squared, and steps quickened. What happened? Were their bodies strengthened with a healthy meal? No. Their minds were nourished with hope.

FOR SOUL. When Saul went to the witch in En-dor, he was looking for hope in his soul. He was in "great distress" because God had turned away from him and answered him no more. When Samuel appeared, perhaps to the witch's surprise, Saul asked Samuel to tell him what to do. In reply, Samuel asked rhetorically why he was seeking advice from one he had made an enemy. Then he repeated the last words he had spoken to Saul: "The Lord has torn the kingdom out of your hand and given it to your neighbor" (compare v. 17 with 1 Sam. 15:28). Finally, he told Saul that he and his sons would die the next day, and the Israelite army would be defeated. Saul found no strength for his soul. Whatever spiritual strength Saul may have had left was then exhausted, and Saul collapsed on the ground.

FOR BODY. Perhaps due to his spiritual distress, and perhaps due to the intense preparations for battle, Saul had not eaten anything all day. He needed physical strength too. Although the woman could not provide him with any spiritual strength, she did provide physical strength with food she prepared and set before him. After eating, he rose and went his way. We read no more of Saul until he is mortally wounded on the battlefield the next day. The last meal Saul ate was probably from the hand of the witch of En-dor.

David is excluded from the Philistine army
1 Sam. 29:1-11

RUMORS

> Rumor doth double, like the voice and echo,
> The numbers of the feared.
> -- William Shakespeare

The Philistines marched north to try to take control of the prosperous Valley of Jezreel, which was also a critical part of the trade route from Mesopotamia to Egypt. Saul and the Israelite army were on Mt. Gilboa, which protected the critical pass from the Jordan Valley to the Valley of Jezreel. Achish insisted that David accompany him with the other Philistine forces. David and his men marched at the rear of the Philistine army, and rumors spread quickly among the Philistines and the Israelites.

A RUMOR FEARED. When Achish joined the other Philistine commanders at Aphek about 10 miles east of Joppa in the territory of Ephraim, they immediately asked (v.3), "What are these Hebrews doing here?" They were afraid David's men might turn against them during the battle. Years before when Saul had been powerless to stop the Philistine raiding parties, many Israelites had joined the Philistine forces. Then when the Philistines fled before Jonathan's bold attack, the Israelites had turned on them and helped Saul's army rout them (1 Sam. 14:20-23). Achish was sure David would not do such a thing saying that David had been loyal to him for more than a year. The other Philistine commanders, however, would not listen to him. They could not dispel the rumor they had heard about David: "Saul has struck down his thousands, and David his ten thousands." Consequently, they refused to give David's men the same opportunity. David and his men rose early the next morning to return the forty miles back to Ziklag.

David receives defectors from Saul's army
1 Chron. 12:19-22

RUMORS (CONTINUED)

A RUMOR DISPELLED. When David marched north with the Philistine armies, news spread among the Israelite soldiers. Seven commanders of thousands from the tribe of Manasseh deserted Saul's army and joined David (1 Chron. 12:19-22). You can imagine the dimensions this story would take as it spread among Israelite troops: David was conspiring with the Philistines to overthrow Saul. In order to dispel any lingering remnants of that kind of rumor, the writer records David's dismissal from the Philistine army and return to Ziklag before the battle in which Saul and his sons died. The seven commanders from Manasseh also accompanied David to Ziklag and helped him against the band of Amalekite raiders who burned Ziklag (v. 21). Neither they nor David participated in the battle on Mt. Gilboa (1 Chron. 12:19). David did not lift his hand against the Lord's anointed either personally or in battle. God took the kingdom from Saul and gave it to David.

Rumors were the news of the day. (Even today, they may on occasion be more reliable than official media.). God used a rumor about David slaying tens of thousands, appropriately exaggerated, to get David dismissed from the Philistine army. But God also saw fit to dispel any rumor that David had conspired against Saul by making sure people knew that he had been dismissed from the Philistine army and had returned to Ziklag before the battle in which Saul died.

David finds Ziklag plundered and burned
1 Sam. 30:1-6

GREAT DISTRESS

No trial has overtaken you that is not faced by others.
And God is faithful: He will not let you be tried beyond
what you are able to bear, but with the trial will also

provide a way out so that you may be able to endure it.
-- 1 Cor. 10:13 NET

Saul and David lived in the same world and faced similar trials, but one found strength in the Lord and the other did not. The difference was not in God, who is impartial, but in the seeker.

SIMILAR TRIALS. Saul was in "great distress" (1 Sam. 28:15) because he and the Israelite army were facing a formidable Philistine army. At about the same time, David was "greatly distressed" (v. 6) because David had found Ziklag plundered and his family taken captives by a marauding band of Amalekites. Both were under added stress because their men and the families of their men were also at risk. Some of Saul's officers had deserted him to go to David, and David's men spoke of stoning him (v. 6). In their distress, both sought the Lord, but only one was strengthened.

ONLY ONE STRENGTHENED. Saul did not find strength in God because he had cut himself off from God by disobedience. He cut himself off from the prophet Samuel when he refused to acknowledge his sin, and he cut himself off from the priests when he murdered an entire family in Nob. Even when he finally sought the Lord in desperation, he was seeking his favor without seeking his will, for he was seeking the Lord in an unauthorized way, through a medium. David, on the other hand, had a dynamic relationship with God. He regularly sought the will of God, and he followed the will of God whether spoken by the prophet Gad or Abiathar the priest. His psalms show that he regularly meditated on God's words and blessings, and praised God in all circumstances. Consequently, when he sought the Lord, he found strength in him.

David rescues his family from the Amalekites
1 Sam. 30:7-20

A GODLY GENERAL

> Enduring setbacks while maintaining the ability to show
> others the way to go forward is a true test of leadership.
> – Nitin Nohria

David could not have faced a greater tragedy than the one he discovered when he returned to Ziklag, and it was multiplied by 600 when including his men. They were all so overwhelmed that they wept until they lost their strength. Then, in their despair, David's men found it easy to make him a scapegoat for what happened, and they talked of stoning David.

After finding strength in the Lord, David showed the signs of godly leadership which put his men to work in the constructive effort of regaining their families.

1. DAVID INQUIRED OF THE LORD (v. 8). Despite David's vast knowledge of the region, he knew it was a slim chance that he could find their families before they had been abused, sold, or killed. He needed God's direction, and he sought it. God said to pursue, and God promised that he would overtake the Amalekites and rescue their families.

2. DAVID GAVE HIS MEN DIRECTION (v. 9). David's men were talking of stoning him as if that would somehow atone for their loss, but they knew it really wouldn't. Setting out in pursuit of the Amalekites, however, gave them real hope of recovering their loss.

3. DAVID SHOWED MERCY TO THE EXHAUSTED (v. 10). David did not allow tragedy to harden his heart. He did not chastise the men who could not cross the brook Besor as weaklings. He understood their exhaustion after marching more than 40 miles in less than three full days, and on the third day discovering that their families had been taken captive. He assigned them the task of guarding the luggage so that the remaining men could travel more quickly.

4. DAVID SHOWED KINDNESS TO OUTSIDERS (vv. 11ff.). David didn't have time for interruptions from strangers, and it would have been quite natural to be suspicious of a foreigner in time of war. David could have isolated himself in own little group, but David remembered the Law, which commanded that the Israelites show kindness to aliens (Lev. 19:34). When he found a hungry, thirsty Egyptian in the desert, he took time to offer him food and water. When he did so, he found the guide God had sent to lead him and his men to their families.

David's leadership reminds us of Jesus. When faced with opposition, Jesus sought the will of his Father, and found strength in him (Luke 22:42-43). He gave people a new direction, a new purpose in life. He offered forgiveness to those who opposed him and mercy to those who abandoned him. Jesus showed kindness to outsiders: to publicans and sinners, to the sick and disabled, to a Roman centurion and a Samaritan woman. Those people, in turn, changed the world.

David shares the spoil
1 Sam. 30:21-31

GENEROUS IN VICTORY

> Show yourself in all respects to be a model of good
> works.
> -- Titus 2:7a

The Egyptian led David and his men to the Amalekites who had raided
their village. It was evening, and the Amalekites were celebrating their
victories with drunken revelry. David led the attack against them, and the
battle raged for a whole day. In the end, they saved the lives of all their
families, recovered their own possessions, and took an enormous amount
of additional plunder. Despite the victory, trouble was brewing.

CREDIT WHERE DUE. When David returned after the victory to the
men who had remained at the brook Besor, certain troublemakers among
his soldiers wanted to cut the quitters loose and send them away. The
troublemakers wanted to take all the credit for themselves and destroy the
group that David had assembled, but David did not let them (v. 22).
First, he gave credit to God. The plunder was the gift of God, and God
had both protected them and given them victory (v. 23). Second, he gave
credit to those who stayed behind. Even though they did not participate
in the battle itself, they had protected the supplies that were left behind
while pursuing the enemy (v. 24). Accordingly, it was appropriate to share
both the joy and the blessings of God with those who stayed behind.
David did not allow wicked men to bite and devour one another. David
maintained a spirit of unity and a bond of peace.

FRIENDS REWARDED. David still had enemies in Judah. Recall that
several towns in Judah had either been ungrateful or spiteful toward
David. Among them were Keilah (1 Sam. 23:12), Ziph (1 Sam. 23:19),
Maon (1 Sam. 23:25), and Carmel (1 Sam. 25:2). Though these had
forced him to flee Judah, David also had those in Judah who had
befriended him while fleeing from Saul (vv. 26-31). At his first
opportunity, David acknowledged and strengthened them. Among them
were the inhabitants of Hebron where he would soon be proclaimed king
over the whole tribe of Judah. Godly leaders are grateful to all who help
them.

David showed himself a godly example to his men not only in recovering
from tragedy and in pressing the attack during battle, but also in being

generous in victory. Just as God permitted the Israelites to keep the plunder from Ai after devoting all of the initial plunder of Jericho to destruction (Josh. 6:17-18; 8:2), so God allowed David to keep and distribute plunder from the Amalekites though the initial plunder taken by Saul was to have been devoted to destruction.

Saul dies in battle
1 Sam. 31:1-13 [1 Chron. 10:1-14]

DEAD END

When the battle was finally engaged, the Philistines prevailed and overtook Saul and his sons on Mt. Gilboa. His sons were killed, but Saul continued to fight. He himself was not overpowered in hand-to-hand combat, but archers found their mark and Saul was badly wounded. "Badly wounded" suggests that he was writhing in great pain (BDB, *hûl*, p. 296-97) and so was unable to continue fighting. In that condition, he feared that before killing him, the Philistines would mistreat, abuse, or humiliate him because he could no longer defend himself.

A LIFE SHORTENED. Knowing that he was unable to defend himself and fearing the agonies of torture and ridicule more than death, Saul asked his armor-bearer to kill him. The armor-bearer, however, was greatly afraid to kill the king whom he was bound by devotion and duty to defend (contrast him with the armor-bearer who killed Abimelech whose skull had been cracked when a woman threw a millstone from a tower – Judges 9:54-55). Saul then fell on his own sword, and his armor-bearer did the same.

A DREAM SHATTERED. Saul's death was premature not only because he died by his own hand, but also because he died without fulfilling the dream of Israel when they made him king. They wanted a king to give them victory on the battlefield. God gave them Saul, and told Samuel, "You shall anoint him to be prince over my people Israel. He shall save my people from the hand of the Philistines" (1 Sam. 9:16). Saul showed promise of fulfilling the dream against the Philistines (1 Sam. 14:47-48), but then he acted presumptuously and lost the Lord's blessing (1 Sam. 13). He became indecisive, but Jonathan took the initiative and won a great victory (1 Sam. 14). On another occasion, he was afraid, but David slew Goliath and initiated a great victory (1 Sam. 17). His final battle was a disastrous defeat. When the victorious Philistines returned to the battleground the next day to strip the dead, they found Saul's body. They cut off his head and sent it with messengers to their cities as evidence of their great victory. They hung Saul's body and the bodies of his sons from the walls of Beth-shan, a city about six miles east of Mt. Gilboa. The dream was shattered.

A FAMILY FALLEN. Not only did a man and a dream die on Mt. Gilboa, but a dynasty also died. Saul fell on his own sword and three of his sons including the valiant heir apparent, Jonathan, died in battle. Only one rather weak son continued as king for a short time. In this way, the book ends much the same way it began. The book begins with the high priest Eli and his sons not giving honor to God as they should. When the Philistines attacked Israel, his sons carried the ark into the battle where they died at the hands of the Philistines. When news of the Philistine victory reached Eli, he fell from his chair and died. His family continued in the priesthood only a short time. As it had been with the high priest who did not honor God, so it was with the king who did not honor God. Their families were no longer allowed to serve God as priests or kings.

David receives news of Saul's death
2 Sam. 1:1-16

A "CONFESSION" GONE AWRY

The young man who brought the news of Israel's defeat on Mt. Gilboa to David was an opportunist. He habitually sought to take advantage of situations to gain wealth or advancement, and he did so without considering whether his actions were right or wrong. Evidences of his opportunistic character are found throughout this episode.

FIRST, the young man said, "By chance I happened to be on Mount Gilboa" (v. 6). By neglecting to give his reason for being on Mt. Gilboa, he probably raised David's suspicions about his character. He was not there at the command of an officer. He was not participating in the heat of battle out of loyalty to the king or to Israel. He just happened to be there. He implies he was behind the line of battle because the wounded king saw him when he "looked behind him." He was probably a human vulture at the battle site merely to profit from any opportunity that might present itself.

SECOND, the young man was an opportunistic liar. Although David had no way of knowing that the messenger was lying, we know from 1 Sam. 31:3 ff. that he was lying. Saul could not have been "leaning on his spear"

(v. 6) after he and his armor-bearer had fallen on their swords. What the Amalekite saw was a dead king. No armor-bearer was there to defend the king's life or honor. Accordingly, when he saw the dead king, he thought it would be to his advantage to confess to David, "I killed him." He thought he could obtain honor and advancement because he had lived in Israel long enough to know that Saul was the only obstacle to David becoming king.

THIRD, the messenger brought Saul's crown and arm-band to David (v. 10). If he had killed Saul out of a sense of mercy as he implied, he would have tried to restore the crown to the royal family, or at least to one of Saul's army officers, without claiming to have killed him. Instead of doing that, he made a much longer journey to take the crown to David. So the crown and arm-band were not only evidence that Saul was dead, but they were also conclusive evidence of the Amalekite's opportunism.

FOURTH, the young man told David he was the son of an alien or sojourner (v. 13). His father was an Amalekite, a member of the nomadic, warlike tribe that David had been destroying in obedience to God's command. Perhaps many in his family were opportunists who chose to sojourn in Israel merely to save their lives. (If you can't beat them, join them.) However, aliens who obeyed Israel's laws received rights and protections from those laws, so David could not execute the Amalekite merely because he brought bad news.

FIFTH, the Amalekite showed no respect for "the Lord's anointed." The messenger's claim to have killed the king showed that he had no loyalty to Israel's law or Israel's rulers. As such, the young man could not claim the protection of that law. In fact, he would fall under the condemnation of that law. His "confession" did not bring him the advancement and honor he anticipated. Instead, it convicted him and brought him swift destruction.

David mourns for Saul and Jonathan
2 Sam. 1:17-27

FUNERAL ORATION

When Anthony gave Julius Caesar's funeral oration, his rhetoric was crafted more by political considerations than his personal devotion to Caesar. He was not looking back upon the life of Caesar, but looking forward to who would rule now that Caesar was gone. When David heard of the deaths of Saul and Jonathan, he composed a lament for them that he taught to Israel. It is perhaps natural to ask, "Did David express his genuine feelings or were his words politically motivated?"

BRAVE. Saul had been a valiant soldier and successful commander. He fought successfully against Moab, the Ammonites, Edom, the kings of Zobah, and the Philistines (1 Sam. 14:47-48). Jonathan had also been a brave soldier. David compared them to eagles and lions (v. 23). Indeed, Saul was swifter than an eagle when he saved the men of Jabesh Gilead from Nahash, the Ammonite king (1 Sam. 11:1 ff.). Jonathan was stronger than a lion when he put the whole Philistine army to flight (1 Sam. 14:1 ff.). David's refrain was fitting: "How the mighty have fallen!" David was expressing genuine grief when he wrote this lament.

GRACIOUS. It is a little harder to see why David praised both Saul and Jonathan as "loved and gracious" (v. 23 NIV; ESV has "loved and lovely"). Saul certainly had not been gracious in his treatment of David. Nevertheless, if the people prospered when Saul protected them from their enemies, then Saul might be considered generous. It could then be said that Saul had clothed the daughters of Israel in scarlet and finery and adorned them with ornaments of gold (v. 24). Furthermore, both Saul and Jonathan had loved David at one time (1 Sam. 16:21), and David evidently loved both of them. So even though Saul later treated David maliciously, David managed to remember the good in Saul and always showed him great respect. David's praise was not motivated by a desire to be king.

LOVED. It is easier to understand David's grief over the death of Jonathan, who had been a close friend for years. Their shared faith and courage made them kindred spirits. They were comrades in arms. Their devotion to each other was born of fighting Israel's enemies together, enduring hardships together, and overcoming obstacles together. They knew they could depend on each other in whatever physical or spiritual battle they were fighting. Their shared devotion was different in kind than the love of man for a woman. In the midst of battle, that devotion was also greater than the love of man for a woman. David's lament for Jonathan was not politically motivated.

Part Four: Hebron

1009–1003 B.C.; age 31-37; regnal years 1-7

David is proclaimed king over Judah in Hebron
2 Sam. 2:1-7

CHANGING ALLEGIANCE

After receiving news of Saul's death, David inquired of God whether he should return to Judah. God told him to go to Hebron, which was located in the hill country about 15 miles south of Bethlehem. As a city of refuge (Josh. 20:7) and a city designated for priests (Josh. 21:13), Hebron was probably the leading city in Judah at the time. When David arrived in Hebron, the men of Judah gathered there and anointed him a second time making him king over the house of Judah. When David finally became king of all Israel, he had been anointed three times. What was the significance of each anointing?

CHOSEN OF GOD. At God's command, the prophet Samuel anointed David privately the first time. David had not yet reached adulthood, and he was not proclaimed as king to Israel. The anointing did, however, signify that God had chosen him to replace Saul as king (see 1 Sam. 16:1-13).

RECOGNIZED BY THE ELDERS OF JUDAH. When David went up to Hebron from Ziklag, the men of Judah anointed him as king. This probably was not merely a declaration of their choice as king, but a recognition that God had chosen him to be their king (see 1 Sam. 25:30).

BROADER RECOGNITION SOUGHT. Although David was chosen of God to be king of all Israel, he did not seek to subdue the other tribes through force of arms. Instead, he sought their favor. One of David's first official acts as king was to promise to show the people of Jabesh Gilead the same kindness Saul had as king, and announced that Judah had already anointed him. He introduced this offer by praising them for taking the bodies of Saul and Jonathan down from the walls of the Philistine outpost at Beth-shan and giving them a proper burial. Eventually, David did win the favor of the rest of Israel and was anointed a third time when all Israel recognized him as the king God had chosen (2 Sam. 5:1-3).

GOD'S CHOICE IGNORED. The three kings over united Israel, Saul (1 Sam. 10:1), David (1 Sam. 16:13), and Solomon (1 Kings 1:39), were anointed privately as an indication of God's choice. After these three, a private anointing occurred only once when Jehu was appointed to destroy the house of Ahab (1 Kings 19:16; 2 Kings 9:6; 2 Chron. 22:7). Gradually, tradition (publicly anointing the oldest son of the king in Judah) and expediency (publicly acknowledging the strongest rival in Israel) became the norm, and little consideration was given to the kind of person God would want to be king.

God's choices don't depend on human recognition. God chose many prophets whom men persecuted, and he chose Jesus whom they killed. Jesus chose twelve apostles without seeking men's recognition, and God gave special spiritual gifts to some people according to his own will (Heb. 2:4). Although God's choices don't depend on human recognition, God does desire our recognition of his chosen leaders. The apostles told the brothers in Jerusalem to choose seven men whom God had filled with the Spirit and wisdom (Acts 6:3). These leaders upon whom God had bestowed his favor were chosen by men to care for the widows in the church. Similarly, elders are chosen from among those whose lives are demonstrations of God's workmanship (1 Tim. 3:1-7). How we recognize leaders should never become a mere tradition. Instead, we should seek and recognize those whom God has chosen.

David fathers sons in Hebron
2 Sam. 3:2-5 [1 Chron. 3:1-4]

CULTURAL APPROVAL

Cultural approval does not equal divine approval. The former makes the will of mankind the measure of acceptance and the latter makes the will of God the measure of correctness. God may accept some things that are culturally approved, but he may reject others. David was a man with a godly heart, but when it came to marriage, he did what was culturally acceptable even though it violated God's law.

MANY WIVES. The Scripture names six sons who were born to David in Hebron, each by a different wife. A man of power and wealth could marry several wives with cultural approval. The marriages confirmed the man's power and gave him leverage in asserting that power. After Saul gave Michal to another man, David married two women from Judah, one from Jezreel and the other from Carmel, confirming his growing power in Judah. The hometowns of the last three wives are not known.

FOREIGN WIVES. One of the six sons born in Hebron was the son of Maacah. She was the daughter of the king of Geshur, a country east of the Sea of Galilee. Again, marriage to the daughter of a neighboring king was culturally approved. The marriage guaranteed an alliance between David and the king of Geshur, and put pressure on Ish-bosheth, who then had allied enemies to the north and the south.

VIOLATED LAW. Even though they were culturally approved, David's marriages violated Mosaic Law. First, they violated the law concerning kings, which said the king must "not acquire many wives for himself, lest his heart turn away" (Deut. 17:17). Second, the marriage to the daughter of the king of Geshur violated God's explicit command to Israel not to intermarry with the idolatrous nations of the land (Deut. 7:3). Geshur was a territory that the Israelites failed to conquer during the days of Moses and Joshua (Josh. 13:13) so that its people lived among the Israelites for many years.

David is opposed by Ish-bosheth
2 Sam. 2:8-11

WHAT'S IN A NAME?

> A good name is to be chosen rather than great riches,
> and favor is better than silver or gold.
> -- Prov. 22:1

After Saul was killed and Israel defeated on Mt. Gilboa, Saul's cousin Abner (1 Sam. 14:50), who was captain of his army, regathered his forces at Mahanaim, a town east of the Jordan on the border between Gad and the half tribe of Manasseh (Josh. 13:24-31). There he proclaimed Saul's son Ish-bosheth king over Israel, probably after he regained control of the territory west of the Jordan perhaps four or five years later. Thus, the civil war between the house of Saul and David would not have begun until David's fourth or fifth year and ended with Ish-bosheth's death two years later when David had been king for six or seven years.

THE SURVIVING SON. Ish-bosheth was not, of course, mentioned among Saul's sons who were slain on Mt. Gilboa. Those sons were Jonathan, Malki-Shua, and Abinadab (1 Sam. 31:2). Surprisingly, Ish-bosheth does not appear in any other lists of Saul's sons. In 1 Sam. 14:49, they are listed as Jonathan, Ishvi, and Malki-Shua. In 1 Chron. 8:33 and 9:39, they are listed as Jonathan, Malki-Shua, Abinadab, and Esh-Baal. The names of Jonathan, Malki-Shua, and Abinadab are consistent. Accordingly, it appears that Ish-bosheth was the same person as Ishvi and Esh-Baal because all include the same root "Esh/Ish."

AN AMBIGUOUS NAME. Many suggest that Saul named his son Esh-Baal (Youngblood, 1992, p. 823). He probably intended the name to mean "Man of the Lord" as "baal" could mean "lord" as well as "husband" or "master." However, "baal" could also refer to the Canaanite god worshipped in the region. In order to avoid that association, he was called Ishvi in 1 Sam. 14:49. Ishvi means "Man of Yahweh" (**Nelson's Quick Reference Topical Bible Index**, 1995, p. 324). Ishvi would mean the same as Esh-baal, but it would not have the idolatrous associations of the latter name.

AMBIGUITIES MULTIPLIED. Ish-bosheth may have arisen in a similar way. In this case, scribes substituted "sheth," meaning "shame," for "baal" to show their abhorrence of anything associated with idolatry (Youngblood, 1992, p. 823). Ish-bosheth, therefore, would mean "Man of Shame." On the other hand, some have suggested recently that Ish-bosheth means "Man of Strength" where "strength" refers to a divine attribute (Wood, et al., 1996, **New Bible Dictionary**, p. 518). Even if this were true, it would not have eliminated the ambiguous associations created by the name, but would have multiplied them: Esh-Baal would mean "Man of the Lord/Baal," and Ish-bosheth would mean "Man of Strength/Shame." Perhaps the ambiguity of his names suggests the weak, wavering character of Saul's son who became king for two short years.

Today, the associations that gather around our names during our lives are more important than the meanings of the names themselves. We would do well to reflect on what people think when they hear our names.

David wins initial victory at Gibeon
2 Sam. 2:12 - 3:1

FOR LOVE OF BATTLE

All the men who gathered at the pool in Gibeon, just north of Judah's border and eight miles NW of Jerusalem, were brothers. So why did they fight? Three factors contributed to this fight among friends. First, there were divided loyalties. Those with Abner were loyal to Saul's house, and those with Joab were loyal to David. Second, there was a perceived threat. Joab undoubtedly considered it a threat to David when Abner moved his army to Gibeon. At the same time, Abner may have considered David's growing strength to be a threat to the property of Saul's family in Benjamin. Still, the two armies did not seem overly anxious to fight. The third factor may have simply been the male desire for a contest in which one may prove his superior strength or prowess.

THE GAME. The contest began when Abner proposed that twelve men from each side "compete before us" (v. 14). His idea was that the men would "hold a contest" (NASB) in a kind of sporting event for the entertainment of the onlookers. Undoubtedly, the proposal had been preceded by a contest of words: boasts and insults being shouted between the camps. When the taunting had escalated, the words had to be backed up with actions. The twelve men did not hesitate to accept the challenge. Each one armed with a sword but carrying no shield, grabbed his opponent with a free hand and stabbed him with the other. The "game" ended in a draw.

PRESSING THE ADVANTAGE. None were satisfied with a draw, so the two armies were soon fully engaged in battle. Abner's men suffered heavy losses and fled before David's men. Joab's brother Asahel, a son of David's older sister Zeruiah, soon found himself pursuing Abner. Abner, an older and more experienced soldier, was better armed, but Asahel was faster. Abner suggested either that Asahel give up his pursuit long enough to better arm himself by stripping a fallen soldier (Bergen, 1996, p. 304) or that he be satisfied fighting a younger soldier more his equal (J.E. Smith, 2000, p. 353). Asahel knew his advantage was his speed and refused to change either his strategy or his objective. Without turning to face his pursuer, Abner thrust backward with the butt of his spear. Asahel's momentum carried him into the spear which passed through his stomach and out of his back.

VICTORY. David's men who saw the body of Asahel were shocked at the death of one of David's mighty men (2 Sam. 23:24; 1 Chron. 11:26), and their pursuit of Abner's men was abruptly stopped. The course of the battle, however, was not changed because the other soldiers continued their pursuit and surrounded Abner's men on a hill east of Gibeah. Abner, who had suggested that twelve men from each side begin the fighting, called upon Joab to end the fighting. Joab accepted the truce because the victory had been decisive. Only twenty of David's men had died, but 360 of Abner's men had been killed.

CAUSE FOR REVENGE. When Joab accepted the truce, he apparently did not know that his brother Asahel had been slain. After the dead were identified, he made a quick trip to Bethlehem to bury his brother and returned with the other soldiers to David at Hebron. Abner crossed the Jordan River and returned to Mahanaim, but Joab did not forget him. Despite Judah's victory that day, Joab was determined to avenge his brother's death just as Abner knew he would be (v. 22).

David accepts Abner's offer
2 Sam. 3:6-21

POWERS BEHIND THE THRONE

Politics is the maneuvering of people with power for a position of supremacy. Over a period of about two years, David had been growing stronger than Saul's son Ish-bosheth. The power struggle involved many people behind the scenes, people not sitting on either throne.

ABNER. Abner was Ish-bosheth's commander-in-chief. Four or five years after the Philistine victory over Saul on Mt. Gilboa, Abner was able to proclaim Ish-bosheth, Saul's surviving son, king of the northern tribes. He managed to accomplish this even though many of Israel's elders wanted to make David their king (see v. 17). Ish-bosheth was a weak and incompetent monarch, so Abner became ambitious strengthening his own position.

RIZPAH. Ish-bosheth saw Abner's power growing and suspected that Abner had asserted it by sleeping with Rizpah, one of the concubines in the royal harem. Whether Ish-bosheth was paranoid about the success of his military commander as Saul had been, or Abner had in fact slept with Rizpah, Abner was insulted. Abner suddenly found it convenient to appeal to God's promise to David, and he openly declared that he would establish David as king over all Israel. Although Abner openly proclaimed his treasonous purpose, Ish-bosheth was so afraid of Abner that he could not even speak, let alone order his execution.

MICHAL. When Abner sent emissaries to David, he quickly learned that Michal was more important to David than he was. David declared that he would not negotiate with Abner or allow Abner in his presence unless he brought "Michal, daughter of Saul" with him (v. 13). The importance of Michal was reinforced when David sent messengers directly to Ish-bosheth demanding that he order the return of "my wife Michal" (v. 14).

In this way, David rejected secrecy in Abner's negotiations, required public transfer of Saul's daughter to David's family reasserting his right to the throne, and insisted that Ish-bosheth publicly acknowledge that his father Saul had no legal right to give David's wife to another man. (Paltiel was heartbroken, but the heartbreak was of his own making because he had married another man's wife.)

ELDERS OF ISRAEL. The elders of Israel and Benjamin played a key role in who would rule all Israel. For a long time, they had wanted to make David their king, and perhaps Abner sensed that he could not deliver their support to Ish-bosheth much longer. At Abner's urging, the elders cast their support to David. Abner undoubtedly felt the euphoria of a power broker, but it was the support of the elders that David wanted, not merely the support of Abner.

GOD. David's throne was actually God's throne, and God would give it to whom he wished despite all human schemes. Saul had tried to cut David off from claiming the throne by driving him out of the country and giving his daughter, David's wife, to another man. Abner had tried to retain royal power for Saul's family and his own power within that family even though he knew God had chosen David. Michal was a pawn in the hands of those who wanted power, and the elders of Israel followed the lead of Abner despite their private desire to make David their king. Whatever human powers were involved in the politics of the time, God was the real power behind the throne, and he made David king of all Israel.

Joab kills Abner
2 Sam. 3:22-27

POWER PLAY

Just as a hockey team tries to take advantage of extra players on the ice in a power play, so David's nephew Joab used every advantage he could create to avenge his brother Asahel's death (2 Sam. 2:23). He operated on the principle that the end justifies the means.

SUSPICION. Joab was wise in the ways of the nations. His strategies included deception and spying on others. Accordingly, when he heard that Abner had seen David and left peacefully, he accused Abner of spying on David and deceiving him. Perhaps malice made him suspicious of treachery, or perhaps Joab was also trying to make others suspicious to justify what he was about to do to Abner.

ABUSING TERMS OF PEACE. Having decided to kill Abner, Joab took advantage of David's promise of peace and secretly recalled the unsuspecting Abner, whom his men found at the well or cistern of Sirah about two miles north of Hebron. Of course, Joab was defying the king, but he was doing so for the good of the king. The end justified the means in his own mind, and hopefully also in the minds of others.

(UN) LAWFUL VENGEANCE. The real reason Joab secretly defied the king and deceived Abner was his desire to avenge the death of his brother, Asahel, whom Abner had killed in battle. Even though Abner had been in battle, had not wanted to kill Asahel, had tried to dissuade Asahel from pursuing him, and had killed Asahel in self-defense (2 Sam. 2:23), Joab took advantage of the Law which allowed a kinsman to avenge a death until the killer sought protection and a trial in a city of refuge (Num. 35:9 ff.; Deut. 19:1 ff.). When Abner returned to Hebron, a city of refuge, Joab took him aside at the city gate and stabbed Abner in the stomach so that he died of the same kind of wound that killed Asahel. Whether Joab actually killed Abner outside the gate of Hebron is open to question just as his justification for killing Abner is open to question. Nevertheless, Joab seems to have schemed to retain the protection of the Law even while seeking revenge. He bent the Law to protect himself from being accused of unlawful revenge. For him, the end justified the means.

David curses Joab and honors Abner
2 Sam. 3:28-39

END GAME

In chess, the end game begins when the opposing armies have been depleted and one or both kings begin to face repeated threats to their safety. So it was in Israel. There were two kings, and over a period of two years, David's forces had gained strength while Ish-bosheth's had weakened. Ish-bosheth was in serious danger of losing his authority over the northern tribes because his military commander, Abner, had decided to deliver those tribes to David.

BIG BLUNDER. The northern tribes sent Abner to David as an emissary to propose making David their king. An agreement had apparently been reached between David and Abner when Joab murdered Abner to satisfy a personal desire for revenge. Suddenly, the allegiance of the northern tribes was no longer assured. They could not be sure that David would treat them justly or that there would be no further bloodshed. Joab's action seemed to guarantee that hostilities would continue.

DAMAGE CONTROL. David had to assure the northern tribes that he would treat them justly, so he had to deal with Joab. David could not punish him for exercising his legal right to avenge the blood of his brother, but Joab's motive had been evil, and his method devious. Therefore, David could and did heap upon Joab the curses that God placed on those who did not keep the law (compare 2 Sam. 3:29 with Lev. 26:14-39 and Deut. 28:15-68). Then David shamed Joab by forcing him to participate in the funeral for Abner, while David lavished great honor upon Abner both in burying him in the royal city and by composing a lament for him. Thus, David assured the northern tribes that he and his kingdom were innocent of the blood of Abner, and that evil would not be tolerated even when it was not punishable by law. He and his kingdom would abide by both the letter and the spirit of the law.

TURNING WEAKNESS TO STRENGTH. This section ends with David saying something that is understandable but perplexing when read in the KJV or NIV. He said that though he was king he was actually weak and that Joab and Abishai were too hard for him (v. 39 KJV) or stronger than he was (NIV). The statement is understandable in that David's hands seem to have been tied in dealing with Joab and his brother, but it is perplexing because it would be unsettling to the northern tribes. How could they hope for security under David if Joab was stronger than the king? While there may have been a hint of frustration in David's statement, he may have been saying something much more profound. The English Standard Version translates verse 39 this way:

> And I was gentle today, though anointed king. These
> men, the sons of Zeruiah, are more severe than I. The
> Lord repay the evildoer according to his wickedness!

David was assuring the northern tribes that he was not a severe or cruel monarch like the sons of Zeruiah would have been. God would repay them. Instead, he had conducted himself with gentleness and compassion toward Abner, his former enemy, and he would deal with the northern tribes with the same gentleness and compassion (see Bergen, 1996, p.

315). God would bless that gentleness, so David turned weakness to strength. Everything David did pleased the people.

We often forget that gentleness is stronger than severity. Jesus said, "Blessed are the gentle, for they shall inherit the earth" (Matt. 5:5 NASB). Jesus, our king, is a gentle monarch. Matt. 12:18-21 (NIV) says of him,

> Here is my servant whom I have chosen,
>   the one I love, in whom I delight;
> I will put my Spirit on him,
>   and he will proclaim justice to the nations.
> He will not quarrel or cry out;
>   no one will hear his voice in the streets.
> A bruised reed he will not break,
>   and a smoldering wick he will not snuff out,
> till he leads justice to victory.
>   In his name the nations will put their hope.

David punishes Ish-bosheth's murderers
2 Sam. 4:1-12

POLITICAL FAVORS

Politicians often publicly disassociate themselves from political action groups that operate illegally and slander their opponents, but they secretly welcome that help and even reward the lawbreakers when they win an election. David was not that kind of man.

FAVORS LOST. Baanah and Recab were from Beeroth, a town belonging to the Gibeonites (Josh. 9:17) in the territory of Benjamin (Josh. 18:25) near Saul's hometown. Sometime before this, the Gibeonites had fled Beeroth, possibly when Saul killed many of them (2 Sam. 21:1-2). After they fled, Saul may have given their lands to Benjamites such as the father of Baanah and Recab (cf. 1 Sam. 22:7). Whatever favors they had received from Saul and from Ish-bosheth as captains of his raiding bands, they no longer expected those favors to continue.

NEW FAVORS EXPECTED. Baanah and Recab knew Ish-bosheth had no real power without Abner and that the people were eager to make David king. They were sure that Ish-bosheth would lose the throne and probably his life also. Why not make the best of a bad situation?

Accordingly, they went to the royal residence and found Ish-bosheth sleeping at midday. They killed him, cut off his head, and took it to David hoping to win a reward when they presented the evidence of his rival's death. They obviously expected to win David's favor when they reminded him that Ish-bosheth's father had tried to kill him. David would surely be impressed that they had acted as God's agents in avenging "my lord the king this day on Saul and on his offspring" (v. 8). They confidently awaited new favors from the new king.

JUST REWARD. Their reward was not what they expected because David was not a man whose judgment could be impaired by political favors. He did not need the help of lawless men. He had the help of the Lord who had delivered him out of every adversity (v. 9). Accordingly, David not only disassociated himself from these men who murdered his rival, but he also gave them their just reward. He executed the men who thought that favors could be purchased with wickedness.

David is proclaimed king of all Israel
2 Sam. 5:1-5 [1 Chron. 11:1-3]

THE INAUGURATION

In the United States, inaugural activities begin with the president-elect attending a morning worship service. He then proceeds to the Capitol, where he takes the oath of office required by the Constitution. Following that, there is a luncheon, parade, and finally in the evening, an inaugural ball. The inaugural activities culminate a selection process, they focus both on the president's promise to uphold and defend the Constitution and on his appointment to preside over the government, and finally they celebrate fresh leadership in fulfilling the hopes and dreams of the nation. Although the times were different, David began his reign over all Israel in a similar way.

SELECTION. For a long time, the leaders of Israel had wanted to make David their king (2 Sam. 3:17) because even while King Saul had been alive, David had been the most successful military commander against their enemies (2 Sam. 5:2). So, the leaders of Israel went to Hebron determined to make him king (1 Chron. 12:38). Nevertheless, they did not select David merely because he was successful. They also chose him according to the guidelines of Mosaic Law:

You may indeed set a king over you whom the LORD
your God will choose. One from among your brothers
you shall set as king over you. You may not put a
foreigner over you, who is not your brother.
-- Deut. 17:15

When all Israel came to David in Hebron, they affirmed that they were the same "bone and flesh," that is, they were brothers. Furthermore, they cited evidence that God had chosen David: the Lord had told David that he would be shepherd and prince over Israel (v. 2). Hence, what happened in Hebron was the culmination of a selection process that included both Israel and God. After Solomon, there is no record of the people seeking the Lord's choice for king. The next king chosen of God was Jesus.

COVENANT. When all Israel came to David in Hebron, he made a compact or covenant with them (2 Sam. 5:3). The exact nature of the covenant is not known, but Samuel wrote the regulations concerning the kingship on a scroll when Saul was anointed (1 Sam. 10:25). Samuel's regulations were probably based on Deut. 17:14-17 and designed to prevent the abuses Samuel foresaw in a kingship (1 Sam. 8:10-18). The covenant between David and Israel may have included some positive aspects as well because God had designated David to be "shepherd of my people Israel" (v. 2). One positive aspect, related to shepherding, would be that he promised to lead, tend, and defend Israel with compassion. Another positive aspect, related to Israel being God's people or flock, would be that he agreed to be faithful as a steward of God. No other covenants between the king and the people are mentioned until Joash became king in 2 Kings 11:17. Today, Christ, a descendant of David, reigns as the Good Shepherd over God's people on the basis of a new covenant.

ANOINTING. David had previously been anointed both privately and again in the presence of the elders of Judah. This third time, he was anointed in the presence of the elders and leaders of all Israel. Anointing signified more than selection. It signified consecration or devotion to serving the Lord with undivided purpose and energy. Today, Jesus is God's anointed, and Jesus reigns with undivided purpose and energy until God's will is accomplished on earth.

CELEBRATION. 1 Chron. 12:39-40 tells us that Israel's leaders remained in Hebron for three days eating and drinking because there was great joy in Israel when David was anointed king. The bounty and joy shared at this three-day feast were a foretaste of God's blessings that would follow in a faithful Israel ruled by a king who had a heart like God's.

Armed men gather to David
1 Chron. 12:23-40

THE ARMY OF THE LORD

> Be watchful, stand firm in the faith, act like men, be strong.
> -- 1 Cor. 16:13

TRIBES. All twelve tribes and the Levites were present to make David king over all Israel. Two tribes (Judah and Simeon) were present from the south. Seven and a half tribes (Benjamin, Ephraim, half Manasseh, Issachar, Zebulun, Naphtali, Dan, and Asher) were present from the north. Two and a half tribes (Reuben, Gad, and half Manasseh) were present from the east. In addition to the twelve tribes, the Levites also sent representatives to make David king. Just as all the tribes made David their king, so today all who come to Jesus make him their Lord (Rom. 10:9).

NUMBERS. The soldiers who came under David's command at Hebron numbered 340,800 men. (Some have suggested that only the officers, commanders of thousands and hundreds, were present for the anointing in which case a total of 398 officers from the twelve tribes are enumerated in text; see Payne, 1988, p. 378). This number under David's command were about a quarter of all the men of fighting age in David's kingdom at the time he took the census toward the end of his reign. All of these, however, were the core of the army which would give Israel victory over the people of the land and the surrounding nations. Today, God gives us victory over all the power of Satan through our Lord Jesus Christ (1 Cor. 15:57).

READINESS. These soldiers were experienced and equipped for battle. They bore "shield and spear," and they were "equipped for battle with all the weapons of war." They were "mighty men of valor," troops "seasoned" and "ready for battle." Some were men who had "understanding of the time, to know what Israel ought to do," but all came with singleness of purpose to make David king. Today, Christians are soldiers called to serve Jesus, the son of David. We who given our lives to Christ should have a single of purpose – to please the one who enlisted us (2 Tim. 2:4). We should be equipped having taken up the whole armor of God. Being equipped, we should be ready to engage the enemy standing firm in our opposition to all spiritual forces (Eph. 6:13).

Part Five: Jerusalem

1002 – 994 B.C.; age 38-46; regnal years 8-16

David conquers Jerusalem
2 Sam. 5:6-10 [1 Chron. 11:4-9]

OBEDIENCE AND BLESSING

David desired in his heart to fulfill God's purposes as stated by Moses. Even while in Ziklag to avoid Saul, David was destroying the Amalekites in accordance to God's command (Deut. 25:17-19), and God blessed David. When David became king of all Israel, David continued to pursue the will of God, and God continued to bless him.

MOVING THE CAPITAL. David needed a capital that was more centrally located, not associated with Judah alone, and more defensible than Hebron. Jerusalem was an ideal site. It lay between the two most powerful tribes of Ephraim to the north and Judah to the south. Although it was in territory assigned to Benjamin (Josh. 18:16; 18:28), it bordered Judah (Josh. 15:8), which was the base of David's power. Furthermore, Jerusalem was quite defensible because on three sides it could be approached only by ascending a steep hill. The major obstacle to making it his capital was that it was still in the hands of the Jebusites.

UNFULFILLED MANDATE. The Jebusites were "inhabitants of the land," a phrase that often described the people, including the Jebusites, whom the Israelites were to drive out (Ex. 23:31; Num. 33:52; and Deut. 7:1). Although Jerusalem belonged to Benjamin, the Benjamites had never driven them out (Judges 1:21). Consequently, David was not merely achieving a personal ambition when he conquered Jerusalem, but he was fulfilling God's mandate to possess the land promised to Abraham's descendants.

CONQUERING JERUSALEM. Conquering Jerusalem was no easy task. The Jebusites were so confident of their defenses that they tried to insult David by boasting that even the blind and the lame could defend the city against David. David resolved to defeat the insolent "blind and lame" inhabitants. He scouted the city's defenses and discovered that the city obtained its water from a source outside the city walls through a narrow shaft in the rock upon which the city was built (2 Sam. 5:8). Having discovered the passageway, he called for a volunteer to enter the city through the water shaft and promised the command of the army to the man who first entered the city. Joab accepted the challenge and enabled David's army to capture the city (1 Chron. 11:6).

BLESSED OF GOD. After David conquered the city, he lived in the fortress (stronghold) and built up its supporting terraces (Millo) and city walls while Joab took charge of rebuilding the rest of the city (1 Chron. 11:8). David did not conquer and beautify the city by his own ingenuity and strength. Rather, he did so because "the LORD, the God of hosts, was with him" (2 Sam. 5:10).

David builds a palace
2 Sam. 5:11-12 [1 Chron. 14:1-2]

GRACE FOR THE HUMBLE

> One's pride will bring him low,
> but he who is lowly in spirit will obtain honor.
> -- Prov. 29:23

Success makes people arrogant, but David resisted the temptation. Though he was established as king over Israel, he understood that it was the Lord who had done so. Though the kingdom had been exalted, he understood that God had exalted it "for the sake of his people Israel," and not merely for his sake. As long as David kept a humble spirit, God blessed him.

David fathers other sons in Jerusalem
2 Sam. 5:13-16 [1 Chr. 14:3-7] [[1 Chr. 3:5-9]]

ROYAL ANCESTRY

Two of David's sons born in Jerusalem have a part in the continuing story of the Bible. Solomon, who became the ancestor of the royal line, was the ancestor of Joseph, the husband of Mary (Matt. 1:6-16). Nathan became an ancestor of Mary, the mother of Jesus (Luke 3:23-31). Both Solomon and Nathan were sons of Bathsheba (Bath-shua). None of the other sons born in Jerusalem play any role in the story that follows.

David defeats the Philistines in Rephaim Valley
2 Sam. 5:17-25 [1 Chron. 14:8-17]

KING OF THE MOUNTAIN

Because of his higher position, the king on the mountain enjoys a great advantage over his rivals. However, the rivals are more numerous and with time can dislodge the king at the top. But then, the new king on the mountain suddenly finds that his allies have turned against him. His success does not bring rest. Instead, it invites attacks from all sides. David's elevation to the throne over all Israel antagonized the Philistines, who like David had been counted enemies by Saul's house. They were troubled because David had become their chief rival. They gathered their forces and marched toward Jerusalem from the southwest. They occupied the fertile Valley of Rephaim (Isa. 17:4-6) midway between Bethlehem, where they had established a garrison (2 Sam. 23:14), and Jerusalem. Before the Philistines gained complete control of the countryside around Jerusalem, David took a small force to Baal-perazim, where he could observe the movement of Philistine troops between Philistia and the Valley of Rephaim.

THE LORD BREAKS FORTH. Although David was accompanied by brave and proven soldiers, he inquired of the Lord before attacking the Philistines. After receiving God's approval, David attacked the Philistines near Baal-perazim with such suddenness that they abandoned their idols. David and his men carried off the idols (2 Sam. 5:21) and burned them (1 Chron. 14:12) according to the Lord's command (Deut. 7:5, 25). After the battle, David noted that the Lord had "broken through my enemies before me like a breaking flood." Still, one battle seldom wins a war, and the Philistines returned with reinforcements.

THE LORD GOES IN FRONT. Again David inquired of the Lord, and God instructed David to circle around the Philistines and attack from the rear in a guerrilla-style ambush. The "sound of marching in the tops of the balsam trees" signaled that the Lord had gone out before them "to strike down the army of the Philistines." Perhaps the sound in the treetops masked the sound of his men as they moved into position or misled the Philistines with regard to the direction of the attack. Since David had circled around behind the Philistines, they could not flee down the valley westward when they were attacked. Instead, they had to go north over the hills five or six miles to Gibeon and then westward 15 miles to Gezer on the border of Philistia.

Twice the Philistines had attacked, twice David inquired of the Lord, twice the Lord had led the way, and twice David and the Israelites won the victory. When Israel sought the Lord's will and obeyed his command to destroy the idols in the land, the Lord blessed Israel and gave them victory.

David makes plans to bring the ark of God to Jerusalem
1 Chron. 13:1-4

NEGLECT AND HASTE

> Haste makes waste.
> -- Ben Franklin

The area west of Jerusalem had often been under Philistine control, but twice now David's army had defeated them. David had taken and burned their idols, and driven them to Gezer some miles to the west. Within the area now freed from Philistine domination was Baale-judah (Kirjath-jearim) where the ark had been for two generations after being returned from Philistia (1 Sam. 7:1). It had been neglected there in the house of Abinadab during the reign of Saul (v. 3). (Chronicles places the first attempt to move the ark to Jerusalem before the battles with the Philistines, but Samuel's order is to be preferred.)

David consulted his commanders, and they decided to call the army together again to bring the ark to Jerusalem. David appears to proceed cautiously because he suggests that they do so only if 1) "it seems good to you," and 2) if it is "from the Lord our God." David and his military commanders were "can do" people. In their haste to accomplish the task, they failed to consult those who would know how the ark should be moved. Consequently, they would waste resources, energy, and even a life before the task was accomplished.

David's procession is abruptly halted
2 Sam. 6:1-11 [1 Chron. 13:5-14]

INSUFFICIENCY OF GOOD INTENTIONS

> Good intentions may do as much harm as malevolence if
> they lack understanding.
> -- Albert Camus

David's intentions were good. He recognized the moving of the ark as an opportunity to refocus Israel on their God, on his presence among them, and on the covenant He had made with them. David and those who accompanied him demonstrated their good intentions in several ways.

AN HONOR GUARD. David took thirty thousand "chosen" soldiers to accompany the ark of God to Jerusalem. The best in all Israel gave honor to the God of their fathers.

A NEW CART. David did not use some farmer's old cart that would have defiled the holy ark set upon it. Rather, out of sincere respect, he prepared a "new cart" for this sacred chest, but in so doing, he did no better than the Philistines years before (1 Sam. 6:7).

WHOLEHEARTED CELEBRATION. Rejoicing with thanksgiving, David and the people of Israel celebrated with great joy as is appropriate for worshiping God.

CONSCIENTIOUS CARE. When the oxen stumbled on a threshing floor, Uzzah conscientiously reached out to steady the ark lest it fall and be damaged.

Uzzah had good intentions, as did David and all Israel, yet the Lord's anger burned against Uzzah for what he did, and the Lord struck him down so that he died there beside the ark. David reacted as we would: he was angry. What happened seemed a harsh penalty for a person seeking to protect the ark of God. It also seemed an insult to David's intentions. But then David was overcome with reverent fear. We must recognize, as he did, that good intentions are not good enough. We must also seek the Lord's will.

David consecrates Levites to carry the ark
1 Chron. 15:1-16

DUE DILIGENCE

> What we hope ever to do with ease, we must first learn
> to do with diligence.
> -- Samuel Johnson

The Philistines, who did not have God's law, had sent the ark back to Israel on a new cart. David, who did have God's law, did not consult it and also used a new cart to transport the ark. Because those who had his law did not consult it, God was displeased with the first attempt to bring the ark to Jerusalem. This time, David sought the will of God in his Law. Evidence that he consulted the Law is found in three specific preparations he made for the second attempt.

A TENT. David prepared a place for the ark which obviously honored the pattern given by Moses, for David pitched a tent for it (v. 1).

PRIESTS AND LEVITES. David gathered priests and Levites (v. 4) and had them consecrate themselves for bringing the ark to Jerusalem (v. 12) much as they were charged with carrying the sacred furniture by Moses (see Num. 4). Though Uzzah and Ahio, who accompanied the ark during the first attempt, may have been priests or Levites (Abinadab's son Eleazar bore a priestly name, but his genealogy is unknown), the procession had been primarily a military escort for the ark. A whole company of consecrated priests and Levites participated in the second attempt (Deut. 10:8).

COMMAND TO CARRY THE ARK. David commanded that the Levites carry the ark on their shoulders (v. 13) in accordance with God's instructions in Ex. 25:13-14 and Num. 4:15; 7:9. Thus, with the soldiers and people going before and following after the ark carried by the Levites, the procession resembled the procession of the Israelites as they traveled from one place to another in the wilderness (Num. 10:17-28).

David's second attempt to move the ark to Jerusalem proved successful because he diligently sought how God had commanded it to be carried. If we desire success in the Lord's work, we should diligently seek the Lord's will.

David brings the ark to Jerusalem
2 Sam. 6:12-19a [1 Chron. 15:25 – 16:3]

WHOLEHEARTED CELEBRATION

Although moving the ark to Jerusalem required reverence for God and his Law, there remains room for rejoicing because God does show his favor to those who obey him.

THE PROCESSION. David's enthusiasm for the Lord was not diminished when he finally brought the ark to Jerusalem. After the priests carrying the ark had gone six steps, the procession stopped for making sacrifices to the Lord. When the procession resumed, the rejoicing continued to be expressed with shouting, with the sound of the horn and other instruments, and even with dancing.

THE DESTINATION. After the ark had been placed in the tent David had made for it in the city God had chosen (Deut. 12:1-7; 2 Kings 21:7-8), David offered burnt offerings and fellowship offerings. The people shared in the feasting and fellowship. David blessed the people in the name of the Lord and provided a generous gift of food to each one attending the celebration.

This time the journey of the ark was not aborted by a tragic death. Rather, the journey was completed with great rejoicing, and the lives of the people were blessed by God's bountiful favor. We also can celebrate the bountiful favor of God whose holiness requires that we serve him with reverence.

David gives thanks to God
1 Chron. 16:4-43 [2 Sam. 6:19b-20a]

NEGLECTED NO LONGER

The Ark of the Covenant of the Lord had been neglected while in Kirjath-jearim during the reign of Saul (1 Chron. 13:3), and David did not want the Lord to be neglected any longer. The zeal of the Lord that came on him when the Spirit rushed upon him at his anointing and that burned within him when he heard Goliath blaspheming the Lord still burned within him. He wanted Israel not merely to turn to the Lord, but to follow the Lord. Accordingly, he made plans for Israel to continue worshiping of God.

THE ARK OF THE COVENANT. David wanted the worship to continue in Jerusalem (1 Chron. 16:4-6, 37-38) where God had directed him to place the Ark of the Covenant of the Lord. He appointed Asaph to make regular thanksgiving and praise to God with singing and music. He also appointed Obed-Edom and his family as gatekeepers.

THE ALTAR. Although the ark was in Jerusalem, the tabernacle and altar remained in Gibeon where it had been put after Shiloh, the home of Eli, was destroyed (Jer. 7:12-14). David assigned Zadok and his family to serve as priests there and to present offerings regularly as required by the

Law of Moses (vv. 39-40). He also appointed the Levites Heman and Jeduthun to be in charge of the music there. The sons of Jeduthun were gatekeepers there (vv. 41-42).

THE MUSICIANS. The leading musicians appointed by David were godly men. 1) Asaph was a Levite (1 Chron. 6:39-43) and a seer (2 Chron. 29:30). Several psalms are attributed to him or a descendant with the same name (Ps. 50, 73-83). 2) Heman, who served in Gibeon, was a Levite (2 Chron. 5:12) and the grandson of the prophet Samuel (1 Chron. 6:33-34). Like his more famous grandfather, Heman was a seer (1 Chron. 25:5). From the time of Samuel, there had been a close connection between the prophesying and musical accompaniment (1 Sam. 10:5-6; 1 Chron. 25:1). 3) Jeduthun was also a Levite and a seer (2 Chron. 35:15). He is to be distinguished from the father of Obed-Edom. His six sons are listed in 1 Chron. 25:3. Psalm 39, by David, is dedicated to Jeduthun. Psalm 62 and 77 are "according to Jeduthan." These three seers did not act presumptuously when they accompanied worship with instrumental music (1 Chron. 25:1-5). This musical accompaniment was prescribed by the Lord through David and the prophets Gad and Nathan. When Hezekiah restored temple worship years later, the Scripture (2 Chron. 29:25) says that

> And he stationed the Levites in the house of the LORD
> with cymbals, harps, and lyres, according to the
> commandment of David and of Gad the king's seer and
> of Nathan the prophet, for the commandment was from
> the LORD through his prophets.

THE GATEKEEPERS. The gatekeepers, both Obed-Edom in Jerusalem, and Jeduthun in Gibeon, were Levites (1 Chron. 26:1-4). David did not pick their names out of a hat, but before he was king and even before the death of Samuel, he had discussed these appointments with Samuel the prophet (1 Chron. 9:22-23). All of David's steps with regard to worship at Gibeon and Jerusalem were directed by the Lord.

Today, God dwells in a spiritual temple, the church (1 Cor. 3:16-17). Though the church has often been neglected, we should determine to neglect it no more, but make it a house of praise, prayer, and proclamation.

David argues with Michal
2 Sam. 6:20-23

MICHAL'S FOLLY

When the Ark of God entered Jerusalem, the whole city turned out just as it would have if David were returning victorious from battle. At such times, even the women rushed out, mingled with the festive crowd, and participated in the celebration. Normally, the king and army officers would have had the place of honor, but when the Ark entered the city, God had the place of honor, and King David celebrated with the citizens, leaping and dancing with them in the presence of the Lord.

CELEBRATION DESPISED. Michal did not get excited about the arrival of the ark as she would have at an earlier time when David returned from a successful campaign. She did not rush to the street in excitement, but remained haughty and aloof at her window. Just as her father had neglected the Ark during his reign, so she failed to celebrate its arrival in Jerusalem. In fact, when she saw David celebrating with the crowds, she despised him.

HUMILITY MOCKED. Later, David entered his house to bless it, but Michal interrupted the blessing with sarcasm. "How the king of Israel honored himself today," she said (v. 20), "uncovering himself today before the eyes of his servants' female servants!" No, David had not disrobed in public, but he had discarded his royal apparel for the garments worn by the Levites (1 Chron. 15:27) and an ephod (2 Sam. 6:14; 1 Chron. 15:27). Michal's problem was not that David was naked, but that his dress lacked royal dignity. She wanted a king for a husband, not a man who mingled with ordinary citizens.

HUMILITY DEFENDED. David reminded Michal that God had rejected her father, who was not humble before God, and had chosen him instead. No matter how undignified it appeared to Michal, David would celebrate before the Lord. David would humble himself not only before others, but also in his own eyes. David understood that "One's pride will bring him low (as Saul's pride had), but he who is lowly in spirit will obtain honor" (Prov. 29:23). Michal did not understand. As a young woman, she had fallen in love with a brave warrior, but now she was married to a man who gladly humbled himself in order to exalt God.

BLESSING LOST. Michal refused to celebrate the arrival of the ark and interrupted David's blessing with sarcasm. Consequently, she herself missed out on God's blessing. Michal died childless.

David rules with justice and righteousness
2 Sam. 8:15-18 [1 Chron. 18:14-17]

GOOD GOVERNMENT

> The single most exciting thing you encounter in
> government is competence, because it's so rare.
> -- Daniel P. Moynihan

David was not only a great military leader, he was also a good ruler. A single, often overlooked verse (2 Sam. 8:15) notes his greatness as a ruler, and his reign set the standard by which all later reigns were judged and most often found deficient.

ACTIONS. During David's reign, he "administered justice and equity." "Administered justice" meant not only that he and all the courts throughout the land made correct judgments (see Deut. 16:18-20; 17:8-13; and 19:15-21), but also that all in his administration thought and acted in accordance with right judgments (see BDB, *šepeṭ*, p. 1048). "Administered equity" meant that all those in authority acted in accordance with an ethical or moral standard (TWOT, #1879). Government did not function one way for the wealthy and another way for the poor. Hence, every function of government was carried out according to Mosaic Law. Later, God called David "my servant" because he "kept my commandments and my statutes" (1 Kings 11:34).

ADVOCACY. A part of the Mosaic Law which David carried out was advocacy for the poor. Even before he was king, the distressed, the debtors, and the discontented found refuge with him (1 Sam. 22:2). When he became king, he continued to do what was just and right "to all his people," for the poor, the weak, and the alien, as well as the rich (2 Sam. 8:15). David was bound to defend the poor by the Law. He did this not through government programs but through judicial regulation and priestly instruction. He faithfully administered the Law, which did not allow anyone to oppress the alien (Ex. 23:9) or take advantage of the widow and orphan (Ex. 22:22-24); instead, it required generosity to be shown to the poor (Deut. 15:7-11). It required that runaway slaves be given refuge (Deut. 23:15-16). It did not permit the people to charge their fellow

Israelites interest (Ex. 22:25; Deut. 23:19-20), or to take a person's means of livelihood as a pledge for a loan (Deut. 24:6), or to keep a cloak as pledge overnight, or to enter a house to obtain a pledge (Ex. 22:26-27; Deut. 24:10-13). It required that wages be given to a laborer at the end of each day (Deut. 24:14-15) and that corners of fields and fallen grain be left for the poor (Deut. 24:19-22). It prevented cheating in the market by requiring merchants to keep but one scale and to use it for both buying and selling (Deut. 25:13-16).

APPOINTMENTS. Part of the reason that David succeeded in promoting justice and righteousness is because he gave priests and Levites prominent positions in his government. The priests and Levites had been appointed by God to teach the people all that God commanded in the Law (Lev. 10:11; Deut. 17:8-13; Malachi 2:7). Three of the men mentioned as a part of David's government were Zadok and Ahimelech, who served as priests, and Benaiah, a Levite (see 1 Chron. 27:5) who promoted what was just and right in the military. Thus, justice and righteousness were promoted in all institutions by priests and Levites, whom Saul had alienated along with God's prophets.

ASPIRATION. The kings who came after David often did not follow his example of doing what was just and right. Isa. 5:7 notes the failure of later kings:

> For the vineyard of the LORD of hosts
>   is the house of Israel,
> and the men of Judah
>   are his pleasant planting;
> and he looked for justice,
>   but behold, bloodshed;
> for righteousness,
>   but behold, an outcry![1]

Because their ways were evil, God admonished them in Isa. 1:16-17 to return to the just and right ways practiced by David:

> Wash yourselves; make yourselves clean;
>   remove the evil of your deeds from before my eyes;
> cease to do evil,

---

[1] NIV "cries of distress."

> learn to do good;
> seek justice,
>> correct oppression;
> bring justice to the fatherless,
>> plead the widow's cause.

Few kings lived up to the ideal established by David. Accordingly, the prophets and the righteous who listened to them looked for a king, the Messiah, who would again aspire to justice and righteousness. Isa. 9:6-7 foresaw that king:

> For to us a child is born,
>> to us a son is given;
> and the government shall be upon his shoulder,
>> and his name shall be called
> Wonderful Counselor, Mighty God,
>> Everlasting Father, Prince of Peace.
> Of the increase of his government and of peace
>> there will be no end,
> on the throne of David and over his kingdom,
>> to establish it and to uphold it
> with justice and with righteousness
>> from this time forth and forevermore.
> The zeal of the LORD of hosts will do this.

David shows kindness to Mephibosheth
2 Sam. 9:1-13

UNUSUAL KINDNESS

The justice and righteousness of David's reign was demonstrated in his treatment of Mephibosheth, who might lay claim to the throne, though he was lame, because he was the grandson of King Saul. Saul, of course, had become the mortal enemy of David and had driven him out of his homeland. If David had modeled his reign after the kings of the nations, he would have killed Mephibosheth and never looked back. But David did not do that.

COVENANT LOYALTY. Instead, David remembered his covenant with Mephibosheth's father, Jonathan. David and Jonathan had been best friends even while Saul was consumed with jealousy knowing that God had chosen David to be the next king. They had agreed that regardless of what happened they would show kindness to the other's offspring (1 Sam.

20:42; 24:21-22). Accordingly, David wanted to show loyal kindness to any descendants of Jonathan who might yet be living. Such loyalty and kindness was a supreme virtue among God's people.

LAWFUL OBEDIENCE. When Mephibosheth appeared before David, he was understandably afraid. His uncle, Ish-bosheth, had been king for two years and was murdered by traitors trying to please David. David, however, never sought revenge against Saul, and he would not punish Saul's descendants for the sins of their father in accordance with the Law which stipulated, that "Fathers shall not be put to death because of their children, nor shall children be put to death because of their fathers" (Deut. 24:16).

COMPASSION. So David did not kill Mephibosheth or banish him, but he showed him kindness by restoring to him the property that had originally belonged to his grandfather, King Saul, and assigning Saul's steward, Ziba, to manage the property for him. Furthermore, he gave Mephibosheth a permanent invitation to dine at the royal table even though it might be inconvenient to accommodate a person who was lame in both feet. David showed not only faithfulness to a covenant and obedience to the law, but also genuine kindness to a person with disabilities. David showed that he still had the heart of God.

David appeases the Gibeonites
2 Sam. 21:1-14

A LAND POLLUTED BY BLOODSHED

Sometime during the reign of David after he had moved to Jerusalem from Hebron, a famine came upon the land for three years. David sought the face of the Lord so that the Lord might look favorably on Israel again.

THE OFFENSE. God told David that the problem was that Saul and other members of his house (family) had killed the Gibeonites (v. 1). The Gibeonites were not Israelites, but they lived in several villages in Benjamite territory. Joshua had made a treaty with them promising not to kill them, and the Israelite leaders had confirmed the treaty with an oath (Josh. 9:15). Saul, however, in his zeal for Israel had plotted against them and tried to annihilate them (v. 2). Many had been killed (v. 5), and others had fled their homes to save their lives (see also 2 Sam. 4:2-3 which reports that the Gibeonites of Beeroth had fled to Gittaim and lived there as aliens). They had not been able to live anywhere in Israel safely (v. 5).

THE ATONEMENT. When David asked the Gibeonites how atonement or reconciliation could be made, they said they had no right to demand money or to put anyone to death. Such a statement, however, was the beginning of a bargaining process (cf. Ephron's negotiations with Abraham in Gen. 23:11 and 2 Sam. 24:22-23). When asked again, they requested that seven male descendants of Saul be killed before the Lord. David turned over seven male members of Saul's family to the Gibeonites who executed them at the beginning of the barley harvest.

FAMINE'S END. The Gibeonites exposed the bodies of those they executed, and Rizpah, the mother of two of them, protected their bodies from the birds and wild beasts until the rains came. At that time, David retrieved the bodies of Saul and Jonathan from Jabesh-gilead and buried them in the family grave in Benjamin along with those who had been executed. After atonement had been made for the land, God heard Israel's prayers and lifted the famine.

A PROBLEM. Although Canaanite law apparently permitted killing the children of a person who had violated a covenant (Youngblood, 1992, p, 1054), God's law stipulated that children could not be punished for the sins of their fathers (Deut. 24:16). Had these descendants of Saul participated in the slaughter of the Gibeonites? Possibly they had for verse one indicates that Saul's family had participated in the bloodshed. However, the text also says that David spared Jonathan's son Mephibosheth not because he was innocent (he was only five at the time of Saul's death – 2 Sam. 4:4) but because of the oath David had made to Jonathan. Furthermore, Merab did not marry Adriel until after David slew Goliath (1 Sam. 18:19), so her sons, who could not have been more than teenagers at the time of Saul's death, probably did not participate in the slaughter. (A textual problem complicates the issue of which daughter of Saul was mother of five of the men. While some Hebrew and Greek manuscripts read "Merab" in 2 Sam. 21:8, most read Michal. However, Saul gave Michal to Palti in 1 Sam. 25:44, and David recovered her from him in 2 Sam. 3:15. Saul gave Merab to Adriel in 1 Sam. 18:19.) Whatever the solution to this problem, God revealed to David that Saul's sin had led to the famine, and God accepted the atonement and blessed the land again.

Part Six: Military Conquests

1002–994 B.C.; age 38-46; regnal years 8-16

David defeats the Philistines at Metheg Ammah
2 Sam. 8:1 [1 Chron. 18:1]

PHILISTINE PESTS OVERPOWERED

This final, decisive defeat of the Philistines is recorded after David brought the Ark of the Covenant to Jerusalem. The reference to Metheg-ammah (2 Sam. 8:1) is puzzling. The words may be taken as a place name (as in ESV and KJV), but no such place is mentioned elsewhere. Another possibility is that the words refer to the "reins of the forearm." This alludes to the way a person controls a horse and suggests that David wrested from Philistia the reins of the land, that is, control of the land between the Mediterranean Sea and the Jordan River (Hertzberg as reported in Youngblood, 1992, p. 903). The NASB takes them as a description: "the chief city" (literally, the bridle of the mother city) meaning that David took the control of Philistine villages out of the hands of the mother city, which was Gath. 1 Chron. 18:1 may support this view when it says that David took "Gath and its surrounding villages (literally, daughters) out of the hands of the Philistines."

David conquers the Moabites
2 Sam. 8:2 [1 Chron. 18:2]

BLESSING AND CURSING

God promised Abraham that from his descendants there would come one who would bless all nations. In order to guarantee that promise, he resolved to bless those who blessed Abraham's descendants and curse those who cursed his descendants. Egypt enslaved Abraham's descendants, the Israelites, and so experienced God's curse. When Israel approached the Promised Land to enter it, the Moabites refused to give them bread or even water, and hired the prophet Balaam to curse Israel (Num. 22:1 ff.). In so doing, they brought God's curse on themselves.

REFUGE ABANDONED. When David was running from Saul, he had taken his parents to Moab, the homeland of his great-grandmother Ruth, for safety. His parents stayed with the king of Moab "all the time that David was in the stronghold" (1 Sam. 22:4). However, Moses had forbidden making any peace agreement with Moab (Deut. 23:3-6), so the prophet Gad advised David to return to Judah, and David left his stronghold in Moab immediately. David's parents apparently left Moab safely at the same time even though an old Jewish tradition says that the king of Moab murdered them (Kirkpatrick in Youngblood, 1992, p. 903).

VICTORY FORESEEN. The text gives no clue about the immediate cause of David's war against Moab. Perhaps the king of Moab had been offended when David had neither left his parents in Moab nor made a peace agreement with him. He may have found that sufficient reason to attack David when he became king. Whatever the cause of the conflict, the war was fought and Moab was crushed by a king from Judah just as God had foretold through Balaam, the prophet Moab had hired to curse Israel (Num. 24:17).

SOLDIERS SPARED. When David fought the Amalekites, he left none alive in accordance with God's command regarding the Amalekites (Deut. 25:19), but when he defeated the Moabites, he spared one third of the soldiers because God had forbidden the Israelites to occupy Moab (Deut. 2:9). Killing two thirds of the soldiers probably guaranteed that Moab would not raise a formidable force against Israel in the near future, but it did not exterminate the people. Thereafter, the Moabites became subject to David and paid tribute to Israel.

The Ammonites insult David's messengers
2 Sam. 10:1-5 [1 Chron. 19:1-5]

SUSPICION AND INSULTS

> Never insult an alligator until you've crossed the river.
> -- Cordell Hull

The Ammonites lived just north and east of the Dead Sea. Like the Moabites, they were descendants of Lot. The king of Ammon had been Nahash (perhaps the son of the king who had threatened the town of Jabesh in Gilead during Saul's reign — 1 Sam. 11:1 ff.). His son, Hanun, became king some time after David had established himself in Jerusalem. The two young kings were polar opposites.

FIDELITY VS SUSPICION. When King Nahash died, David sent emissaries to deal "loyally" or "kindly" with his son Hanun. The ESV uses "kindly" in the Chronicles parallel, but the word often suggests covenant loyalty (J.E. Smith, 2000, p. 413). In other words, David wanted to maintain the same friendly relations between himself and Hanun as he had had with Nahash, his father. Hanun's advisors, however, planted suspicions in his mind. "Perhaps," they said, "David is not really honoring your father but spying out our defenses. David intends to overthrow us just as he did the Moabites" (paraphrase). Consequently, Hanun became skeptical of David's loyalty and motives, and he refused David's offer of sympathy.

INSULT VS EMPATHY. Hanun wanted to send an emphatic "No" to David's offer of friendship, so he chose to insult David's emissaries. He cut off their beards on one side of their faces, cut their garments off short enough to expose their buttocks, and sent them away. Not only did he humiliate the emissaries, but he also forced them to be in violation of God's Law (see Lev. 19:27 and Num. 15:38-39). When David was told what Hanun had done, he understood that the emissaries were humiliated and gave them permission to remain in Jericho until their beards had grown back. When Hanun insulted the emissaries, David understood how they felt and allowed them to save face rather than returning home immediately.

The Ammonites insulted an alligator, and they still had to cross the river.

David's army prevails over Ammon's allies
2 Sam. 10:6-14 [1 Chron. 19:6-15]

HIRELINGS HUNG OUT TO DRY

> He who is a hired hand and not a shepherd, who does
> not own the sheep, sees the wolf coming and leaves the
> sheep and flees, and the wolf snatches them and scatters
> them. He flees because he is a hired hand and cares
> nothing for the sheep.
> -- John 10:12-13

Mercenaries are hirelings. They care nothing for the ones who hired them. They care only for the money. If they have already received the money, woe to those depending on them.

HIRELINGS. After Hanun insulted David's messengers and rejected David's offer of friendship, he realized that he was not prepared for war. Accordingly, he hired an army of 33,000 Aramean soldiers with about 37 tons of silver. (The ESV follows the KJV and LXX in calling the Arameans Syrians, a name not used until Hellenistic times. The commentary will use Aramean.) These Aramean soldiers, from the area east of the Sea of Galilee and northward, went to join the Ammonite army which had occupied Medeba (see 1 Chron. 19:7), a town belonging to Reuben (Josh. 13:15-16) on the plateau southeast of Mt. Nebo.

CITIZENS. When David heard that the Arameans had joined forces with the Ammonites, he could not ignore the combined forces. He sent Joab with his army to Medeba. When Joab arrived, he found himself trapped between the Ammonites in front of the city gate and the Arameans behind. Joab took the best troops to fight against the Arameans, and put Abishai over the rest who were to fight the Ammonites. Before the battle began, Joab encouraged his soldiers with these words:

> Be of good courage, and let us be courageous for our
> people, and for the cities of our God, and may the LORD
> do what seems good to him.
> -- 2 Sam. 10:12

When David's men turned on the hireling Arameans behind them, they fled, and the Ammonites took refuge inside the city.

Joab did not pursue the battle with the Ammonites at the time. Perhaps he did not wish to besiege an occupied city such as Medeba because it contained many Reubenites. Rabbah, the capital of the Ammonites some 20 miles to the north, was so well defended that it was seldom besieged (George M. Landes, "The Material Civilization of the Ammonites," *The Biblical Archaeologist Reader*, 2, p. 76). Joab returned to Jerusalem while the Arameans returned home to plan their return.

David's army is victorious over Ammon's allies again
2 Sam. 10:15-19 [1 Chron. 19:16-19]

SPILLED LEMONADE

Someone once said that when life gives you a lemon, make lemonade. Joab gave Hadadezer and his Aramean army a lemon at Medeba. Hadadezer decided to make lemonade, though he probably had more than lemonade in mind. He hoped to make sure that Ammon remained his vassal and perhaps even hoped to gain control over Israel. God dumped his pitcher of lemonade.

EMBARRASSMENT REPEATED. After the embarrassing defeat at Medeba, Hadadezer king of Zobah (2 Sam. 8:3) sought reinforcements from his Aramean kinsmen on the other side of the Euphrates River. Shobach, Hadadezer's commander, led this army south to aid the Ammonites a second time, but David led his army out to meet Hadadezer at Helam just east of the Sea of Galilee and well north of Ammon. When the two armies clashed, the Arameans again fled before David. This time David's army did not retire to Jerusalem but pressed their advantage and killed a large number of foot soldiers, horsemen, and charioteers. (See any of the commentaries listed regarding the different numbers of the slain in Samuel and Chronicles.) Furthermore, they killed Shobach, the commander of the combined armies.

VASSAL STATES LOST. When the kings who were Hadadezer's vassals, saw that David had defeated Hadadezer decisively, many of them abandoned Hadadezer and made peace with David becoming subject to him. This alliance with the kings immediately north of Israel gave David an additional source of revenue and strengthened his control "over the Via Maris and the King's Highway, the two most important international roads of that region" (Bergen, 1996, p. 361).

AMMONITE ALLIANCE CANCELLED. Hadadezer lost a large part of his army and the allegiance of several vassals in the battle at Helam. Consequently, Hadadezer was unwilling to come to the aid of the Ammonites any more. The Ammonites lost the alliance they were depending on and for which they had paid about 37 tons of silver. The next time the Ammonites faced David, they would face him alone.

David conquers Zobah and Damascus
2 Sam. 8:3-8 [1 Chron. 18:3-8] cf. 1 Kings 11:23-24

THE LORD'S VICTORIES

> All the king's horses and all the king's men
> Couldn't put Humpty together again.
> -- Nursery Rhyme

After Hadadezer king of Zobah lost two battles while trying to give support to the Ammonites, some of the kingdoms who had been his vassals or allies gave their support to David. Other kingdoms subject to him decided to throw off his fetters and be independent. Hadadezer felt compelled to reestablish his control over these kingdoms along the Euphrates River; however, he was doomed to failure because he was fighting against the promise of God.

GOD'S PROMISE. David attacked Zobah, Hadadezer's homeland about 60 miles north of Damascus. God gave David victory over the Arameans of Zobah and over the Arameans of Damascus when they tried to come to Hadadezer's rescue. Consequently, David put garrisons in Damascus, and all the Arameans became subject to David and sent him tribute. In this way, David extended Israel's control to the Euphrates River in accordance with God's promise (Gen. 15:18; Ex. 23:31; etc.).

Hadadezer was not able to put his kingdom back together again.

David dedicates gifts and plunder to the Lord
2 Sam. 8:9-12 [1 Chron. 18:9-11]

CREDIT WHERE DUE

> And the LORD gave victory to David wherever he went.
> -- 2 Sam. 8:6, 14

When a person is successful, he often takes credit for it assuming that there is something about himself that makes him superior to anyone else. Consequently, this successful person thinks that the spoils are rightfully his. He thinks that no one else deserves them. In contrast to this, David never forgot that his success was really the work of God (2 Sam. 8:6). Consequently, he did not keep the spoils of war for himself, but dedicated them to the Lord.

GOD'S PLUNDER. Moses had forbidden Israel's kings to accumulate gold and silver (Deut. 17:17), so David dedicated the plunder, tribute, and gifts to God rather than amassing greater and greater wealth for himself. David recognized God's superiority over idols and expressed his gratitude to God for giving Israel victory. He wanted this immense wealth (more than 3,000 tons of gold and 30,000 tons of silver according to 1 Chron. 22:14) to be used to build a temple for God. He proved superior to his son Solomon, who used the tribute brought to him to increase his personal wealth (1 Kings 10:14-23). Unlike Solomon, David never wavered in his faith and gratitude to God.

OBEDIENCE BETTER THAN SACRIFICE. Nevertheless, it is sobering to observe that even while he was dedicating these resources for a temple for God in Jerusalem, David committed adultery and plotted the death of Uriah. As David later recognized, God was not nearly as pleased with the gifts and sacrifices that David brought as He would have been with a humble heart and obedient life (Psalm 51:16-17).

David conquers the Edomites
2 Sam. 8:13-14 [1 Chron. 18:12-13]
cf. 1 Kings 11:15-18; title of Psalm 60

THE NOOSE TIGHTENS

Rabbah, the capital of the Ammonites about 40 miles east of Jerusalem, was so well defended that it was seldom besieged (George M. Landes, "The Material Civilization of the Ammonites," *The Biblical Archaeologist Reader*, 2, p. 76). Not wanting to besiege Rabbah as long as allies could come to its aid, David decided to cut the city off from the Edomites, who could assist it from the south.

THE ENEMY. The Hebrew text, followed by the KJV and NASB, says that David struck down Arameans in the Valley of Salt, but the LXX and the parallel passage in 1 Chron. 18:12, followed by the ESV, say that he struck down Edomites there. The title to Psalm 60 also mentions a slaughter of Edomites in the Valley of Salt after Joab returned from fighting in Aram-Zobah. Although the exact location of the Valley of Salt is not known, it was undoubtedly south of Jerusalem near the Edomite homelands, so David's enemy here appears to be the Edomites. The difference in writing Aram and Edom are the characters R and D, which look very much alike in Hebrew and could easily be misread by a copyist.

THE SLAUGHTER. Apparently, while Joab was fighting against Aram, Abishai went out and defeated the Edomites (1 Chron. 18:12). When Joab returned from Aram (Psalm 60, title), he joined forces with Abishai, and stayed in Edom for about six months for clean-up operations (1 Kings 11:15-16). Although a great number of Edomites were killed at this time, Israel never occupied Edom because God had given that country to Isaac's son Esau/Edom (Deut. 2:5). Nevertheless, David did place garrisons there, as he had in Damascus, and the Edomites were subject to him (see Gen. 25:23).

THE KING'S HIGHWAY. The King's Highway was a major trade route which came from Aram, passed south through Rabbah in Ammon, and continued south through Moab and Edom. The Ammonites had sought help from Aram to the north, but David defeated them and set up garrisons in Aram taking control of the King's Highway to the north. Then David's victory over Edom took control of the King's Highway to the south. (He had already defeated Moab.) Not only did David's victories in Aram and Edom strangle Ammon economically, they also cut off the routes over which military assistance might come to Ammon. An impassable desert was east of Ammon, and David's armies were to the west.

For perhaps three years after insulting David's emissaries, Ammon's capital, Rabbah, had escaped the wrath of David. However, during that time, David cut Rabbah off from all economic and military aid. Ammon was isolated, and the noose began to tighten around Ammon's neck.

The giant killers
2 Sam. 21:15-22 [1 Chron. 20:4-8]

GIANT KILLERS

During the course of the Philistine wars, David's men killed four giants. The first (omitted in Chronicles) was Ishbi-benob whose spearhead weighed almost eight pounds, half the weight of Goliath's spearhead. He was threatening David, who had become weary, when Abishai, David's nephew, came to his rescue and killed the giant. Abishai was also one of his mighty soldiers (see 2 Sam. 23:18-19), greater than the thirty but not as great as the three. Sibbecai killed the second giant named Saph at a place called Gob. Elhanan killed a third giant who is called Goliath here, but he is called Lahmi the brother of Goliath in 1 Chron. 20:5. Finally, David's nephew Jonathan killed the fourth Philistine giant, who was an unusual man with six fingers on each hand and six toes on each foot.

These exploits remind us that a Christians we must sometimes stand alone against the multitudes opposed the knowledge of our God and our Savior and be willing to face the giants who would harm us. God gives the victory to those who are faithful even to death.

Three mighty men
2 Sam. 23:8-17 [1 Chron. 11:10-19]

HALL OF FAME (PART ONE)

Major League Baseball and the National Football League both have a Hall of Fame where the careers and feats of famous athletes are memorialized. The exploits of David's special forces unit known as The Three are recounted in the summaries at the end of his life, but those exploits probably occurred during the wars with the Philistines before the fall of their principle city, Metheg-ammah (Gath), mentioned in 2 Sam. 8:1.

MIGHTY MEN. The first of The Three was Josheb-basshebeth (or Jashobeam, 1 Chron. 11:11), who killed 800 men in one encounter. The second of David's three mightiest men was Eleazar. When David's men retreated before the Philistines, he refused to flee and fought alone until his hand was "frozen" to his sword. When David's men returned, they found that he had already won the victory. The third of David's mightiest men was Shammah, who by himself defended a field of lintels against the raiding Philistines when the other Israelites had fled. (Chronicles omits Shammah's name and apparently confuses the deeds of Eleazar and Shammah.) Through these men who dared to stand when all others fled, God turned the tide of the battle and gave Israel the victory.

GRATEFUL TO THE LORD. The Three, who apparently members of The Thirty at the time, came to David when he was at the cave of Adullam (2 Sam. 23:13). David had once hidden from Saul there (1 Sam. 22:1), and later he defeated the Philistines at Baal-perazim in the Valley of Rephaim near the cave, which may have been his stronghold before attacking the Philistines (2 Sam. 5:20). Perhaps on this latter occasion, these three soldiers demonstrated their devotion and bravery after David expressed his desire for a drink from the well at Bethlehem, which was occupied by Philistines. They undertook the dangerous mission, broke through the Philistine lines, and brought David water from the well at Bethlehem. David was so overwhelmed by their devotion and bravery that he could not drink it. Instead, he poured it out as an offering to the Lord (2 Sam. 23:13-17; 1 Chron. 11:15-19).

Abishai and Benaiah
2 Sam. 23:18-23 [1 Chron. 11:20-25]

HALL OF FAME (PART TWO)

Abishai was the brother of Joab and son of David's sister Zeruiah (1 Chron. 2:13-14). He had gone with David by night into Saul's camp (1 Sam. 26:6-9). He had plotted with his brother Joab to kill Abner to avenge the death of Asahel (2 Sam. 3:30). Whenever Joab divided the army, Abishai often commanded the second part (2 Sam. 10:10). He had also slain the giant Ishbi-Benob when he was about to kill David (2 Sam. 21:17). Here, he is remembered for killing 300 men with his spear, a feat comparable to the feats of the three mighty men. Abishai became commander of "The Thirty" (ESV and Syriac; Hebrew "three").

Benaiah's father, Jehoiada, was a priest and the commander of the soldiers from the family of Aaron who had gone to Hebron with the northern tribes when they made David king of all Israel (1 Chron. 12:27). As a priest, Benaiah had participated in bringing the ark to Jerusalem (1 Chron. 15:16 ff.). Although of a priestly line, Benaiah was a brave soldier. He had slain two of Moab's best soldiers, killed a lion in a pit on a snowy day, and armed with only a club, he had disarmed an Egyptian and killed him with his own spear. At one time, Benaiah was commander of "The Thirty" (1 Chron. 27:6), but later David put him in charge of his bodyguard and made him commander of the standing army in the third month (1 Chron. 27:5-6).

Thirty mighty men
2 Sam. 23:24-39 [1 Chron. 11:26-47]

HALL OF FAME (PART THREE)

Those who visit the Vietnam War Memorial often are looking for one specific name, perhaps a father, brother, or son. Most of the other names on the wall are unknown to them, yet the list of names adds something to the meaning of the one name they are looking for. Similarly, relatives of the men in David's special forces unit known as The Thirty may not have known everyone in the unit, but those relatives would have taken great satisfaction that one of their own family was included at one time or another.

Soldiers in the unit undoubtedly changed over time. Consequently, more than thirty names are found in the lists in Samuel and Chronicles. David's special forces unit also had different commanders from time to time. Known commanders included Ishmaiah (1 Chron. 12:4), Amasai (1 Chron. 12:18), Benaiah (1 Chron. 27:6), and finally Abishai (2 Sam. 23:18-19 ESV).

The following names in 2 Sam. 23 are listed elsewhere in the story of David: 1) Asahel and 2) Joab, David's nephews. Asahel (v. 24) was killed by Abner during the war between the house of Saul and David. Joab (v. 37) led the attack on Jerusalem and became commander of David's army. 3) Naharai, Joab's armor-bearer (v. 37). 4) Jonathan (v. 32), the son of Shammah, who was one of the Three (2 Sam. 23:11-12). 5) Eliam and 6) Uriah the Hittite. Eliam (v. 34) was the son of Ahithophel the Gilonite, who was one of David's most trusted advisors (2 Sam. 15:12). Eliam was also the father of Bathsheba (2 Sam. 11:3). Uriah the Hittite (v. 39) was the husband of Bathsheba.

Each month of the year, David had a different division of his army on active duty. Each division consisted of 24,000 men. Several of the thirty mighty men were commanders of these divisions: Helez (2 Sam. 23:26) was commander of the division on duty during the seventh month of the year (1 Chron. 27:10), Ira the son of Ikkesh (2 Sam. 23:26) was commander of the division on duty during the sixth month of the year (1 Chron. 27:9), Abiezer (2 Sam. 23:27) was commander of the division on duty during the ninth month (1 Chron. 27:12), Maharai (2 Sam. 23:28) was commander of the division on duty on duty during the tenth month (1 Chron. 27:13), and Benaiah the Pirathonite (2 Sam. 23:30) commander of the division on duty during the eleventh month (1 Chron. 27:14).

Part Seven: Favor and Forgiveness

992-990 B.C.; age 47-50; regnal years 17-20

David desires to build a temple for God
2 Sam. 7:1-17 [1 Chron. 17:1-15]

DAVID'S DREAM

David brought the Ark of the Covenant into Jerusalem with celebrations and thanksgiving, and he placed it in a tent he prepared for it. He dreamed of eventually reuniting the altar in Gibeon with the ark in Jerusalem so that all Israel could worship God in the place God had chosen. When God gave him victory over Israel's enemies, David dedicated the plunder to the Lord because his dream was growing.

DAVID'S OATH. David compared the tent where the ark was with his own palace and was perhaps embarrassed. He wanted something better for God. He dreamed of building a house for "the name of the Lord my God" (1 Chron. 22:7). Psalm 132:1-5 reveals the intensity of his dream when it says that David had vowed that he would not rest until he had found a dwelling for the Lord:

> Remember, O LORD, in David's favor,
>   all the hardships he endured,
> how he swore to the LORD
>   and vowed to the Mighty One of Jacob,
> "I will not enter my house
>   or get into my bed,
> I will not give sleep to my eyes
>   or slumber to my eyelids,
> until I find a place for the LORD,
>   a dwelling place for the Mighty One of Jacob."

GOD'S DENIAL. Nathan's initial response to David's dream was favorable, but Nathan had not consulted God on this matter. He was merely expressing his own private opinion. God had different plans. God told Nathan that night that he had never asked anyone before David to build him a house, and that he was not asking David either. God did not require a majestic temple as a dwelling place. What God really wanted was to dwell in David's heart and in the hearts of every Israelite.

For thus says the One who is high and lifted up,
 who inhabits eternity, whose name is Holy:
"I dwell in the high and holy place,
 and also with him who is of a contrite and lowly
 spirit,
to revive the spirit of the lowly,
 and to revive the heart of the contrite."
-- Isa. 57:15

GOD'S BLESSINGS. After God refused to allow David to accomplish his dream, God set about reviving his heart. First, he enumerated what he had already done for David (vv. 8-11). He had taken him from the pasture and made him ruler. He had cut off his enemies and made his name great. He had given Israel rest from foreign oppressors. A secure homeland had already been won through David's military conquests recorded in 2 Sam. 8 and 10.

GOD'S COVENANT. Second, God declared what he would do for David in the future (12-17). He said he would build a house, or dynasty, for David by causing his seed, one who was yet to be born, to succeed him. Three promises were made concerning this seed. He would build a house for God. He would be treated as a son; when he sinned God would not reject him but would discipline him. Finally, his kingdom would be established forever. Each promise has reference to both Solomon (the first of his seed to reign) and to the Messiah (the last of his seed to reign). Solomon would build the temple in Jerusalem, and the Messiah would build a spiritual temple of lowly and contrite people in whom God would dwell (Matt. 16:18; 1 Pet. 2:4-6; 1 Cor. 3:16; 2 Cor. 6:16; Eph. 2:21). When Solomon and his descendants departed from following God, God often disciplined them as sons removing the peace and security he had given them through David and causing them to be oppressed by their enemies. The Messiah, too, was God's Son (Luke 1:35), and though he did not sin, he still learned obedience by the things that he suffered (Heb. 5:8). And finally, when Judah was carried into Babylon captivity, it was not clear how David's kingdom would be eternal until the Messiah took his seat upon the throne at the right hand of God (Luke 1:32-33; Acts 2:32-36; Eph. 1:20-21).

There was evidently more to God's denial than recorded here because David told Solomon that God did not permit him to build the temple because he had shed much blood and fought many wars (1 Chron. 22:8).

David gives thanks to God
2 Sam. 7:18-29 [1 Chron. 17:16-27]

GOD'S GRACE.

David dreamed of building a house for God, but God promised to make a lasting house for David. He promised to make his seed king and establish his throne forever. The promise had certain similarities with the promise God made to Abraham about his seed, and David responded by addressing God as Sovereign Lord, the same name used by Abraham to address God when he reaffirmed the covenant in Gen. 15. Not once in his prayer did David express any disappointment with not being allowed to fulfill his own dream.

UNWORTHY. David expressed no disappointment because he was overwhelmed with the magnitude of God's undeserved gifts (vv. 18-19). His family was insignificant, yet God had made him king of Israel. Such unmerited favor was beyond comprehension. In v. 19 where the ESV has a statement, the NIV has a question in which David continues to express his wonder at God's grace when he asked, "Is this your usual way of dealing with man, O Sovereign LORD?" All Scripture demonstrates that grace is God's usual way of dealing with men who seek him.

REDEEMED. David expressed no disappointment because God had redeemed Israel (vv. 22-24), that is, he had paid a price to make Israel his own possession. God had purchased Israel when he did great and awesome wonders to deliver Israel from Egyptian slavery and drive out the nations before them. David marveled that the Great and Sovereign Lord had become their God, and that they had become his possession.

LONGING. David confessed that what God promised him fulfilled the deepest longings of his heart (vv. 26-25). He urged God to do as he promised, not because he was afraid God would fail to keep his word, but because he so earnestly desired for all to know that "The LORD of hosts is God over Israel!"

COURAGE. Because God had revealed his compassion and mercy through this covenant, David found courage to pray to God, not only to thank him, but to ask him for greater and more precious promises than he could have imagined on his own (vv. 27-29). Without the promises God made to him, David would have been satisfied with asking for much less!

Joab lays siege to Rabbah
2 Sam. 11:1 [1 Chron. 20:1a]

PROTECTING THE KING

Several years had passed since Hanun, king of Ammon, had insulted David's messengers. David first cut them off from their northern allies, the Arameans whom Hanun had hired to help defend him against David. Then David cut off any hope of aid from the south by defeating the Edomites. Ammon was then isolated between a vast desert to the east and David's army to the west. Having isolated Ammon from all assistance, David sent Joab against Rabbah, the capital city.

David himself did not march with his army to attack Rabbah. In an earlier war with the Philistines when the giant Ishbi-benob had pressed the battle against David so vigorously that he was threatening to kill David, Abishai had come to his rescue and slain the giant. After that, David's men vowed that he would no longer go out with them to battle (2 Sam. 21:16-17). He apparently had not accompanied his army in the earlier battle with the Ammonite and Aramean allies (2 Sam. 10:7) or in the conquest of Edom (1 Chron. 18:12).

David commits adultery
2 Sam. 11:2-5

A TRAGIC SIN

> Therefore let anyone who thinks that he stands take heed
> lest he fall.
> -- 1 Cor. 10:12

Few sins related in the Bible are as tragic as David's sin. David had made a name for himself as a warrior who trusted in the Lord and so defeated Israel's enemies. Rabbah, the capital of Ammon, was about to fall. Plunder from Aram, Moab, and Edom had already been dedicated to God. He had hoped to build a house for God in Jerusalem, and he had established a just and righteous government. He was at the peak of his career. But at that very moment when David appeared to be standing firm, he fell. He acted like one of the kings of the nations. Samuel had warned that such kings would take the daughters of Israel to be perfumers, cooks, and bakers (1 Sam. 8:13), but David did much worse.

UNBRIDLED PASSION. From the rooftop of David's palace, David could see inside the walled, private residence of Uriah where Bathsheba was bathing. Instead of retiring quickly from the rooftop until the bath was over, he lingered to gaze at her beauty and then inquired about her. He foolishly allowed his physical desires to gain control of his thoughts and entice him to sin (James 1:14).

BROKEN LAWS. David's informant told him that the woman's name was Bathsheba, and that she was the wife of Uriah. This information should have served as a warning. She was a neighbor's wife. The Law was explicit: "You shall not covet your neighbor's wife" (Ex. 20:17). But David paid no heed. He sent messengers to get her, and he slept with her breaking a second command which said "You shall not commit adultery" (Ex. 20:14).

BETRAYED FRIENDSHIPS. David's deeds were treacherous. He betrayed Bathsheba's husband, Uriah (2 Sam. 23:39), who was one of his Thirty Mighty Men. Furthermore, he betrayed her father, Eliam (called Ammiel in 1 Chron. 3:5 where the syllables are reversed), another of his trusted mighty men (2 Sam. 23:34). Finally, David betrayed Bathsheba's grandfather Ahithophel, who was one of David's trusted advisors (2 Sam. 15:12; 23:34). David's sin could not be excused or white-washed. He had betrayed three loyal and honored servants: one the husband, one the father, and another the grandfather of Bathsheba.

DAMNING EVIDENCE. If David thought he was too big to fail, or above the law, his delusion did not last long. Bathsheba sent him a message: "I am pregnant" (2 Sam. 11:5). Soon Bathsheba's whole family would know she was pregnant: her husband, father, and grandfather. Because Uriah had gone to war against Rabbah, they all would suspect something was amiss. Furthermore, David knew that Bathsheba had not been pregnant when he slept with her because she had been purifying herself from her monthly uncleanness when he saw her. David could not escape the conclusion that he himself was the father of Bathsheba's child.

David tries to hide his sin
Samuel 11:6-13

DRUNKEN SOLDIER, SOBER KING

> The iniquities of the wicked ensnare him,
> and he is held fast in the cords of his sin.
> -- Prov. 5:22

After Bathsheba informed David that she was pregnant, David attempted to remove any suspicions that he was the father of her child. David's attempts soon impaired his sober judgments.

A CONSCIENTIOUS SOLDIER. David recalled Uriah from battle with hopes that Uriah would go home and spend a night or two with his wife. In that way, Uriah might assume that he was himself the father when a child was born several months later. Even if he had suspicions, nothing could be proved, and David would be free from any consequences for his sin. Uriah, however, slept where David's servants slept at the entrance of the palace. When David asked why he had not gone home, Uriah said he could not in good conscience enjoy homemade cooking or lie with his wife at home while his fellow soldiers and the Ark of God were camped on a battlefield.

A SOBER KING. If at first they don't succeed, even kings try again. David asked Uriah to stay another day and dine with him. David made Uriah drunk hoping he would forget his scruples and go home for the night, but Uriah again slept at the entrance of the palace. Uriah drunk remained more pious than David sober (Ackroyd in J.E. Smith, 2000, p. 424). Although David was not intoxicated with wine, his thoughts were impaired by a consuming desire to hide his sin. Sobriety failed him.

Like an insect caught in a spider's web, the more David tried to hide his sin, the more he became ensnared in it.

David has Uriah killed
2 Sam. 11:14-26

WHITE-WASHED SEPULCHER

> For everyone who does wicked things hates the light and
> does not come to the light, lest his works should be
> exposed.
> -- John 3:20

David did not want his sin exposed. He was afraid of the consequences. Therefore, he committed even fouler deeds to keep his dark secrets hidden.

BRAZEN. David, the man who restrained his own men from killing Saul and who punished Recab and Baanah for murdering an innocent man in his bed, decided to have a faithful and innocent soldier killed and brazenly sent the death warrant by the hand of Uriah himself. David, the leader who mourned the death of Jonathan, brazenly commanded Joab to act imprudently in war so that not only was Uriah killed but also several other innocent soldiers. All this he did to hide his adultery. God's light had gone out in David's heart.

PHONY. Because his heart was darkened, David became a pretentious phony. After word came of Uriah's death, David told Joab not to get discouraged because "the sword devours now one and now another" as if what happened was merely a matter of chance. He even pretended piety when he allowed Bathsheba to observe the usual thirty days of morning (see Num. 20:29 and Deut. 34:8) before taking her as his wife. David had become a white-washed sepulcher concealing the bones of dead men.

Nathan rebukes David
2 Sam. 12:1-12

SEVERE MERCY

We all know that God was merciful to David and forgave him, and we usually assume that God's mercy reduced the severity of his punishment. While God's mercy certainly removed completely the eternal punishment of his sin, God did not in his mercy reduce the severity of the consequences of sin. God's severe mercy is justified by the parable Nathan told David.

THE PARABLE. The parable stresses three things. First, it stresses the great difference in the wealth of two men. The rich man had "very many flocks and herds," but the poor man had a single ewe lamb that he had bought. Second, the story stresses the intimacy between the poor man and his ewe lamb. It lived in his house like a pet. It ate his food, drank from his cup, and lay in his "arms" ("bosom" – KJV). The lamb was like a daughter (Heb. *bat*, which is the same as the first syllable of *Bathsheba*). Finally, the story emphasizes the rich man's heartless treatment of the poor man. The rich man had no pity and slaughtered the poor man's dear pet to feed a traveler.

THE KING'S JUDGMENT. David was enraged because the rich man had no regard for the feelings of the poor man. David declared, "As the LORD lives, the man who has done this deserves to die, and he shall restore the lamb fourfold." The fourfold restoration for the sheep required by the Law (Ex. 22:1), which guided David's final judgment, could not restore the object of the poor man's affection. The Law's penalty was woefully inadequate for the callous act (Youngblood, 1992, p. 943). David's declaration that the man deserved to die recognized the inadequacy of even fourfold restoration and left him no room to protest the Lord's judgment.

GOD'S JUDGMENT FOR MURDER. As soon as David gave his verdict and noted its inadequacy, Nathan declared, "You are the man who had no pity; you are the man who deserves to die. You are the rich man who had many wives while your poor neighbor had but one. Nevertheless, you killed Uriah with the sword (in other words, in battle, for he was killed by archers on the wall) and took his wife. Therefore, the sword will never depart from your house" (2 Sam. 12:7-9 paraphrase). The actions set in motion by David's sin could not be stopped with David's death. The sword would not devour one man, David, but many in David's family instead. David's earlier reply to Joab, "the sword devours now one and now another," would haunt him repeatedly as the swords of lust, revenge, rebellion, and selfish ambition devoured his own sons. David learned that the God whose law he had despised, was the God who said, "I the LORD your God am a jealous God, visiting the iniquity of the fathers on the children to the third and the fourth generation of those who hate me" (Ex. 20:5). What a great punishment God handed down!

GOD'S JUDGMENT FOR ADULTERY. After sentencing David for murder, God turned to the charge of adultery. Just as David had taken the wife of a man close to him, so one close to him would take his wives and lie with them openly. What David had done to Uriah would be done to him, "wound for wound, stripe for stripe (Ex. 21:23-25), but with a painful twist. Not merely one of his wives would be taken, but many; furthermore, they would not be taken secretly, but openly. What a dreadful thing it is to fall into the hands of the living God!

David repents and is restored
2 Sam. 12:13-23

GENUINE REPENTANCE

Nathan's rebuke occurred about nine months after David's sin. Although David was occupied with the final assault on the Ammonites during those nine months, he had not been able to hide from his own guilt. Undoubtedly, his guilt weighed heavily on his heart as when he wrote Psalm 32:3-5a:

> For when I kept silent, my bones wasted away
>   through my groaning all day long.
> For day and night your hand was heavy upon me;
>   my strength was dried up as by the heat of summer.
>   Selah
> I acknowledged my sin to you,
>   and I did not cover my iniquity;
> I said, "I will confess my transgressions to the LORD,"

NO EXCUSES. David was quick to acknowledge his sin and accept full responsibility for it when confronted by Nathan. He said quite simply, "I have sinned against the Lord." He was not like Saul who at first denied his sin (cf. 1 Sam. 15:13, 20) and blamed others (cf. 1 Sam. 15:21). Neither was he like Saul who, even after he reluctantly acknowledging his sin, still excused it (1 Sam. 15:24) and asked to be honored as if there were no shame in his sin (1 Sam. 15:30). David knew he could not hide his shame from God. In Psalm 51:4, he confessed, "Against you, you only, have I sinned and done what is evil in your sight."

FORGIVENESS. In his repentance, David did not desire honor before men, as Saul had, but God's mercy, compassion, and forgiveness.

> Have mercy on me, O God,
>   according to your steadfast love;
> according to your abundant mercy

blot out my transgressions.
Wash me thoroughly from my iniquity,
    and cleanse me from my sin!
-- Ps. 51:1-2

FELLOWSHIP. Forgiveness was the means to an even greater desire, that his fellowship with God might be renewed.

Create in me a clean heart, O God,
    and renew a right spirit within me.
Cast me not away from your presence,
    and take not your Holy Spirit from me.
-- Ps. 51:10-11

FREELY GIVEN. God freely forgave and restored fellowship to the penitent king. Though God did not change the consequences of the sin, David saw the death of the son not as God's refusal to forgive but as evidence of God's faithfulness. If God said he was forgiven and his son would die, and if God kept his word with regard to his son, then he was assured God kept his word with regard to his own forgiveness (Bergen, 1996, p. 376). He washed and went to worship the Lord. His fellowship with the Lord was restored, and the Lord would sustain him in the troubles he would face.

David takes Rabbah of the Ammonites
2 Sam. 12:26-31 [1 Chron. 20:1b-3]

THE FALL OF THE PROUD

When Hanun, king of Ammon, insulted David's messengers, he knew he would make David his enemy, but he may also have felt confident that he could defend himself against any resulting aggression. Historians tell us that during six centuries of Ammonite rule in Rabbah, its defenses were breached only once, and that by David's army (George M. Landes, "The Material Civilization of the Ammonites," *The Biblical Archaeologist Reader*, 2, p. 76). David's accomplishment followed a thorough, if slow, preparation. David defeated Ammon's allies to the north and south, took control of the King's Highway from Aram to Edom, and isolated Rabbah behind its city walls. After two or three years of preparation, David sent Joab out to besiege Rabbah in the spring of the year (1 Chron. 20:1).

THE SIEGE. Even after such thorough preparations, Rabbah did not fall immediately. It was at least a year before Joab captured the "royal city" ("royal citadel" – NIV), perhaps a separate walled section of the city where the king lived. Joab sent messengers to David saying he had captured the "city of waters," suggesting that the "royal city" protected the water supply. Then the messengers urged David to come and direct the final capture of the city.

THE CAPTURE. The city fell into David's hands like a ripe plum, and he took a great quantity of plunder from the city. One of the notable items was a crown of gold weighing 75 pounds. It is hard to imagine a king lifting, let alone wearing, a crown weighing 75 pounds, so from ancient times it has been suggested that the crown sat on the idol of the Ammonite god Milcom or Molech (both king and Molech are spelled "mlk" in Hebrew). The crown, or a jewel from the crown, was placed briefly on David's head as a symbol of David's power over the Ammonites (J.E. Smith, 2000, p. 434).

THE PUNISHMENT. The price for insulting David's messengers was steep. David put the Ammonites of Rabbah and the surrounding towns to work with stone-cutting saws, picks, and axes and in making bricks. All of these tasks, which require heavy manual labor, are related to building walls and other large structures which David may have used to strengthen the defenses of many Israelite cities (see Bergen, 1996, p. 378). (Some translations such as the KJV and NASB suggest that David tortured and killed the Ammonites with these instruments, but the language is not clear. The ESV and NIV say that David sentenced them to hard labor with them.)

Solomon is born
2 Sam. 12:24-25

A CHILD OF PROMISE

After Bathsheba's son died, David comforted her, and she bore a second son who would later sit on his father's throne in Jerusalem. The names given to her second son are significant.

SOLOMON. David named his son Solomon, which means something like "His [Yahweh's] Restoration/Peace" (Bergen, 1996, p. 376). By giving his son this name, David expressed his confidence that God had forgiven him and restored the relationship that had been broken by his sin (TWOT, #2401: "The general meaning behind the root š-l-m is of completion and fulfillment—of entering into a state of wholeness and unity, a restored relationship.)

JEDIDIAH. The Lord confirmed that Solomon was a special son. He sent a message by Nathan the prophet to give Solomon a second name, Jedidiah, which means "beloved of the Lord" (see footnote in ESV). Hence, this son would build a house for God, and God would love him as his own son and establish his throne forever (2 Sam. 7:12). Solomon had older brothers who would try to usurp the throne, but Nathan the prophet would be an advocate for God's choice and help anoint Solomon as the next king.

The Lord renews his mercies every day!

Part Eight: Family Trouble

989-977 B.C.; age 51-63; regnal years 21-33

Amnon rapes Tamar
2 Sam. 13:1-22

FODDER FOR A FAMILY FEUD

> Happy families are all alike; every unhappy family is
> unhappy in its own way.
> -- Leo Tolstoy, **Anna Karenina**, first sentence

Family feuds have a cast of characters. Some cause trouble, some find trouble, some feed trouble, some are victims of trouble, and some stumble into trouble. Amnon's behavior was fodder for a family feud that David was unable to contain. It ripped through his sons and daughters, their cousins and uncles, and even his own wives killing some and wounding all.

CARNAL SON. Amnon was David's firstborn, the son of Ahinoam from Jezreel in Judah (2 Sam. 3:2). Being the son of a powerful king whom he would probably succeed made Amnon a privileged person. Despite his privilege, he lusted for his beautiful half-sister Tamar, a woman who was forbidden to him by law (Lev. 18:9), just as his father had lusted for a woman forbidden to him. Amnon's lust for Tamar so consumed him that several people guessed his thoughts. Absalom had observed his lustful looks and immediately knew the cause of Tamar's grief after Amnon raped her (v. 20). Jonadab watched his unsatisfied lust turn to self pity and suggested a way for him to satisfy it. Amnon's lust was not love for Tamar. He did not hesitate to use his strength to overpower Tamar despite her protests. Then when he had proved her weak and vulnerable, he loathed her even more than he had desired her. He threw her out of his house and barred the door. The consequences of his sin proved him to be the fool that Tamar saw him to be.

SHREWD COUSIN. Jonadab was David's nephew, the son of Shimeah (Shammah), who was the third of Jesse's sons (1 Sam. 16:9). He was a shrewd judge of human weakness. He observed Amnon's self pity, and knew David to be a doting father. He was willing to exploit the moral weakness of his uncle and to purvey sexual fantasies to his cousin knowing full well that Amnon would not stop at watching Tamar lustfully but would also rape her.

VIRTUOUS SISTER. Tamar was the daughter of Maacah, the daughter of the king of Geshur and mother of Absalom. Tamar begged Amnon not to do anything wicked saying, "No, my brother, do not violate me, for such a thing is not done in Israel; do not do this outrageous thing.… You would be as one of the outrageous fools in Israel" (2 Sam. 13:12-13). She pled with Amnon so that her virtue might be preserved: "As for me, where could I carry my shame?" Finally, in desperation, she begged Amnon to ask the king that she be given to him in marriage. Although this was forbidden by the Law (Lev. 18:9; Deut. 27:22), she saw this as a way of preventing a rape (Deut. 22:28). Her pleas were ignored. After Amnon raped her, she tore her virgin's garment as a sign of sorrow and shame. Though beautiful, she remained desolate in the house of her brother Absalom.

INEFFECTUAL FATHER. Although Jonadab and Absalom had seen lust written on Amnon's countenance, David failed to see it. When asked, he granted Amnon's desire to have Tamar sent to his house failing to see that it was not prudent. David was incapable of preventing his own sin from corrupting his children. Then, after Amnon had raped his sister, David failed to punish Amnon even though David was very angry. Perhaps David was reluctant to discipline Amnon because of his own adultery, or perhaps he was unsure what punishment to mete out according to Law (Deut. 22:28-29; Lev. 18:9, 29). Regardless, David's silence, his total failure to rebuke Amnon, made David an impotent judge in this case. Where there is no justice, wickedness and every evil work prospers.

PENT-UP BROTHER. Absalom provided refuge for his disgraced sister, but he never said anything to his half-brother Amnon. He waited and saw David's silence and impotence, but Absalom's silence was not the silence of impotence. It was the silence of a man who intensely hated his brother and who was intent on revenge (see Alter, 1981, p. 79).

Absalom kills Amnon
2 Sam. 13:23-39

SWEET REVENGE

> Revenge is sweeter than life itself. So think fools.
> -- Juvenal

Absalom waited two years to exact his revenge on Amnon, the heir apparent who had raped his sister Tamar. During that time, he had apparently confided his intention to a few friends, perhaps including Jonadab (2 Sam. 13:32 NIV). He planned his revenge during sheep shearing festivities at Baal Hazor, a mountain about 15 miles NNE of Jerusalem. Absalom's revenge mirrored Amnon's sin in many ways (Bergen, 1996, p. 385).

DECEPTION. Just as Amnon deceived King David about his intentions, so Absalom deceived the king. When the king declined Absalom's invitation to the feast, no doubt as Absalom expected, he asked that, in lieu of the king being the honored guest, the heir apparent be the guest. David appeared suspicious but relented when Absalom called Amnon his brother.

TRAP. Just as the king had sent Tamar into a trap devised by Amnon, so now the king sent Amnon into a trap devised by Absalom.

VIOLENT MEAL. Just as the little meal Tamar prepared for Amnon turned violent when Amnon overpowered her, so the feast Absalom prepared for Amnon turned violent when Absalom's men killed him. The other sons of David rose in terror and fled.

The first news to reach Jerusalem was that Absalom had killed all the king's sons. Immediately David rose from his throne just as his sons had risen from the feast. Then he tore his clothes just as Tamar and torn her clothes in grief (Youngblood, 1992, p. 970). The king, whose adultery with Bathsheba was mirrored by Amnon's rape of Tamar, and whose murder of Uriah was mirrored by Absalom's murder of Amnon (Youngblood, 1992, p. 969), was overcome with grief. The sword had turned upon his own house. Furthermore, Absalom had just proved himself a fool. Eventually, the sword would consume him also.

DRAMA IN THE COURTROOM

As king, one of David's responsibilities was to judge difficult cases according to law. Sometimes plaintiffs and defendants dramatized their cases, and David had to separate fact from fiction. In 2 Sam. 14, the entire case is a fabrication. A woman of Tekoa acted the part of a widow in a play written by Joab. As a superb actress, she changed David's behavior toward his son Absalom.

BROTHERS IN A FIELD. The woman stated the case quite simply: "Your servant had two sons, and they quarreled with one another in the field. There was no one to separate them, and one struck the other and killed him" (2 Sam. 14:6). Immediately, David would recall the story of Cain, who killed his brother in a field. Although Cain was guilty of murder, God had spared Cain and even protected him from being killed himself (Gen. 4:15). Without denying her son's guilt, the woman artfully prepared the king to make a judgment favorable to her.

CLAN'S QUESTIONABLE MOTIVE. As would be expected, the elders of the clan asked that the remaining son be turned over to them so that they might kill him to avenge the death of his brother (see Num. 35:16-25), but the woman insinuated that the clan was more concerned with profit than justice because they had said that when they got rid of the murderer, then they would "destroy the heir also" (2 Sam. 14:7).

BURNING COAL. Finally, the woman revealed her own motive for wanting to spare her son. He was the only coal she had left. Housewives used a glowing coal from the previous day's fire to start a fire for the coming day. If only one ember was left, it was very important to preserve it until the fire was started for the next day. Her son was her husband's one remaining descendant. If he was executed, her husband would have "neither name nor remnant on the face of the earth" forever.

The woman acted superbly, and she obtained the judgment she desired though at first it appeared half-hearted. Then when she applied her story to Absalom, she also obtained the judgment Joab desired. Joab wanted David to show mercy to his son who had killed a brother just as God had shown mercy to Cain. Joab, through the woman, also insinuated that David's motive for not recalling Absalom may not have been justice so much as a desire to "destroy the heir" so that David could give the throne to young Solomon. David immediately suspected Joab's role in the plot, but he relented. Joab was relieved because he knew he had forced David's hand (J.E. Smith, 2000, p. 447). David sent Joab to recall his son from Geshur.

David forgives Absalom
2 Sam. 14:25-33

PRETENSION AND PROTOCOL

Joab went to Geshur and brought Absalom back to Jerusalem where he was restored to his wife and children. However, David did not accept him in the royal family or as an heir to the throne. David refused to see Absalom personally.

PRETENSION. Absalom had a kingly appearance much like Saul before him. While Saul was praised for his height, Absalom was highly praised for his appearance. But God had warned Samuel not to put confidence in appearance, and the people should not have put confidence in Absalom's appearance. Nevertheless, the people praised him. They were still looking for a king like the kings of the nations around them. Absalom, their choice, was vain about his appearance and especially his hair. Nevertheless, the appearance of virility was an illusion. Though he had three sons, they all died before Absalom himself (2 Sam. 18:18). In the end, even his hair would become his undoing just as it was the undoing of Samson.

PROTOCOL. Absalom felt his position in Jerusalem was intolerable. It stood in the way of his ambitions. After two years, he was tired of being treated as an inferior. He sent servants to fetch Joab as a member of the royalty might call an inferior. The commander of David's army did not think the demand fit proper protocol; he did not feel compelled to answer the summons of one not admitted into the royal family. At the same time, Absalom, who felt his rightful position was heir apparent, was not about to go crawling to Joab, so he commanded his servants to set fire to Joab's barley fields. Though he would probably be required to pay for the burned fields (see Ex. 22:6), he anticipated that the benefits of his action would far outweigh the costs. As Absalom foresaw, Joab came personally to see him. Through Joab, Absalom was able to get an audience with the king. He acted according to protocol himself. He bowed down with his face to the ground before David, and David kissed him.

Absalom acted according to protocol when he met his father, but his actions were pretentious. He didn't merely want the king's recognition. He wanted the king's crown. Restored to the royal family, Absalom would soon be acting the part of a king. Soon, people would be bowing down to him, and he would kiss them.

Absalom wins the favor of the people
2 Sam. 15:1-6

A CONSUMMATE POLITICIAN

> In order to become the master, the politician poses as
> the servant.
> -- Charles de Gaulle

Absalom was a keen observer of how David's government operated. He saw an opportunity to exploit the system to undermine his father and advance his own royal ambitions, which he exhibited by riding in a chariot and sending fifty men to run ahead of him just as Samuel had warned that kings would do (1 Sam. 8:11).

FINDING GRIEVANCES. Absalom observed that people unhappy with decisions of their city elders brought their complaints to the king. Absalom decided to greet these people before they got to the king. Greeting the people in this way would make them feel that they were important.

PRETENDING SYMPATHY. Not only did Absalom make the people feel important, but he also assured them that their complaint was important and just. Nevertheless, he warned the people that the king didn't even have any representatives to hear their complaint. Indeed, the people may have had a hard time getting a hearing if they had not been sent by their city elders because they themselves considered the case difficult (Deut. 17:8-10). If for any reason a hearing was denied or delayed (to collect evidence, gather witnesses, or consult city elders), then these people would think favorably of Absalom who not only met them but also said he would immediately rule in their favor.

STEALING HEARTS. Absalom identified himself with the people. He did not allow the people to bow down to him. Instead, he reached out to them, gave them a hearty hug and kissed them. His informality and intimacy contrasted with the formal greeting given royalty. In this way he "stole" the hearts of the people. In other words, he took their hearts with stealth or secrecy (TWOT, #364). Furthermore, Absalom could always "prove" that he had no aspirations to the throne because he refused to allow the people to bow down to him (see Bergen, 1996, p. 397).

Absalom proclaims himself king in Hebron
2 Sam. 15:7-12

COUP D'ÉTAT

After Absalom had gained sympathizers throughout Israel, he began to carry out his plan for a coup d'état. He went to his father and asked permission to fulfill a vow by worshiping God in Hebron. David suspected nothing and sent Absalom away with his blessing, "Go in peace."

PLACE. Hebron was an ideal city from which to launch the coup. It was far enough away from Jerusalem (20 miles) that Absalom could carry out his plan without immediate detection, but close enough that he could launch a surprise attack on David's capital. Furthermore, Hebron was the leading city in Judah, perhaps the most influential tribe in Israel. It had been David's former capital, and may, therefore, have resented its loss of influence when David moved the capital to Jerusalem. With Hebron on his side, Absalom removed David's oldest base of support.

PEOPLE. Absalom invited 200 citizens of Jerusalem to Hebron. Although they were unaware of Absalom's plot, they played an important role. Even if none of them could be won over, their presence would give the appearance of popular support and guarantee that their families in Jerusalem would be reluctant to resist Absalom when he attacked the city. In addition, Absalom called Ahithophel, who had been one of David's trusted advisors, from Giloh, his hometown near Hebron. Because Ahithophel was called from his hometown instead of Jerusalem, he may have already left his position as David's advisor (see J.E. Smith, 2000, p. 454). Ahithophel may have joined the coup because he was Bathsheba's grandfather (2 Sam. 11:3; 23:34) or because he wanted to restore Judah's influence in the kingdom (J.E. Smith, 2000, p. 454 footnote). His presence gave Absalom's regime legitimacy.

PLAN. The sacrifice that Absalom planned in Hebron was really a coronation feast. Absalom sent messengers throughout Israel so that trumpets might be sounded throughout the land coinciding with the coronation feast. When the trumpets sounded, the messengers would announce Absalom's ascension to the throne of Israel.

Absalom was declared king at a sacrifice just as his father David was anointed at a feast, but their careers bore little resemblance thereafter. The Spirit rushed powerfully on David (1 Sam. 16:13), but Absalom's "conspiracy grew strong" (2 Sam. 15:12). David waited patiently for the throne and refused to raise his hand against King Saul. Absalom seized the throne as soon as possible, raised an army against King David, and publicly insulted David's concubines in Jerusalem. David's reign thrived on righteousness, but Absalom thrived on disorder and wickedness because he was motivated by selfish ambition. As James 3:16 notes, "Where jealousy and selfish ambition exist, there will be disorder and every vile practice."

David flees Jerusalem
2 Sam. 15:13-23

HURRIED FLIGHT

Soon after Absalom had been proclaimed king, a messenger came and told David, "The hearts of the men of Israel have gone after Absalom." David immediately decided to flee from Jerusalem. Why would he abandon Jerusalem?

LACK OF TROOPS. God had given Israel peace from the surrounding nations, so David had sent the militia to their homes. The messenger's report suggested that the hearts of many who served in the militia were now with Absalom (The phrase "men of Israel" in verse 13 appears to refer to the militia in Judges 7:23; 20:11 ff.; 1 Sam. 7:11; 14:24.). David's only force in Jerusalem was his personal bodyguard consisting of the Kerethites and Pelethites along with 600 Gittites.

FAMILY DANGER. God had promised David would be followed on the throne by a son whom God would love. When God had made it clear that he loved David's son Solomon, David had promised Bathsheba that Solomon would be the next king (see 1 Kings 1:13). Absalom was not the one God had chosen, and if he was willing to depose his father, he would not hesitate to kill Solomon. David fled with his family to protect his heir from intrigue and murder.

DOUBTFUL LOYALTY. If David had remained in the city, he could not have depended on the loyalty of those within the city walls. Two hundred men of Jerusalem had gone with Absalom to Hebron, so David could not be sure of the loyalty of their families. If the citizens were divided, some supporting Absalom and some David, danger could be as great inside the city as outside. David had been well aware of this kind of danger earlier when he fled Keilah (1 Sam. 23:12-13). Therefore, David fled with only those absolutely loyal to God and himself. Even Ittai, a Philistine warrior from Gath, swore loyalty to David, much as his great-grandmother Ruth had sworn loyalty to Naomi, before he was allowed to go with David.

Fleeing Jerusalem was probably the best for David himself, but that was not the major reason he fled. He was actually thinking more of others than himself (Phil. 2:3-4). By fleeing, he saved the city from civil strife. By fleeing, he protected God's chosen heir to the throne.

David leaves agents inside Jerusalem
2 Sam. 15:24-37

GRACE FOR THE HUMBLE

> Humble yourselves before the Lord, and he will exalt
> you.
> -- James 4:10

David had to swallow his pride to flee from his son Absalom and allow him to occupy the royal city. Not only did David swallow his pride, but he also humbled himself before God.

RESPECT. David showed the utmost respect for God when he sent the Ark of the Covenant back to Jerusalem. The ark was the symbol of God's presence in Israel. When Israel had been traveling from Egypt to Canaan, the ark went with them. Indeed, it led them. But now God had given Israel their inheritance and no longer led Israel from place to place. Now he had chosen Jerusalem as his dwelling place (2 Kings 21:7-8). David respected God's choice, and he believed that God could bring him back to Jerusalem if he found favor in God's sight. Therefore, he commanded Zadok, "Carry the ark of God back into the city" (2 Sam. 15:25).

HUMILITY. Moreover, David was willing to accept whatever God chose for him. As he left the city, he wept. He did not weep for what he was leaving behind, but he wept in humble repentance knowing that God was disciplining him for his sin. Therefore, he covered his head and removed his sandals as he ascended the Mount of Olives just as Moses had hid his face and removed his sandals at the burning bush on Mt. Sinai.

PRAYER. As David was leaving the city, he was told that his trusted advisor Ahithophel had joined Absalom's conspiracy. Ahithophel had a reputation for giving counsel that was like the counsel of God (2 Sam. 16:23), so David knew that he had to depend on God to nullify Ahithophel's advice. Showing his dependence on God, David prayed, "O LORD, please turn the counsel of Ahithophel into foolishness" (2 Sam. 15:31).

PROVISION. God saw David's humility before he fled the city or knew his need, so God had already made provision for him. God's priests, Zadok and Abiathar, had remained loyal to David. David was able to send them back into the city where they could collect valuable information and relay it on to David. When David prayed that God would turn Ahithophel's advice to foolishness, God had already planned for Hushai, another of David's wise counselors, to meet him. David sent Hushai back to Jerusalem to infiltrate Absalom's inner circle, nullify Ahithophel's counsel, and pass Absalom's plans to the priests Zadok and Abiathar, who would then inform David.

David did not depart the city a proud and defiant man. He did not stand at the top of the Mount of Olives overlooking the city and vow, "I shall return." In his humility, he left his future in the hands of God. God saw his humility and chose to lift him up. David wisely used the help that God gave him.

Ziba slanders Mephibosheth
2 Sam. 16:1-4

STEALING FROM A LAME MAN

> For the love of money is a root of all kinds of evils.
> -- 1 Tim. 6:10

Ziba had managed Saul's estate for years. He managed it after Saul's death, and he continued to manage it when David gave Saul's estate to Saul's grandson Mephibosheth (2 Sam. 9:1-12) to keep a promise he had made to Jonathan. Ziba's life was in the estate, and his heart was in it, too. The only problem was that it was not his. In this episode, Ziba revealed himself to be both shrewd and greedy. His greed led him into sin.

SHREWD. If Absalom was able to secure the throne, he would undoubtedly confiscate Saul's property and make it part of his royal estate. Ziba astutely perceived that the best hope for preserving the estate was to gamble that the rebellion would fail, so he cast his lot with David. He quickly gathered donkeys and supplies that would be useful during flight and brought them to David. In this way, he obtained David's favor. Ziba knew that "A man's gift makes room for him and brings him before the great" (Prov. 18:16).

GREEDY. What Ziba really wanted was to make the estate his own, and he saw his opportunity in the confusion of the moment. In David's hurry to leave Jerusalem, he would not have time to investigate an accusation thoroughly, so Ziba slandered Mephibosheth accusing him of staying in Jerusalem in hope that Saul's kingdom would be given to him (cf. 19:26-27). He guessed correctly. David gave the estate to Ziba without a second witness or thorough investigation as required by Law (Deut. 19:15; see also Prov. 18:17; 25:2).

It would have been absurd for Mephibosheth, crippled as he was, to expect restoration of the throne to Saul's family, but Ziba's accusation was believable because a pathetic character like Mephibosheth might be expected to entertain such a fantasy. Furthermore, Ziba gambled that, in the confusion of Absalom taking over the city, Mephibosheth would be killed or neglected and left to die. Hopefully, when David finally returned to the city, no one would be able to prove his slander, and the estate would be secured for himself and his children forever.

Shimei curses David
2 Sam. 16:5-14

STICKS AND STONES

The old saying, "Sticks and stones may break my bones, but words will never hurt me," is not entirely true. Although words do not damage the physical body, they do cause emotional pain. Consequently, self-control and faith are required to keep from retaliating when attacked verbally. David exemplified that self-control and faith when Shimei cursed him as he fled Jerusalem.

INSULTS. Shimei yelled at David like one would chase away a troublesome dog, "Get out, get out!" Then he called David a "man of blood" equating him with a common murderer for the way he had treated Saul's family (a false accusation, by the way). He also called him a "worthless" man. "Worthless" is Belial in Hebrew, a word that would later become a name for Satan. When David didn't respond, Shimei threw stones at him and threw dust in the air as if David was a fleeing dog. Shimei felt justified in his verbal and physical insults because he saw what was happening as the Lord repaying David for his evil deeds.

SELF-CONTROL. In response, Abishai requested permission to kill Shimei, whom he called a "dead dog." David refused to retaliate. He did not have the vengeful disposition of his nephews. Perhaps, David recognized that Shimei's curses were part of God's discipline, not for his treatment of Saul's family, but for his sin with Bathsheba, which was the cause of his family problems with Absalom. He himself would not punish Shimei if all this was the Lord's doing.

TRUST. Instead of retaliating, David chose to trust God. He thought that perhaps God, seeing the evil accusations that he endured patiently, would repay him with good. David entrusted himself to the Lord, who judges justly. God did repay him with good, and brought him back to Jerusalem. When he returned, Shimei met David in humble submission, like a dog with his tail between his legs.

David was patient and self-controlled partly because he knew his afflictions were the Lord's discipline and, more importantly, because he trusted the Lord to do what was right. His promised descendant, Jesus, who was without sin, also endured affliction patiently leaving us an example that we should follow.

> For to this you have been called, because Christ also
> suffered for you, leaving you an example, so that you
> might follow in his steps. 22 He committed no sin, neither
> was deceit found in his mouth. 23 When he was reviled,
> he did not revile in return; when he suffered, he did not
> threaten, but continued entrusting himself to him who
> judges justly.
> -- 1 Pet. 2:21-23

Hushai infiltrates Absalom's inner council
2 Sam. 16:15-19

MEANING IS IN THE EAR OF THE LISTENER

> Through pride we are ever deceiving ourselves.
> -- Carl Jung

The proud person thinks that he is the most important person on the earth, so it naturally follows that he thinks all praise and honor belongs to him. His first inclination upon hearing words of praise and honor is that they are directed to him. Herein is the potential for the proud person to be deceived. Hushai, David's loyal friend (2 Sam. 15:37; 1 Chron. 27:33), deceived Absalom precisely because Absalom could not imagine anyone else receiving the praise Hushai gave.

KING. When Hushai met Absalom, Hushai said, "Long live the king! Long live the king!" Of course, those words are usually said when meeting a king, and Absalom naturally thought Hushai was recognizing him as king even though Hushai had never mentioned his name. For his part, Hushai was undoubtedly thinking, "Long live King David!" Certainly, he would work to that end. Absalom, however, could hardly believe his good fortune in attracting another of his father's best counselors. Laughing inwardly he asked, "Is this your loyalty to your friend? Why did you not go with your friend?" (Absalom could have been suspicious, in which case his deception was delayed a short time.)

CHOSEN. Hushai replied with more apparent flattery. "No," he said, "for whom the LORD and this people and all the men of Israel have chosen, his I will be, and with him I will remain." He seemed to imply that recent events had convinced him that God and the people had chosen Absalom (J.E. Smith, 2000, p. 462), and Absalom absolutely loved it. Inwardly, however, Hushai was proclaiming his loyalty to David whom God had truly chosen (David was often called God's chosen, but Absalom never. See Youngblood, 1992, p. 1006). As for the people and leaders of Israel, they also had chosen David, and many of them were still loyal to him (2 Sam. 15:23).

SERVE. Hushai continued with a rhetorical question, "Whom should I serve? Should it not be his son?" However, the real question is how he would serve the son. Hushai said he would serve Absalom "as I served your father." How had Hushai served the father? As a friend of the king. How would he serve the son? As a friend of the king. Absalom, blinded by his ego and Hushai's flattery, could conceive of no one but himself being king, but in Hushai's mind David was still king. He actually told Absalom, though ambiguously, that he would serve him as a loyal friend of David (Bergen, 1996, p. 410).

The Scripture says that pride goes before destruction (Prov. 16:18). In Absalom's case, it not only went before his destruction, it also set him up for destruction. His egotism blinded him to the danger posed by Hushai who never wavered in his loyalty to David in word or deed.

Absalom disgraces David's concubines
2 Sam. 16:20-23

ACHILLES' HEEL

The counsel Ahithophel gave Absalom to lie with his father's concubines on the roof of David's house was brilliant, but it had a fatal weakness.

BRILLIANCE. The advice was brilliant because it gave a sense of justice being done for a royal crime that appeared to have been ignored. It was an "eye for an eye, tooth for a tooth" kind of justice which the public understood. It may also have made Absalom a hero. Furthermore, when Absalom disgraced David's concubines, he made it clear he was not merely seeking to be named heir or designated coregent. He was acting like the king. Finally, Absalom had made himself such a stench to David that reconciliation was impossible. He declared he would be king, and nothing less. Such a bold action was sure to embolden Absalom's supporters.

WEAKNESS. Although Ahithophel's advice was brilliant, it had an Achilles' heel. It flaunted the basic principles of morality. First, it paid no heed to the example of Reuben, who slept with his father's concubine, and forfeited the inheritance of the firstborn as a consequence (Gen. 35:22; 1 Chron. 5:1-2). Absalom's right as the oldest living son to sit on David's throne would go to another. Second, Ahithophel's' advice also gave no heed to the Law, which designated a death penalty for the son who had lain with his father's wife (Lev. 20:11). Before many days had passed, Absalom himself would be dead.

> There is a way that seems right to a man,
>   but its end is the way to death.
> -- Prov. 14:12

Hushai opposes Ahithophel's advice
2 Sam. 17:1-14

PAMPERING A SUPERSTAR

If superstars don't demand pampering, someone will pamper them for their own purposes. Absalom was a superstar, and his advisers spent a lot of time pampering his ego. Absalom's swollen ego led to his downfall.

AHITHOPHEL. Absalom was already basking in the adulation of the multitudes. Although some had fled with David, Ahithophel assured Absalom that they too would return to him if David were dead. "Let me," he advised, "choose twelve thousand men, and I will arise and pursue David tonight. I will come upon him while he is weary and discouraged and throw him into a panic, and all the people who are with him will flee. I will strike down only the king, and I will bring all the people back to you as a bride comes home to her husband." Ahithophel's advice was brilliant because David had not yet joined up with Joab, who was apparently on the other side of the Jordan, but had only a small bodyguard protecting himself and his family. Ahithophel's advice won initial approval, but it had one weakness: the fame for killing David, a fierce and crafty warrior, would go to Ahithophel instead of Absalom.

HUSHAI. Hushai assured Absalom that on previous occasions Ahithophel's advice had been good, but "this time," he said "the counsel that Ahithophel has given is not good." Although David and his men were backed into a corner, they were fierce, experienced warriors who would prepare for ambush and fight like a bear robbed of her cubs. Hushai suggested a better strategy for meeting such a foe. He told Absalom (paraphrase), "You yourself should gather and lead such an immense army against David that neither David nor his men will be able to escape alive." In giving this advice, Hushai appealed to Absalom's pride and raised questions about Ahithophel's motives without making any direct accusations. (Actually, Ahithophel's offer to lead the troops to kill David was probably motivated less by ambition and more by wanting to insure that Absalom defiled David's concubines.)

ADVISERS. Normally, it is good for kings to have many advisers. After hearing Ahithophel, Absalom also sought out Hushai in accordance with Prov. 24:6, which says, "By wise guidance you can wage your war, and in abundance of counselors there is victory." In this case, seeking additional advice backfired because "the LORD had ordained to defeat the good counsel of Ahithophel, so that the LORD might bring harm upon Absalom" (2 Sam. 17:14). Hushai was actually David's agent, and he cleverly appealed to Absalom's vanity to overturn Ahithophel's advice so that David might have time to escape and gather an army. When Absalom approved of Hushai's advice, his advisers proved to be "yes men" instead of astute advisers. Unlike David, Absalom had no prophets or priests among his advisers who were unafraid to confront his sin or expose his vanity.

Hushai sends a secret message to David
2 Sam. 17:15-23

A TREACHEROUS CITY

We don't know when Psalm 55 was written, but it describes quite well how David felt when he fled the Jerusalem with Shimei cursing him, pelting him with rocks, and throwing dust in the air.

> Give ear to my prayer, O God,
>   and hide not yourself from my plea for mercy!
> Attend to me, and answer me;
>   I am restless in my complaint and I moan,
> because of the noise of the enemy,
>   because of the oppression of the wicked.
> For they drop trouble upon me,
>   and in anger they bear a grudge against me.
> -- Psalm 55:1-3

David's primary concern was to find a place of rest and safety for himself and his family.

> My heart is in anguish within me;
>   the terrors of death have fallen upon me.
> Fear and trembling come upon me,
>   and horror overwhelms me.
> And I say, "Oh, that I had wings like a dove!
>   I would fly away and be at rest;
> yes, I would wander far away;
>   I would lodge in the wilderness; Selah
> I would hurry to find a shelter
>   from the raging wind and tempest."
> -- Psalm 55:4-8

JERUSALEM, JERUSALEM. The city David left behind was a treacherous place. Many within its walls were allied with Absalom and looked at others suspiciously. David's friends were in danger, so he prayed,

> Destroy, O Lord, divide their tongues;
>> for I see violence and strife in the city.
> Day and night they go around it
>> on its walls,
> and iniquity and trouble are within it;
>> ruin is in its midst;
> oppression and fraud
>> do not depart from its marketplace.
> -- Psalm 55:9-11

FRIENDS. Hushai, David's friend, faced great danger. He had infiltrated Absalom's council of advisers to learn Absalom's plans and disrupt them if possible. If his real mission were exposed, he would surely have been executed. Zadok and Abiathar, priests of God, also faced danger. They were longtime allies of David both in worship and in war. They were also ears and intermediaries between Hushai and David. Jonathan and Ahimaaz were messengers who would carry the intelligence gathered in the city to David. Their mission was so dangerous they could not risk being seen in the city. They hid by a spring outside the city walls. A servant girl relayed the information from the priests to the messengers near the spring. Her life was at risk. When the messengers were seen by a friend of Absalom, they fled and hid in a well on the far side of the Mount of Olives near Bahurim. The owners of the well covered it with grain spread out to dry in the sun. By hiding the messengers, they put their lives in danger.

FOES. David's primary foe was Absalom, his own son. David's most dangerous foe was Ahithophel, who had formerly been one of his closest advisers. In anguish, David cried out,

> For it is not an enemy who taunts me—
>> then I could bear it;
> it is not an adversary who deals insolently with me—
>> then I could hide from him.
> But it is you, a man, my equal,
>> my companion, my familiar friend.
> We used to take sweet counsel together;
>> within God's house we walked in the throng.

Let death steal over them;
    let them go down to Sheol alive;
    for evil is in their dwelling place and in their heart.
-- Psalm 55:12-15

God answered David's prayer. God confused the wicked (Psalm 55:9) and turned the counsel of Ahithophel into foolishness (2 Sam. 15:31). In a short time, death would claim Absalom by surprise. For Ahithophel, who had betrayed God's chosen king, death came even sooner. When he saw his advice had not been followed, he went home, put his affairs in order, and hung himself. Centuries later, another man who betrayed God's chosen king would also go out and hang himself.

Blessed are those who are faithful to God's chosen king. No risk is too great; they remain faithful in the midst of treachery.

David finds refuge in Mahanaim
2 Sam. 17:24-29

ACTIONS LOUDER THAN WORDS

When a friend is in trouble, don't annoy him by asking if
there is anything you can do. Think up something
appropriate and do it.
-- Edgar Watson Howe

A DESPERATE NEED. David had been a fugitive when he was young, a shepherd boy turned soldier. He was a fugitive again as a mature man, a king who had been settled in a palace ruling a vast territory. Israel's army, which he had formerly led to numerous victories, was camped in Gilead ready to attack him. Judah, his own tribe, had given their support to Absalom at Hebron. Jerusalem, his city, was divided and no longer safe. Many of his own family now opposed him: Amasa, David's nephew, was commander of Israel's mutinous army, and Absalom, his own son, had proclaimed himself king. David had fled leaving most of his household possessions behind. He and his family were hungry and tired.

APPROPRIATE ACTIONS. More than sympathetic words, David needed helpful actions, and God sent true friends who proved helpful (see Psalm 55:22). Mahanaim, a fortified city which had served as Ish-bosheth's capital after Saul's death (2 Sam. 2:8 ff.), gave David and his family refuge. Still, David's large family, which fled its home hurriedly, needed bedding, kitchen utensils, and a pantry full of food. Three friends anticipated these needs and generously supplied them. None of these friends were close relatives. Makir and Barzillai were from cities in Gilead and probably belonged to the tribe of Manasseh. Shobi was an Ammonite from the royal family of Nahash. They didn't merely offer their sympathy and say, "If there is anything you need, let us know." They demonstrated their sympathy by doing something appropriate.

> If a brother or sister is poorly clothed and lacking in daily
> food, [16] and one of you says to them, "Go in peace, be
> warmed and filled," without giving them the things
> needed for the body, what good is that?
> -- James 2:15-16

Joab defeats and kills Absalom
2 Sam. 18:1-18

DIVINE CONSPIRACY

> Many are the plans in the mind of a man,
> but it is the purpose of the LORD that will stand.
> -- Prov. 19:21

Absalom had big plans. He was going to trap David in Mahanaim like a caged bird, pull down the city's walls, and kill his father so that he would be the undisputed king of Israel. God had different plans. He had determined to bring disaster on Absalom (2 Sam. 17:14).

POWERLESS TO SAVE ABSALOM. Although King David was fighting to save himself and his family from Absalom, he did not want to destroy his son. He instructed his army commanders, "Deal gently for my sake with the young man Absalom." However, David's wishes were unable to save Absalom. The army of Israel had answered Absalom call to arms, but Israel's army could not save Absalom. One of David's soldiers who had heard David's instructions to the commanders refused to kill Absalom, but even that did not save him. God's purpose would prevail.

DEADLY PROVIDENCE. Absalom's army never attacked Mahanaim because David's army attacked his forces in the Forest of Ephraim where the forest happened to consume more of Absalom's army than the sword. Absalom fled, but he happened to meet some of David's men. He tried to escape from them on his mule, but as he rode through the trees, his head happened to get caught in the branches. The mule did not stop, and

Absalom was left hanging from the tree like one cursed of God (Deut. 21:23). Unarmed and defenseless, he died like a criminal rather than a soldier. What happened was not mere coincidence; it was determined by God.

ABSALOM'S MEMORIAL. David's soldiers took Absalom's body down from the tree, threw it into a pit, and covered it with stones. The heap of stones over Absalom's body was a more fitting memorial for a rebellious son (Deut. 21:18-21) than the pillar Absalom had erected for himself earlier in the King's Valley near Jerusalem.

David mourns for Absalom
2 Sam. 18:19-33

A KING'S GRIEF

> Would I had died instead of you, O Absalom, my son,
> my son!
> -- King David, 2 Sam. 18:33

The agonized sobbing of David as he climbed the stairs to the room over the gateway to the city of Mahanaim is one of the most memorable scenes in the life of David. It evokes both pity for the man who had been a great warrior and king, and perhaps even contempt for his weakness and failure. Yet, in the scene, there remains a hint of the divine love that would characterize his son, Jesus.

INCONSOLABLE. The messengers brought the good news that David's enemies had been defeated, but when David understood that Absalom was dead, David's body trembled uncontrollably, and he left sobbing, "O my son Absalom, my son, my son Absalom!" His inconsolable grief stands in stark contrast to his reactions to both the death of Jonathan and the death of Bathsheba's first son. In the first case, he composed a tribute to his friend and taught the song to Israel, and in the second case, he rose from his mourning, washed himself, worshiped the Lord, and ate. Why was David so inconsolable in this case?

ALIENATED. David grieved because he had alienated his son. David had not provided justice for Absalom's sister, Tamar, when Amnon raped her. After Absalom avenged the rape of his sister by murdering Amnon, he fled to Geshur where he lived in exile for 3 years (2 Sam. 13:38). David eventually recalled Absalom from exile, but he still refused to see

Absalom for two more years (2 Sam. 14:28). Absalom finally forced an audience with David (2 Sam. 14:33), and David kissed him, but the effort was too little and too late. Absalom's resentment continued to grow. David had not treated either him or his sister fairly. Absalom felt he was more capable of providing justice than David (2 Sam. 15:4). Alienation led to resentment and rebellion, and rebellion had led to death. Death cut off the possibility of reconciliation forever. David mourned for this reason.

UNRECONCILED. Reconciliation escaped David because he learned the depth of reconciling love too late. His love was too shallow to make him willing, even eager, to forgive in order to achieve reconciliation. Recalling Absalom from exile yet refusing to see him did not communicate that willingness. Furthermore, his love was too shallow to seek forgiveness by confessing his own offense. David had not confessed his own failure to punish Amnon for raping Tamar, and his failure remained a hindrance to reconciliation. But now, too late, he understood that he desired reconciliation so much that he would have been willing to die in Absalom's place. "Would I had died instead of you, O Absalom, my son, my son!"

Joab rebukes David
2 Sam. 19:1-8

THE KING SPOILS A VICTORY CELEBRATION

David was a highly emotional person who experienced both great despair, as when he was hiding from Saul in the Desert of Ziph (1 Sam. 23:16), and great elation, as when he brought the ark to Jerusalem (2 Sam. 6:14-16). Both emotions molded a great part of his lyric poetry and music in the Psalms. Often, he was able to express his emotions in a way that comforted, encouraged, or motivated Israel, but on this occasion, his inconsolable grief over the death of Absalom nearly cost him the kingdom.

CELEBRATIONS CANCELED. David's victorious army returned to Mahanaim only to find David weeping uncontrollably above the city gate. No parades or celebrations greeted them. Instead, David's grief shamed them so that they entered the city like defeated, cowardly soldiers afraid to show their faces. Their "enthusiasm was soon depleted" (Bergen, 1996, p. 425). Unless David changed his behavior quickly, those who stole into the city would steal out of the city and leave David and his family deserted and vulnerable.

SAVED LIVES FORGOTTEN. David's army had saved David's life, the lives of his sons and daughters, the lives of his wives, and the lives of his concubines, but instead of rejoicing with his army over the many lives they had saved, David mourned for a single life that had been lost. The army, neither congratulated nor feeling appreciated, would soon slip away unless David showed them his gratitude.

LOYAL LOVE SPURNED. David's army had served him loyally with the love they had covenanted with him when he became king, but David appeared more devoted to a rebel who had renounced not only covenant love but filial love as well. Joab put it more bluntly, "You love those who hate you and hate those who love you." Those he "hated" might soon oppose him unless David returned to them the covenant love they had shown him.

Joab was a pragmatic and blunt military officer who had no time for David's sentimentality. He reacted to situations immediately with necessary actions as he judged them. While David was pouring out his soul in grief, Joab saw that the kingdom was slipping away. Putting aside all protocol, he intruded on the king's private grief, rebuked him, and commanded him to go out and express his appreciation to his army. David regained his self-control and greeted his faithful soldiers.

Israel and Judah recall David
2 Sam. 19:9-15

PUTTING HUMPTY TOGETHER AGAIN

Although David's men had defeated Absalom, David did not march back to Jerusalem with his victorious army to reclaim the throne. Instead, he waited for popular support to arise because he wanted the people to bring him back. Like Solomon after him, he knew that "without people a prince is ruined" (Prov. 14:28).

ISRAEL. Support arose for David first in the northern tribes. Those who wanted to bring David back began making their case. "Who," they asked, "could be a better choice than David? He is the one who delivered us from our enemies, and Absalom is now dead" (paraphrase). David was encouraged by Israel's desire to restore him as their king and anxiously waited for news from Judah.

JUDAH. Surprisingly, David's own tribe did not ask him to return. They had been the first to give their support to Absalom, and may have feared reprisals. Accordingly, David asked Zadok and Abiathar to assure them of his favor. Through them, David reminded the men of Judah that he was from their tribe and offered to remove Joab from being commander of his army and to replace him with Amasa, who had been Absalom's commander. This move not only pleased the men of Judah but also punished Joab for disobeying his command regarding Absalom. The men of Judah asked David to return as their king and to bring his men with him.

MERCY. So why didn't David march back to Judah and punish those who joined Absalom's rebellion? David knew by experience that Humpty Dumpty cannot be put back together with a hammer. When he had sinned, God had shown him great mercy. Though he suffered the consequences of his sin, God had forgiven him, restored him to fellowship, and given him a beloved son. As one who had experienced God's mercy, he knew he should show mercy to others (see Matt. 18:33). He knew that mercy could put the nation together again but that cruelty never would:

> A man who is kind benefits himself,
>   but a cruel man hurts himself.
> -- Prov. 11:17

When Jesus, the son of David, came to this earth, people often asked him for mercy (Matt. 9:27; 15:22; etc.). His mercy reunites us with him. We love him because he first loved us.

Shimei meets David at the Jordan
2 Sam. 19:16-23

EATING HUMBLE PIE

When David fled Jerusalem, Shimei had cursed him and pelted him with stones. Shimei assumed that David had lost the throne and would never return. Now David was returning again as king. Shimei had two choices. One was to hide from the king, but that would have been nearly impossible because he lived so near Jerusalem. The second was to try to make amends.

SERVICE. When the men of Judah went to bring King David back across the Jordan, Shimei and a thousand other Benjamites went with them. When they got to the Jordan, Shimei and his men did not hesitate. They rushed across the Jordan to bring the king's household back across the river and do whatever else the king wished. Shimei tried to make amends by providing useful services to the king.

SUPPLICATION. While the men with Shimei were helping the king's household across the Jordan River, Shimei found the king and fell prostrate before him, acknowledged his guilt, and begged forgiveness. He made no excuses. He ate humble pie.

SUPPORT. Finally, Shimei noted that he had been the first of the "whole house of Joseph" (i.e. the northern tribes) to meet the king, to welcome him back, and to give him his support. Certainly, he hoped that his zeal in gathering support for David would help make amends.

Shimei had a good recipe for humble pie. Even though Abishai tried to dissuade the king, David promised on oath that Shimei would not die.

Mephibosheth meets David at the Jordan
2 Sam. 19:24-30

DIVIDING A CANDY BAR FAIRLY

When we were young, Mom would occasionally divide a candy bar between my brother and me. When she did, we often argued over which one got the biggest piece. I am sure this annoyed Mom because when we were old enough to cut the candy bar ourselves, one of us cut the candy bar, and the other got first choice. Something about that process eliminated the arguing. King David had to settle a conflict between two of his subjects: Mephibosheth and Ziba. He divided Saul's lands between them equally. We may never know exactly what dividing the lands accomplished, but this we do know,

> As the heavens for height, and the earth for depth,
>   so the heart of kings is unsearchable.
> -- Prov. 25:3

SUSPICION.   Like Shimei, Mephibosheth rushed out with the other Benjamites to meet the king at the Jordan River. Also like Shimei, he had reason to fear the king's return. As a sign of distress and sorrow, he had not taken care of his feet, trimmed his mustache, or washed his clothes since David fled the city. David immediately asked him, "Why didn't you go with me?" With the exception of his personal agents whom he had left in the city, all David's household had fled with him. Because Mephibosheth ate at David's table, he expected Mephibosheth to go with him. Accordingly, David was suspicious when Mephibosheth failed to do so.

EXPLANATION. Mephibosheth explained that he had desired to go with David, and had even asked Ziba to bring his saddled donkey for him to ride, but Ziba had misled him and never returned with his donkey. Not only that, but Ziba had gone to the king and slandered Mephibosheth, saying that he was hoping to become king in place of David.

DILEMMA.   David   remembered   Ziba's   accusations   against Mephibosheth,   and   he   remembered   that   he   had   given   all   of Mephibosheth's lands to Ziba. So, who was telling the truth? David seemed annoyed and refused to make further investigation. He abruptly directed that the lands be divided between Ziba and Mephibosheth. Was this a judgment or a test? If a judgment, it seems unfair. Was David afraid to alienate Ziba and the other Benjamites who had come to support him? If a test, like Solomon's command to divide the living son and to give a half to each of the women (1 Kings 3:16-28), it lacks a conclusion.

Whether judgment or test, Mephibosheth's response was important. When he said, "Let him (Ziba) take everything, now that my lord the king has arrived home safely," he made it clear that he had no personal ambitions. Like the woman who begged Solomon to spare the child, so Mephibosheth wished to preserve David's kingdom.   Saul's family supported David and would never entertain royal ambitions. It played no role in the developing rift between the house of Joseph and the tribe of Judah which would become apparent soon.

David parts from Barzillai
2 Sam. 19:31-40

HOSPITALITY AND GRATITUDE

The scene near Gilgal where the entire royal family was trying to cross the Jordan River was chaotic. Two groups were seeking bragging rights for being the first to welcome the king, others were trying to atone for previously insulting the king, and one was trying to save himself from slander. In the midst of this confusion is a tender story of loyalty and love.

HOSPITALITY. Barzillai had provided for David and his family while they were in Mahanaim. Providing room and board for a large, royal family would have required great resources, but Barzillai was both willing and capable for he was a wealthy man. Then despite his 80 years, he accompanied his guests from Mahanaim to the Jordan crossing near Gilgal. The distance Barzillai accompanied his departing guests, at least 20 miles, was a measure of his great respect for them.

TACT. At the Jordan River crossing, David said to Barzillai, "Cross over with me and stay with me in Jerusalem, and I will provide for you." Barzillai tactfully rejected the king's offer saying that his age prevented him from enjoying the pleasures of the court and would make him a burden to David. In addition, residence in Jerusalem would remove him from his home where he wished to die and be buried. Still, Barzillai suggested two ways he was willing to acknowledge David's gratitude. First, he would accompany David across the Jordan a short way. Then he would send Kimham, probably a son, to accept David's gratitude saying that David could do for him whatever he wished.

GRATITUDE. David was pleased to show his gratitude to Kimham, and promised to do for him whatever Barzillai wished while still insisting he would do for Barzillai himself whatever he desired. Then when Barzillai had crossed the river, David kissed Barzillai and blessed him. Barzillai returned to his home, and Kimham continued with the king to Jerusalem.

Part Nine: National Problems

976-973 B.C.; age 64-67; regnal years 34-37

Conflict arises between Judah and Israel
2 Sam. 19:41 - 20:2

WAR OF WORDS

The welcoming celebration for the king had been unplanned, and the northern tribes were underrepresented when it occurred. Words were spoken, accusations made, feelings hurt, and the northern tribes went home in disgust instead of escorting David back to Jerusalem.

ACCUSATION OF STEALING. Perhaps the northern tribes should have been embarrassed that more of them had not met the king, but instead of faulting themselves, the northern tribes directed attention on the tribe of Judah. "Why," they asked David, "did our brothers, the men of Judah, steal the king away and bring him and his household across the Jordan?" By using the word "steal," they hoped to remind David that they had been first to call him back as king, and they implied that Judah wanted to separate the king from the rest of Israel.

JUSTIFICATION. Of course, the men of Judah overheard. They responded that there was nothing unusual about their eagerness to welcome the king because they were more closely related to David, who was of the tribe of Judah. They asked (paraphrase), "Why are you angry? Have we used our relationship to the king for any selfish or unscrupulous purpose?"

ACCUSATION OF SHOWING CONTEMPT. The northern tribes responded that they had ten shares in the king and therefore deserved more from their relationship to him. Since Judah did not recognize their greater share, they accused Judah of treating the rest of Israel with contempt. Judah's contempt was confirmed, they suggested, by their refusal to credit the northern tribes with being the first to speak of recalling the king.

HARSH WORDS. The men of Judah responded with even harsher words. What had begun as unplanned but joyous welcome for the king became a harsh war of words. Rather than resolving the differences, Sheba, a troublemaker who lived in the hill country of Ephraim (2 Sam.

20:21), convinced the northern tribes to go home while the men of Judah escorted the king to Jerusalem.

> And the tongue is a fire, a world of unrighteousness. The tongue is set among our members, staining the whole body, setting on fire the entire course of life, and set on fire by hell.
> -- James 3:6

Joab murders Amasa
2 Sam. 20:3-13

JEALOUSY AND TREACHERY

David's commanders, Amasa and Joab, were opposites though both were David's nephews. Amasa was promoted to commander even though he lost the only battle he was known to lead. Joab was a successful commander credited with many victories including the capture of Jerusalem. The two men crossed paths while David was trying to prevent Sheba from organizing a rebellion.

AMASA. When the men of the northern tribes became frustrated with the men of Judah, Sheba had convinced them to return to their homes, but he had not yet organized a rebellion. David wished to prevent Sheba from organizing any resistance, so he said to Amasa, his newly appointed commander, "Call the men of Judah together to me within three days, and be here yourself." Amasa, however, was negligent. He failed both to gather the army in three days and to report to David. David could not afford further delay, so he sent Abishai to pursue Sheba after putting him at the head of Joab's men and his own personal bodyguard.

JOAB. Joab was a shrewd man always on guard and ever protective of his own interests. He was inclined to treachery from the beginning of his career to the end. Years earlier while pretending to greet Abner, he had stabbed him in the belly to avenge the death of his brother whom Abner had slain in battle (2 Sam. 3:27). Joab had been a co-conspirator with David in deserting Uriah, one of David's mighty men, in the heat of battle so that the enemy might kill him (2 Sam. 11:14-17). More recently, Joab had ignored David's plea to deal gently with Absalom, and slew him while he hung helplessly from a tree (2 Sam. 18:14). In response, David had demoted Joab and replaced him with Amasa, making them rivals.

THE ENCOUNTER. Amasa joined Abishai's forces at Gibeon where he met Joab, who harbored malice in his heart for the man who had replaced him at the head of the army. Unlike Joab, Amasa was not wary or vigilant. In fact, he might even be called gullible. He was not suspicious when Joab dropped a dagger and picked it up with his left hand. He was not wary when Joab took hold of his beard with his right hand to give him a friendly kiss. While kissing Amasa, Joab stabbed him in the belly and then left him to die while writhing in his own blood.

This act of treachery nearly stalled the pursuit of Sheba. All who saw Amasa wallowing in his own blood stopped. They could not help Amasa, but they could not abandon him either. Finally, a soldier drug Amasa off the road and covered him with a garment so the pursuit could continue. David, however, would not forget what Joab had done (1 Kings 2:5-6). From this time on, Joab was living on borrowed time.

> Whoever hates disguises himself with his lips
>   and harbors deceit in his heart;
> when he speaks graciously, believe him not,
>   for there are seven abominations in his heart;
> though his hatred be covered with deception,
>   his wickedness will be exposed in the assembly.
> -- Prov. 26:24-26

Sheba executed at Abel Beth-maacah
2 Sam. 20:14-22

WAR AND PEACE

> A time for war, and a time for peace.
> -- Ecc. 3:8

David's wise son Solomon observed that there is a time for everything, including war and peace. Sheba had declared himself no longer loyal to David and persuaded the northern tribes to return to their homes instead of accompanying David to Jerusalem. Was this a time for war, or a time for peace?

WAR. David clearly thought it was a time for military action lest Sheba gather support and begin another armed rebellion. Joab had regained control of David's army and was leading it in pursuit of Sheba. Sheba passed through Israel trying to gain support but apparently found none except among the Berites, who followed him. Pursued by Joab, Sheba and the Berites took refuge in Abel Beth Maacah in the far north. Joab put the city under siege, building a siege ramp and battering the walls. Given time, he undoubtedly would have succeeded in destroying much of the city and capturing Sheba.

PEACE. A wise woman of the city discerned that this was not a time for war, but a time for peace. She saw that although the men of the northern tribes had gone home when Sheba sounded the trumpet, they were not in a state of rebellion against the king. Few had followed Sheba. It was senseless to defy the king's army when the city had no argument against the king. The city was a "mother," a leading city in Israel where people sought counsel. Its leaders were wise, peace loving, faithful and loyal. Now was not the time to ruin its reputation with senseless defiance of the king's army which would lead to senseless destruction of a part of the Lord's inheritance. Accordingly, she called for Joab, and sought terms of peace. Learning what Joab wanted, the city leaders wisely executed the rebel Sheba, and Joab went back to the king in Jerusalem.

David's advisors
2 Sam. 20:23-26

CHANGES IN THE KING'S CABINET

David's officers toward the end of his reign were mostly the same as they were midway through it (2 Sam. 8:15-18). Joab was still commander of the army, and Benaiah was still commander of the Cherethites and Pelethites, David's personal bodyguard. The leading priests, Zadok and Abiathar, were still the same (but note the reversal of Ahimelech's and Abiathar's names in 2 Sam. 8:17), and Jehoshaphat was still recorder.

There are three differences in the list. The earlier secretary was Seraiah, and the later one was Sheva. Nothing is known of either. Two differences are more significant. The first difference is that David's sons were no longer priests, but they had been replaced by Ira the Jairite. Because Jair is in the region where David found refuge from Absalom's rebellion, Ira may have become acquainted with David at that time. These "priests" at the end of the lists of officials must be distinguished from the Aaronic priests listed earlier. They were probably "royal advisers" (NIV, see also TWOT, #959a) or "chief officials" as in the parallel passage in Chronicles (1 Chron. 18:17, ESV). This change in officials may be due to failure of David's sons as advisers. 1 Kings 4:5 (ESV) appears to equate this kind of "priest" with the position of "king's friend." Hushai had held the position of "king's friend" when David fled Jerusalem during Absalom's rebellion.

The second difference is that toward the end of his reign David had an additional officer in charge of forced labor. The last people David defeated were the Ammonites, and he set many of them "to labor with saws and iron picks and iron axes and made them toil at the brick kilns" (2 Sam. 12:31). Moses had spoken of putting foreign cities to forced labor (Deut. 20:10-11), and Joshua had actually done so before David (Josh. 9:27; 16:10; 17:13). Furthermore, in preparing for his son Solomon to build the temple, David "commanded to gather together the resident aliens who were in the land of Israel, and he set stonecutters to prepare dressed stones for building the house of God" (1 Chron. 22:2). Accordingly, when he gave his final instructions to Solomon, he could say, "You have an abundance of workmen: stonecutters, masons, carpenters, and all kinds of craftsmen without number, skilled in working gold, silver, bronze, and iron" (1 Chron. 22:15-16a). Adoram was apparently in charge of assembling and overseeing this labor force.

David takes a census
2 Sam. 24:1-10 [1 Chron. 21:1-8]
[[1 Chron. 27:23-24]]

WHAT HAPPENED?

Recently I passed an accident on the highway just as the first patrolman was arriving. Heavy black skid marks slanted from the right lane toward ditch where a vehicle was resting on its side. A half dozen people were milling around it. An 18-wheeler was on the shoulder just beyond the vehicle in the ditch. Soon traffic on the highway would slow as people would try to see. Each would ask themselves, "What happened?" Some would say this, and others that. Many answers might be given. Several might be right, and many would probably be wrong. When we look at the account of David numbering the people of Israel as recounted in 1 Chron. 21 and 2 Sam. 24, we get two explanations as to what happened. 2 Samuel says the Lord incited David against Israel, but 1 Chronicles says that Satan incited David to take a census of Israel. Are these explanations contradictory, or could both be true? What really happened?

FIRST. Satan rose up against Israel (1 Chron. 21:1). This is surely due to his malice against God, against God's people, and even against God's ruler. He tempted them to be dissatisfied with God's rule and to desire to be like the nations.

SECOND. The Lord's anger burned against Israel (2 Sam. 24:1). Israel had displeased the Lord by falling to Satan's temptation. They had rebelled against David, the Lord's anointed, who provided righteous rule, directed their devotion toward God, and gave them safety from their enemies. They had wanted a king like the nations, a king like Absalom.

THIRD. David sinned (2 Sam. 24:10; 1 Chron. 21:7). After the rebellions of Absalom and Sheba, David's faith may have wavered. God tested him. Would he rely on God, or would he be anxious about the strength of his army? Anxiety won over faith. Even though God had not commanded him to take a census as he had commanded Moses on two occasions (Num. 1:2; 26:2), David ordered that the people be numbered. In this, he also would have been thinking like the nations, relying on military strength instead of the Lord. David's command to number the people displeased God (1 Chron. 21:7).

FOURTH. Wrath came on Israel on account of the numbering (1 Chron. 27:24). Israel may have found satisfaction in David's numbering of the people capable of bearing arms. David had started acting like a "real" king in measuring the strength of his army. He had never done this before. The numbering was a way for them to "flex their muscles."

So who incited David to take the census? God tempts no one to sin, but he did test David, and Satan used the occasion to lure both Israel and David into sin. Numbering the people was a sin both for David and for Israel. However, even though Satan meant harm, God would purify Israel with his wrath and establish a place for his name to be glorified through David's confession and intercession.

> Let no one say when he is tempted, "I am being tempted
> by God," for God cannot be tempted with evil, and he
> himself tempts no one. 14 But each person is tempted
> when he is lured and enticed by his own desire.
> -- James 1:13-14

God sends a plague
2 Sam. 24:11-17 [1 Chron. 21:9-17]

A GOOD SHEPHERD

God took David from the pasture where he followed the sheep and said to him, "You shall be shepherd of my people Israel, and you shall be prince over Israel" (2 Sam. 5:2). Indeed, David did shepherd Israel. He protected citizens from marauders, showed compassion to those who were discouraged and in debt, gave hope and courage to soldiers in battle, showed sympathy to the weak and weary, and ruled the people with justice and equity. His treatment of Uriah was the one exception to his just and benevolent rule of Israel, but David repented and was disciplined of God. He was again a man who put the interests of the people above his own (cf. Phil. 2:4).

CHOICE. After David numbered the people, his conscience smote him, and he confessed his sin. Through Gad the prophet, God gave David the choice of three punishments: three years of famine, three months of fleeing before his enemies, or three days of plague. The choice was difficult for as the time diminished from three years to three days, the severity of the punishment increased. In all three, many of the people would die, so David cast himself, and all Israel, on the mercy of God asking only that they not fall into the hands of men. God sent a plague, and seventy-thousand men (soldiers?) died throughout the land.

APPEAL. When the plague was approaching Jerusalem, David was distraught for the people and fell face down before the approaching angel. He prayed to God, "Was it not I who gave command to number the people? It is I who have sinned and done great evil. But these sheep, what have they done? Please let your hand, O LORD my God, be against me and against my father's house. But do not let the plague be on your people" (1 Chron. 21:17). It is especially noteworthy that David shouldered full responsibility for the census even though the people had also done something that angered God!

David offered himself and his family to fall under God's hand in order that the people of Jerusalem might be spared. In this, he demonstrated that he still had the heart of a shepherd who cared for his sheep. He foreshadowed the coming Messiah, who had committed no sin yet gave his life for those who had. He said,

I am the good shepherd. The good shepherd lays down
his life for the sheep. [12] He who is a hired hand and not a
shepherd, who does not own the sheep, sees the wolf
coming and leaves the sheep and flees, and the wolf
snatches them and scatters them. [13] He flees because he is
a hired hand and cares nothing for the sheep.
-- John 10:11-13

David builds an altar
2 Sam. 24:18-25 [1 Chron. 21:18-27]

FRIENDLY FIRE

David was so greatly troubled by the plague ravaging Israel that he offered
himself that the plague might be stopped. If David had been the only one
to sin, his death might have satisfied justice, but David was not the only
one who had sinned. God had been angry with Israel as well (2 Sam.
24:1), so they also had sinned. That being the case, either Israel had to die
or an appropriate substitute found. David, of course, was a sinner who
was himself in need of a sacrifice. He could not be a sacrifice for Israel.
God, however, had a plan whereby both David and Israel could be saved
by a sinless and perfect sacrifice. That plan progressed on the hill where
Araunah was threshing wheat.

AN APPOINTED PLACE. At that time, the altar of burnt offering was
at Gibeon a short distance north of Jerusalem, but David was afraid to go
there because of the angel spreading the plague (1 Chron. 21:29-30). God
had chosen another place, Araunah's threshing floor, as the permanent
site for the altar, and his angel had halted at that place. Gad instructed
David to build an altar there and offer sacrifices. This was the place
where God had provided a sacrifice for Abraham when he came to
sacrifice Isaac (Gen. 22:2). This would become the site of the temple and
the altar of burnt offering (2 Chron. 3:1).

AN APPROPRIATE PRICE. When David approached Araunah to buy
his threshing floor, Araunah offered to give the threshing floor and
animals to David. Such offers were part of the negotiation process (see
Gen. 23:11), so it is not surprising that David insisted on paying even
though he was king. Still, his reason for insisting is significant. He said,
"I will not offer burnt offerings to the LORD my God that cost me
nothing." Sin is costly, and David did not wish to make a sacrifice that
denied that cost.

ACCEPTABLE PROPITIATION. David offered blood sacrifices on the altar that he built, and the Lord showed his acceptance of the sacrifice by sending "friendly fire" from heaven to consume it as he had at Mount Sinai (Lev. 9:23-24) and as he would when Solomon's temple was dedicated (2 Chron. 7:1). God accepted David's sacrifice, not because the blood of bulls and goats could atone for sin (they could not, Heb. 10:4), but because he himself had already planned to provide the perfect sacrifice for sin, his only begotten Son, on this very mountain.

David dedicates land for the house of the Lord
1 Chron. 21:28 - 22:1

THE TEMPLE SITE

David had previously brought the ark to Jerusalem with great rejoicing, set it in a tent he had prepared for it, and offered sacrifices to the Lord (2 Sam. 6:12-19). God showed them favor in bringing the ark to Jerusalem because they carried it properly, but God showed no special favor for the location of the tent at the time sacrifices were made there. When David offered sacrifice on the site overlooking the City of David and called upon the Lord, God showed his favorable response to the prayer and sacrifice by sending fire from heaven to consume the sacrifice. God had previously shown his favor when he sent fire from heaven to consume the sacrifices at the end of the week of consecrating the priests and tabernacle (Lev. 9:24). David understood the sign as an indication not only of God's favorable response to his prayer but also of his acceptance of the place as the site for sacrifice before the temple he was planning for his son to build. This was the place God had chosen for his name to dwell (Deut. 12:10-11).

Part Ten: Transfer of Power

972-970 B.C.; age 68-70; regnal years 38-40

David's health declines
1 Kings 1:1-4

GETTING OLD

David was probably now approaching his 68th or 69th year having reigned 38 or 39 years. He would live but a short time longer, but he evidently had not formally announced his intention to make Solomon the next king, perhaps because he did not wish to offend his older sons (see 1 Kings 1:6) or he feared that Solomon was still too young at about age 20 (1 Chron. 22:5; 29:1). Nevertheless, he needed to do something because he was obviously growing older.

PHYSICAL DECLINE. David was not able to keep warm, so a beautiful girl from Shunem by the name of Abishag was chosen to keep him warm. She attended David in his private quarters not only during the night, but also during the day for it is there that Bathsheba and Nathan went to see David when Adonijah proclaimed himself king (1 Kings 1:15). David apparently was not able to go with those who anointed Solomon the first time (1 Kings 1:33 ff.), and when Solomon actually took the throne, David worshiped on his bed (1 Kings 1:47). Even in 1 Chronicles, which details a national assembly David called to anoint Solomon a second time, David rose to his feet only once (1 Chron. 28:2), and only once addressed the assembled leaders of Israel (1 Chron. 29:10).

NO MENTAL DECLINE. David still acted promptly and decisively when he needed to, and the manner in which he later transferred power to Solomon and addressed the gathered officials showed that he was still able to think and speak in an organized fashion.

> The years of our life are seventy,
>   or even by reason of strength eighty;
> yet their span is but toil and trouble;
>   they are soon gone, and we fly away.
> -- Psalm 90:10

Adonijah proclaims himself king
1 Kings 1:5-10

PLOTTING AGAINST THE LORD

Israel still had a hankering for a king like the nations, one who would conquer the nations and provide them with pomp and pageantry. David's sons Absalom and Adonijah wanted to be such a king.

AMBITION. Like Absalom, Adonijah was handsome and ambitious. Being the oldest living son, he promoted himself by sending chariots, horses, and fifty men to run ahead of him as Samuel warned kings would do (1 Sam. 8:11). Then he secured the support of David's army commander, Joab, and one of the priests, Abiathar, who had been a companion of David from the time Saul killed the priests in Nob (1 Sam. 22:20). Finally, he invited many of the royal family and leading men to a sacrifice at En Rogel, a well not far southeast of Jerusalem, where he proclaimed himself king.

DEFIANCE. Adonijah knew that his father planned to make Solomon king after him, but he defied his father's wishes. He did not invite Solomon or any of David's inner circle including Zadok the priest, Benaiah the commander of David's personal bodyguard, and Nathan the prophet. No doubt Adonijah did not want them to know what he planned before it was done. Once he had been proclaimed king, he apparently felt quite sure that the doting and aging king neither would nor could remove him from the throne.

What Adonijah did not realize is that he wasn't plotting against his father but against the Lord. Because God had chosen Solomon to be the next king, no plan would successfully displace him.

> No wisdom, no understanding, no counsel
>   can avail against the LORD.
> -- Prov. 21:30

Bathsheba and Nathan appeal to David
1 Kings 1:11-27

A PROMISE AND A PROBLEM

Most of us don't like problems that come to us when we are exhausted. David was weak and weary from advanced age, but a problem was developing again within his own household about who would follow him as king. He was unaware of the problem, so Nathan the prophet and Bathsheba found it necessary to inform him.

PROMISE. Through Nathan, God had promised David a son whom the Lord would love and establish on David' throne (2 Sam. 7:14-16). Later, Nathan identified Solomon as that son and gave him the name Jedidiah, which meant "beloved of the Lord" (2 Sam. 12:24-25). David then had promised Bathsheba that her son Solomon would be the next king (vv. 13, 17). This promise was also known within the family and by Adonijah, who ominously failed to invite Solomon to the party he was throwing near En Rogel Spring just outside the city walls.

EXPECTATION. Although David had expressed his intention about the throne within his family, he had never made a public announcement about which son would follow him as king. Because David's health was failing, the nation was anticipating such an announcement at any moment (v. 20; Accordingly, the public assembly in 1 Chron. 29:22 could not have already happened.)

SHOCK AND DANGER. With David's health failing and the nation in expectation, Adonijah decided to preempt the king and proclaim himself as David's successor (vv. 13, 18, 25). With the support of a significant portion of the government, namely Joab the army commander and Abiathar the priest, Adonijah would surely treat Solomon and Bathsheba as criminals because he would see them as endangering his rule and authority (v. 21).

Though weak and weary, David needed to act decisively. He would because he was still a leader at heart.

> Be willing to make decisions. That's the most important
> quality in a good leader.
> -- Gen. George S. Patton

David has Solomon proclaimed king the first time
1 Kings 1:28-40

DECISIVE ACTION

When David learned that Adonijah had proclaimed himself king, he acted promptly and decisively. After reaffirming his promise to Bathsheba, he called in three trusted men to execute his plan.

THE KING'S MULE. David commanded that Solomon be placed on his own mule and ride through the city accompanied by his own servants. Passage through the city would attract the attention of the expectant citizens, and riding on the king's mule would assure them that Solomon had David's blessing.

GIHON SPRING. Solomon's procession ended at Gihon Spring. Because Gihon Spring was nearer the city than En Rogel where Adonijah was celebrating, the news of Solomon's anointing would gain the attention of Jerusalem more quickly than Adonijah's earlier but more distant celebration.

PUBLIC ANOINTING. Zadok the priest anointed Solomon with the oil from the sacred tent showing that Solomon was God's choice rather than man's choice. Nathan the prophet and Benaiah, who was of the priestly family as well as a commander (1 Chron. 27:5), were present to confirm God's choice. The public responded with shouts of "Long live King Solomon" and music and rejoicing that shook the ground.

DAVID'S THRONE. After the anointing, the procession returned through the city gathering larger crowds as it went, and Solomon took his seat on the throne of his father David. Although Adonijah made the first move to claim the throne, Solomon was the first to sit on the throne. In this case, possession was more than nine-tenths of the law because God had chosen Solomon.

Solomon's initial humility and the peace that would predominate during his reign were symbolized by the mule he rode that day. God rejected the pride and war symbolized by Adonijah's chariots and horses.

Adonijah obtains clemency
1 Kings 1:41-53

STRIPPED OF THE CROWN

> An athlete is not crowned unless he competes according
> to the rules.
> -- 2 Tim. 2:5

Between 1999 and 2005, Lance Armstrong won the Tour de France seven times, but in 2012, he was stripped of his titles because he had not competed according to the rules. Similarly, Adonijah had proclaimed himself king, but he did so in defiance of God and King David. He acted secretly without telling Nathan the prophet, Zadok the priest, David the king, or Solomon, whom God had chosen. In essence, he crowned himself. Then while Adonijah dallied at the party he had thrown at En Rogel Spring, he was stripped of all royal glory and honor when David ordered Zadok and Nathan to anoint Solomon. The city rejoiced when Solomon was anointed.

ANXIOUS. Adonijah and his guests were just finishing their feast when they heard the trumpets in the city and the noise of the crowds. Joab, always on guard, immediately asked, "What does this uproar in the city mean?" Adonijah would soon share his anxiety.

ABANDONED. Just at that moment, Jonathan, Abiathar's son, arrived with news from the city. Adonijah was hoping for good news, but Jonathan announced that Solomon had already ascended the throne and that the whole city was rejoicing with him. Adonijah's supporters at the feast, insignificant compared to the population of the city, fled the feast in fear for their lives. Adonijah was abandoned.

ALARMED. In fear of his life, Adonijah fled to the altar (perhaps the altar in Gibeon, but more likely one that had been built in Jerusalem (see 2 Sam. 6:17 and 24:25) where he sought refuge and pardon. Solomon sent for Adonijah when he learned where he was, but Adonijah refused to come until he had been promised safety. Only then did Adonijah leave the altar and go to the throne, but the throne was not his.

Adonijah wanted to be a king like the nations. Adonijah wanted chariots and horsemen to run ahead of him. Adonijah wanted glory and power. He was motivated by selfish ambition, and "where jealousy and selfish ambition exist, there will be disorder and every vile practice" (James 3:16). He crowned himself, but Solomon wore the crown.

David makes plans for building the temple
1 Chron. 22:2-5

BIG PLANS FOR A YOUNG MAN

> For children are not obligated to save up for their
> parents, but parents for their children.
> -- 2 Cor. 12:14

Most of the extensive plans for the temple and the organization of the kingdom recorded in 1 Chronicles had undoubtedly been done in preceding years. He had previously appointed Adoram to assemble and organize the forced labor of resident aliens (2 Sam. 20:24). He had dedicated materials for constructing the temple even while defeating the surrounding nations midway through his reign (2 Sam. 8:11-12). Even before becoming king, he had collaborated with Samuel in the organization of the Levites (1 Chron. 9:22).

David may have been slow to designate Solomon as co-regent because Solomon was young and inexperienced. Solomon could not have been born much earlier than halfway through David's 40-year reign (he was born after the conquest of Ammon). On the other hand, he did have a son before he became king (cf. 1 Kings 11:42 and 1 Kings 14:21), so he was probably about 20 years old. At that age, he was just attaining the age when he could take charge of building a temple for the glory of God. David gave him everything he needed to accomplish the task.

David reveals his plans to Solomon
1 Chron. 22:6-19

SUCCESS PLANNED FOR THE SUCCESSOR

> What you have heard from me in the presence of many
> witnesses entrust to faithful men who will be able to
> teach others also.
> -- 2 Tim. 2:2

One responsibility of leadership is to prepare the way for a successor. Although it appears David was slow to designate Solomon as his successor, he did prepare the way for him.

PURPOSE. David had wanted to build a house for the Lord, but God had forbidden him because he was a man of blood and war. Still, God promised that his son Solomon would be a man of peace and that he would build a house for God. When Solomon had been appointed king, David called him in and charged him to build a house for the Lord. David prepared the way for his successor by giving him a clear objective.

PRAYER. David prayed that the Lord would be with Solomon and give him discretion and understanding, and that Solomon would keep the law of the Lord given by Moses. David prayed for his successor.

ENCOURAGEMENT. David encouraged Solomon not to be dismayed by the large task assigned to him but to be strong and courageous because he had provided plans, materials, and workmen. David encouraged his successor.

ASSISTANCE. Finally, David ordered the leaders of Israel to help Solomon, to seek the Lord, and to build the sanctuary of the Lord. David prepared for Solomon to succeed by giving him dedicated leaders.

David organizes temple service under Solomon
1 Chron. 23:1 - 26:32

AN ENDURING LEGACY

During David's lifetime, David reorganized the Levites including the priests. This reorganization would be fully implemented under Solomon when the new temple was built, and it would be retained after the return from Babylonian captivity and endure to the time of Christ. When David counted the Levites, there were 38,000 over the age of 30. He divided them into four groups. The first supervised the work of the temple, the second acted as officials and judges, the third were gatekeepers at the temple, and the fourth praised the Lord in music at the temple. David called the leaders of the priests and Levites to Jerusalem to introduce them to Solomon, the new king who would build the temple where they would soon serve.

TEMPLE WORKERS (1 Chron. 23:6 – 24:31). David retained the three divisions of Levites, but they were assigned different duties because a temple placed permanently in Jerusalem made their responsibilities in carrying the tabernacle unnecessary (1 Chron. 23:26). Instead, they were put in charge of the courtyards and side courts, of purifying the sacred utensils, of making the bread, of overseeing all measurements, and of praising God (1 Chron. 23:28-31). The priests were divided into 24 courses, 16 descended from Aaron's son Eleazar and 8 from his son Ithamar.

SINGERS (1 Chron. 25:1-31). The singers appointed by David prophesied, gave thanks, and praised God with the accompaniment of harps, lyres, and cymbals (25:1-3). The singers were sons of three men: Asaph, Jeduthun, and Heman, a grandson of Samuel (1 Chron. 6:33). They were divided into 24 groups which corresponded to the 24 courses of priests. They had served at the tabernacle and in Jerusalem since the day David brought the ark to Jerusalem (1 Chron. 6:31-32; 16:39-42). David's instructions for their service in the temple came from the Lord (1 Chron. 28:19; 2 Chron. 29:25).

GATEKEEPERS (1 Chron. 26:1-28). The first gatekeepers were assigned their positions at the Tent by David and Samuel (1 Chron. 9:22-23) and at the ark when it was brought to Jerusalem (1 Chron. 15:23-24). Their duties would be greatly expanded when the temple was built. Treasurers were a special section of the gatekeepers.

OFFICIALS AND JUDGES (1 Chron. 26:29-32). The Levites who served as officials and judges were divided into two groups: one group consisting of 1,700 men served west of the Jordan, and a second group consisting of 2,700 men served east of the Jordan. They all served in matters pertaining to God and in the affairs of the king.

The long lists of names makes it is easy to lose sight of David's accomplishments with regard to the worship of God. What he did was make it easier for Israel to remember their God and transfer that knowledge to coming generations. This is exactly what God wanted.

> He decreed statutes for Jacob
> and established the law in Israel,
> which he commanded our forefathers
> to teach their children,
> so the next generation would know them,

even the children yet to be born,
and they in turn would tell their children.
Then they would put their trust in God
and would not forget his deeds
but would keep his commands.
-- Psalm 78:5-7

David transfers the army, government, and royal property to Solomon
1 Chron. 27:1-34

POWER FORWARD

When the leaders of Israel assembled in Jerusalem, David gave Solomon the reins of power which would enable him to rule Israel. David was able to give Solomon a kingdom and the glory that attended that kingdom because God had blessed him.

In a multitude of people is the glory of a king,
but without people a prince is ruined.
-- Prov. 14:28

OFFICIALS OVER THE ARMY. The army he transferred to Solomon was divided into twelve divisions. Each division, which consisted of 24,000 soldiers, was on duty one month during the year.

OFFICIALS OVER THE TRIBES. The thirteen officials over of the tribes of Israel were put under Solomon's authority. Two tribes, Gad and Asher, were omitted for unknown reasons bringing the number to ten. To these ten, three were added: officers over Levi, Aaron, and the half tribe of Manasseh in Gilead.

OFFICIALS OVER THE ROYAL PROPERTY. Officers over the David's property were put under Solomon's command. His lands included vineyards, fields of olive and sycamore-fig trees, and pastures in the plains of Sharon and the valleys. His herds included camels, donkeys, sheep, and goats. He also had storehouses in Jerusalem and outlying districts. There were also officers over the field workers and over David's sons. David's remaining counselors were also turned over to Solomon.

David commits the plans for the temple to Israel and Solomon
1 Chron. 28:1-21

NATIONAL ASSEMBLY

After Solomon had been anointed king and set on the throne, David called the leaders of the government and the leaders of the Levites to Jerusalem to meet with their new king and put them under his command. Undoubtedly Solomon met with many of these leaders privately, but David also planned a national assembly while the leaders were in Jerusalem. Although David had been weak and confined to his own room in the palace, David rose to his feet on this occasion to address the whole assembly.

GOD SELECTED (28:1-7). First, he explained that he had wanted to build a temple for the Lord, but the Lord had not chosen him for the task. The kingdom was the "kingdom of the LORD" (v. 5), and God would exercise his sovereignty over his kingdom. He had chosen Judah to be a leader in Israel, he had chosen David to be king over all Israel, and he had chosen Solomon to succeed David and build the temple in Jerusalem.

DAVID DIRECTED (28:8-10). David then charged Solomon to follow the Lord's commands carefully, to acknowledge God and serve him wholeheartedly, and to be strong and complete the building of the temple. He promised that if he would do these things, he would possess the land and pass it on as an inheritance to his descendants forever.

DAVID DELIVERED THE PLANS HE HAD RECEIVED (28:11-19). Then David gave to Solomon the plans for the temple which the Spirit had put within him (v. 12 – see KJV and NIV), and which David had put "in writing from the hand of the LORD" (v. 19).

DAVID ENCOURAGED (28:20-21). David encouraged his son with these words, "Be strong and courageous and do it. Do not be afraid and do not be dismayed, for the LORD God, even my God, is with you. He will not leave you or forsake you, until all the work for the service of the house of the LORD is finished" (v. 20).

David collects and dedicates gifts for the temple
1 Chron. 29:1-20

LIBERAL LEADERS

> God loves a cheerful giver.
> -- 2 Cor. 9:7

DAVID GAVE LIBERALLY. David understood that the plans for the temple called for abundant materials because the structure was to reflect the glory not of man but of God, so he gave freely from his own treasures so that Solomon might have the resources to build the temple.

LEADERS GAVE WILLINGLY. David then challenged the leaders. He asked, "Who then will offer willingly, consecrating himself today to the LORD?" The leaders of the people responded favorably and also gave freely for the project, and the people rejoiced greatly at the willing response of their leaders.

THE LORD RECEIVED THE PRAISE. David concluded his address to the national assembly with a song of praise to a majestic and powerful God before whom he and all Israel stood in awe because of their own insignificance.

The public assembly not only solidified Solomon's position as king over all Israel, but it also motivated all Israel to help in building a temple for God.

David has Solomon proclaimed king a second time
1 Chron. 29:21-25

GOD'S CHOICE ACKNOWLEDGED

GOD'S CHOICE. Like Saul and David before him, Solomon was anointed as king both privately and publicly. Solomon was anointed hastily the first time because his brother Adonijah had proclaimed himself king. Zadok and Nathan anointed him as God's chosen and seated him on the throne before Adonijah could claim it (1 Kings 1:38-40). Similarly, Samuel anointed Saul the first time as a sign that God had chosen Saul (1 Sam. 10:1). Likewise, Samuel anointed David privately the first time to declare him as God's choice to replace Saul (1 Sam. 16:12-13).

CHOICE ACKNOWLEDGED. Solomon was anointed a second time before all the leaders of Israel. All Israel (officers, soldiers, and the king's sons) acknowledged Solomon as their king at the second anointing. Similarly, David was anointed again publicly both when Judah acknowledged him (2 Sam. 2:4) and when all Israel acknowledged him as God's chosen king (2 Sam. 5:3). (Saul was also later acknowledged as king, but a second anointing is not mentioned; see 1 Sam. 10:24; 11:14-15.)

JESUS, THE ANOINTED ONE. The Scriptures seldom mention whether later kings were anointed. It seems likely that most in Judah were anointed, but still it is seldom mentioned. However, the Psalms and prophets often speak of an ideal, anointed (messianic) king, and it is this king that was the hope of Israel. Jesus fulfilled the promised hope. He is spoken of as the Christ/Messiah/Anointed One. Jesus said that the words of Isaiah were fulfilled in him:

> The Spirit of the Lord is upon me,
>   because he has anointed me
>   to proclaim good news to the poor.
> -- Luke 4:18

Similarly, Peter declared that "God anointed Jesus of Nazareth with the Holy Spirit and with power" (Acts 10:38). Today, Jesus is God's chosen king. God has anointed him, and we should acknowledge him and submit to him in all things.

David advises Solomon privately
1 Kings 2:1-9

FATHER AND SON

When David was about to die, he had a personal talk with his son Solomon. The future of Israel was now in the hands of his son, and David had a few parting words.

KEEP GOD'S COMMANDS. David began by instructing his son Solomon to observe all that the Lord required of him. If David had not previously taught the Lord's laws and requirements, this last instruction would have been meaningless. Although David had failed to discipline Adonijah (1 Kings 1:6) and perhaps other sons, he began instructing

Solomon at a young age because he knew Solomon would be king after him. Later, Solomon wrote,

> When I was a son with my father,
>   tender, the only one in the sight of my mother,
> he taught me and said to me,
> "Let your heart hold fast my words;
>   keep my commandments, and live.
> Get wisdom; get insight;
>   do not forget, and do not turn away from the words
>   of my mouth."
> -- Prov. 4:3-5

At the beginning of Solomon's reign, he sought the Lord and completed the task of building the temple, which God had given him through David.

RULE JUSTLY. Next, David asked Solomon to finish some business that he had left unfinished. David felt keenly about these matters because they were matters of justice. First, he warned Solomon of Joab's insubordination and violence in avenging "in time of peace" blood that had been "shed in war." Such an insubordinate, violent man would be a threat to Solomon's throne, so David told Solomon to deal with him according to his wisdom. Second, David felt he had not yet shown sufficient kindness to the sons of Barzillai for the loyalty Barzillai had shown him during Absalom's rebellion. Finally, David warned Solomon that Shimei, who had cursed David when he fled Jerusalem, was still a dangerous man though David had not punished him for insulting the Lord's anointed. Again, he instructed David to deal with Shimei wisely.

After David died, Solomon did not immediately have Joab and Shimei executed, but he waited until they displayed disloyalty or disobedience to the king. Then the kingdom was firmly established in Solomon's hands.

David dies
1 Kings 2:10-12 [1 Chron. 29:26-30]

FROM TRAGEDY TO REDEMPTION

At first, David's story might seem to be a tragedy. He was a man of great talent, courage, and faith, but his adultery with Bathsheba led to shame and heartache. Nevertheless, the shame and heartache were not the end of his story. God saw something in David that was worth salvaging. God saw that he could still work in David's life to bring praise, honor, and glory to himself, so he forgave David's sin. Although David was not permitted to build God's temple, God used his psalms of repentance and gratitude for forgiveness to turn Israel to God. Furthermore, God gave his plans for the temple to David knowing he would motivate the priests, Levites, and all Israel to dedicate their wealth and energies to building a place where they could unite in giving praise to God. The story of David's life is not a tragedy; instead, the story of his life is the story of redemption. Because God redeemed and rehabilitated him, the prophet could summarize his life with these words:

> Then he died at a good age, full of days, riches, and
> honor.
> -- 1 Chron. 29:28

Similarly, our lives do not need to end as a tragedy. Whatever evil we have done, whatever terrible consequences have followed, and whatever heartache we bear, God sees something worth salvaging. He can still work in us to accomplish great things which will cause those who see us to glorify God for the redemption he has worked in our lives.

> Blessed is the one whose transgression is forgiven,
>   whose sin is covered.
> -- Psalm 32:1

The last words of David
2 Sam. 23:1-7

AN ORACLE OF SALVATION

David's reign and life became the standard by which all later kings were measured. Despite his failures, he set a high standard which was approached by only two kings, Hezekiah and Josiah. None surpassed him until the coming of the promised son, Jesus the Messiah. David, however, could not have known any of that. God did give him opportunity to contemplate his life before dying, and what he saw was a life filled with many successes and a major failure that cast a shadow over those successes. David undoubtedly felt unworthy, but was he in despair? God did not leave David in doubt before he died. God spoke through David one last time. In this oracle, David found hope both for himself and for the coming Light which would bless the whole world.

THE MAN. David had been insignificant. He was the youngest son of Jesse, a herdsman or farmer from one of the smallest villages in Judah. David was a youth of little importance even within his family until the Most High exalted him above his brothers and the God of Jacob anointed him to lead his people Israel. Any worthy thing David had done could be attributed to the choice and blessing of God. In gratitude, David sang praises to God and taught Israel to praise him, too.

HIS MESSAGE FROM GOD. David received a special message from God which said that when a man rules in righteousness and the fear of God, he will be like the morning light that makes the earth fruitful after a rain. This became the principle by which David lived and reigned. Although he was not perfect, he had ruled in righteousness and the fear of God, and Israel had been blessed with rest from the enemies who surrounded her. Perhaps in the future when the True Light had come into the world, even greater blessings would be enjoyed by the people of God.

HIS HOPE IN GOD'S COVENANT. David knew he had made terrible mistakes, but he found hope in two things. First, he found hope in the everlasting covenant that God had made with him. God had promised him a son to sit on the throne and build a house for God, and David had lived to see his son sit on the throne. When he saw it, he said, "Blessed be the LORD, the God of Israel, who has granted someone to sit on my throne this day, my own eyes seeing it" (1 Kings 1:48). Seeing this, he asked rhetorically (2 Sam. 23:5 NIV), "Will he (God) not bring to fruition my salvation and grant me my every desire?"

HIS ESCAPE FROM GOD'S WRATH. Second, David found hope when he observed that though evil men are cast aside like thorns and burned, he had survived to old age. Further, he had not merely survived, but he had been blessed. He could find comfort and rejoice, not in his own goodness or greatness, but in the grace of God.

POST SCRIPT

Three names occur in Scripture in much greater frequency than any others. Those three names are Jesus (or Christ and any combination of the two names), David, and Moses. Their frequency in the English Standard Version are as follows:

- Jesus – 1251 times
- David – 1141 times
- Moses – 852 times

DAVID AND MOSES. David is the most frequently mentioned person in the Old Testament. His name is mentioned 300 times more often than Moses in the Old Testament (1082 vs. 772). Interestingly, Moses and David are alike in several ways.

- Neither was a firstborn son.
- Both were called by God while tending sheep.
- Both lived as a youth in the palace of a king.
- Both fled the presence of the king.
- Both lived in exile.
- Both returned from exile to deliver Israel from her enemies.
- Both organized the priests and Levites as God directed.
- Both received from God a pattern for a place of worship (Ex. 25:8-9; 1 Chron. 28:11-12, 19).
- Both led the people in giving liberally for building the place of worship (Ex. 35:21; 1 Chron. 29:6-9).
- Both left an unfulfilled dream to a successor (entering the Promised Land and building a house for God).
- Both charged the successor to be courageous and faithful (Deut. 31:7-8; 1 Chron. 22:13).
- Both admonished Israel to obey God's law (Deut. 30:16; 1 Chron. 28:8).

DAVID AND JESUS. Although Jesus was the promised prophet like unto Moses (Deut.), he is more often remembered as the Son of David. Both were from the tribe of Judah, both were anointed by God and filled with his Spirit, both had compassion on the weak and discouraged, and both were kings. However, as David himself acknowledged, his son would be greater than he was.

> The LORD says to my Lord
> "Sit at my right hand,
> until I make your enemies your footstool."
> -- Psalm 110.1

Jesus the Son of David is also the Son of God (Mark 1:1). He reigns over all as King of kings, and Lord of lords (Rev. 19:16).

Notes on Chronology

Note on Part One Chronology

Youngblood (1992, p. 555) places the dates for David's reign from 1010 to 970 B.C. based on Thiele's establishment of 931/30 B.C. as the date for the division of the monarchy after the death of Solomon. Because David began reigning in 1010 B.C. and was 30 years old when he became king (2 Sam. 5:4), he would have been born in 1040 B.C.

Men were not to be called into military service until their twentieth year (Num. 1:3), and David was not yet serving in the army when he killed Goliath. Therefore, he was probably less than 20 years old, perhaps about 17, when he was anointed by Samuel. After turning twenty and becoming a commander in Saul's army, David probably served Saul through at least three raiding seasons (1 Sam. 18:12-16; 18:27-30; 19:8), so David's flight from Saul probably occurred when he was about 24 years old.

Most Bible scholars admit that David's story is not told entirely in chronological order. Even conservative scholars such as Bergen (1996, p. 441) and J.E. Smith (2000, p. 499) understand 2 Sam. 21-24 to be detached chronologically from the rest of David's story. Despite the admission that the story is not entirely chronological, many of those same scholars insist that the first several chapters are chronological. However, when 16:1-18:5 are taken to be entirely chronological, two problems arise. The first appears in 1 Sam. 16 where David is introduced as a man of valor and war (16:18) who quickly becomes one of Saul's armor-bearers (16:21) even though later David is said to be a mere youth (17:33) unfamiliar with military weapons and armor (17:38-39) who relies on a shepherd's sling and staff (17:40). The second problem occurs in 1 Sam. 17 when Saul asks whose son the young boy is who is going out to face Goliath (17:55, 58). All this happens after Saul had called David to serve as court musician, had come to love him, and had made him one of his personal armor-bearers (16:21). It is difficult to understand how Saul could not have known who David was when he had listened to his music, come to love him, sent a message to his father to allow David to stay in his court, and even made him one of his armor-bearers.

H.P. Smith (1898, p. 165) bluntly says, "The most ingenious harmonists have not succeeded in reconciling this paragraph (17:55-18:5) with 16:14-23." Nevertheless, Bergen and J.E. Smith attempt to harmonize the accounts. J.E. Smith (2000, p. 217) suggests that the recommendation of David as "a man of valor, a man of war" (16:18) rests on David's reputation for protecting the flocks from lions and bears, and from Philistine raiders, which is not mentioned in the text. Both Bergen and J.E. Smith contend that Saul did not ask who David was but whose son he was for the purpose of preparing an edict to exempt the family of David's father from taxes. Bergen (1996, p. 198-99) explains Saul's ignorance about David by saying that quite a long period had elapsed between chapters 16 and 17, that David was not an armor-bearer to Saul but merely a personal attendant, that David had been allowed to go home, that David had changed in appearance, and that Saul's mental malady made him forget details about David. Although these suggestions for reconciling the apparent contradictions may be correct, they test one's credulity when a better solution may be found. The statements can retain their apparent meaning if we explain their placement by the method used to compose the story of David.

Like chapter 16, chapter 17 through 18:5 is an introduction to the story of David. Both introduce his father and brothers (16:1; 17:12), both tell us that David was the youngest son (16:11; 17:14), both describe David's physical appearance (16:12; 17:42), and both end with a summary of his subsequent career in Saul's court (16:21-23; 18:2-5). Although Youngblood (1992, p. 690) says that two or more narratives should not be assumed, it certainly appears that chapter 16 is dependent upon one account of David's introduction to Saul's court, perhaps written by Samuel, who anointed David, and that chapter 17 is dependent upon another account, perhaps written by Gad, who accompanied David on his early military campaigns (1 Sam. 22:5). David's life in Chronicles, and most likely in Samuel also, was compiled from the records of several prophets as suggested by 1 Chron. 29:29-30.

> Now the acts of King David, from first to last, are
> written in the Chronicles of Samuel the seer, and in the
> Chronicles of Nathan the prophet, and in the Chronicles
> of Gad the seer, with accounts of all his rule and his
> might and of the circumstances that came upon him and
> upon Israel and upon all the kingdoms of the countries.

Both accounts end with a summary of David's career in Saul's court, but the accounts begin in different places. The writer did not break up the two accounts in order to place all the events in chronological order. The writer simply placed the one with the earliest event first. Since that account ends with a summary of David's career in Saul's court, some of the events in the second account, which also ends with a summary of David's career in Saul's court, must have occurred before the summary of the first account and perhaps before some of the other events as well.

If the slaying of Goliath is placed before David being called into Saul's court as a musician, then the two problems noted previously would disappear. First, Saul's servant who recommended David as a musician would naturally call him a man of valor (16:18) because he had previously slain Goliath. Second, Saul would not have known who David was when he went out to face Goliath (17:55) because David had not yet played the lyre to calm his troubled spirit. David did not enter military service immediately after killing Goliath because he was not yet 20 years old. He was, however, called to be a court musician and then entered Saul's army when he reached the age of 20.

Note on Part Two Chronology

David began his life as an outcast in about his 24th year (See note on Part One). He lived as an outcast in Judah until he was 28 and fled to Philistia where he lived a year and four months (1 Sam. 27:7) before becoming king when he was 30 years old (2 Sam. 5:4). Hence, David lived as an outcast in Judah for about four years from his 24th to his 28th year.

While David was "at his stronghold in the desert," men from Gad, Benjamin, and Judah joined him. David's movements during his life as an outcast were these:

- Ramah (1 Sam. 19:18-24)
- A field near Saul's hometown (1 Sam. 20:1-42)
- Nob (1 Sam. 21:1-9)
- Gath (1 Sam. 21:10-15)
- Cave near Adullam (1 Sam. 22:1-2)
- A stronghold in Moab (1 Sam. 22:3-5)
- The forest of Hereth (1 Sam. 22:5)
- Keilah (1 Sam. 23:5-12)
- Moving from place to place (1 Sam. 23:13)
- Strongholds in the Wilderness of Ziph (1 Sam. 23:14)
- Wilderness of Maon (1 Sam. 23:24-28)
- Strongholds of Engedi (1 Sam. 23:29 – 24:22)
- Wilderness of Paran (1 Sam. 25:1)

- Wilderness of Ziph (1 Sam. 26:2)

It is impossible to know with certainty where David was when the men of Gad joined him. It would be tempting to put it at the time David was in the stronghold in Moab because Gad is east of the Jordan, but the Gadites apparently crossed the Jordan to join David (1 Chron. 12:15). Although the forest of Hereth is neither called a stronghold nor a desert, the Gadites and Benjamites may have joined him there. (Where David's men camped would have been their stronghold, and any desolate or deserted place, even a forest, could be called a desert.) I have placed it at the Forest of Hereth for two reasons.

This time accounts for David's men growing from 400 at the cave in Adullam (1 Sam. 22:2) to 600 when he left Keilah (1 Sam. 23:13)

This time gives reason for Saul to ask his men, "Can David give you fields and vineyards or make you commanders of hundreds and thousands?" If some of his men had defected to David, it would account for his outburst (see 1 Sam. 22:7).

Note on Part Three Chronology

David fled to Philistia when he was about 28 years old, and he lived there for a year and four months (1 Sam. 27:7). He returned to Judah to become king when he was 30 years old (2 Sam. 5:4).

The men of Manasseh who deserted Saul before the battle with the Philistines apparently joined David in time to participate in his raid against the Amalekite raiders who had plundered Ziklag (1 Chron. 12:21).

Note on Part Four Chronology

David was 30 years old when he was proclaimed king over Judah in Hebron, and he reigned in Hebron for seven and a half years (2 Sam. 5:4-5). During the first few years of David's reign in Hebron, the Philistines apparently ruled the northern tribes. Eventually Saul's son Ish-bosheth was proclaimed king over the northern tribes, and he reigned for two years before he was killed (2 Sam. 2:10). David was then proclaimed king over all Israel, and he moved his capital to Jerusalem soon thereafter at about age 38 (2 Sam. 5:1-7).

Note on Part Five Chronology

Beginning at age 30, David reigned in Hebron for seven and a half years (2 Sam. 5:4-5). Therefore, he began reigning in Jerusalem when he was about 38 years old. His reign in Jerusalem began with the capture of the city. By the time he was about 47 years old, David had conquered Jerusalem, had brought the Ark of God into the city, and had been victorious over the surrounding nations in war.

Note on Part Six Chronology

David's military campaigns against the Arameans in chapter 8 can be related to his war with the Ammonites in chapter 10 in one of three ways: 1) The Aramean campaigns were prior to the Ammonite war. 2) The Aramean campaigns occurred during the Ammonite war. 3) The Aramean campaigns followed the Ammonite war. Each will be considered in order.

First alternative: the Aramean campaigns were prior to the Ammonite war. Although this sequence has the advantage of being the order of presentation in the Biblical text, it appears improbable that the Arameans, whom David had thoroughly subjugated in chapter eight, would be hired by the Ammonites in chapter ten to save them from David. Bergen (1996, p. 347), who generally considers the events in Samuel to be presented in chronological order makes no attempt to deal with this problem but acknowledges the debate among scholars about the order of events in chapters 8 and 10-12.

Second alternative: the Aramean campaigns occurred during the Ammonite war. The writer has listed the nations David fought in the order in which they were defeated: Philistia, Moab, Aram, and Edom in 2 Sam. 8 and Ammon in 2 Sam. 10:1 through 12:31 with the story of David's sin taking place when the outcome of that final war was evident. However, the war with Ammon began before the wars with Syria when Ammon hired Hadadezer, an Aramean, to help them against David. David had to deal with the more powerful Arameans before turning his full attention to the Ammonites. H.P. Smith (1898, p. 305) suggests that the Aramean campaign was a part of the war against Ammon recounted in chapter 10.

The Aramean campaigns followed the Ammonite war. Youngblood (1992, p. 904) writes, "It is probably best, however, to understand 8:3–12 as a record of battles that occurred after the campaigns reported in chapters 10–12" However, this alternative does create some problems. It puts a major military campaign after David's sin with Bathsheba, and if God made his covenant with David after giving him peace from his enemies, then this alternative improbably places God's covenant with David after his sin.

The second alternative, which has been adopted in this chronology, proposes the following sequence of events. After David defeated (1) Philistia and (2) Moab (2 Sam. 8:1,2), the Ammonites insulted David's messengers and hired the Arameans to help them (2 Sam. 10:1-6). David defeated the Arameans twice, once at Medeba (2 Sam. 10:7-14) and once at Helam (2 Sam. 10:15-19), while they were attempting to help the Ammonites. After Hadadezer was defeated at Helam, he was afraid to help Ammon anymore. At that time, some of his vassal kings allied themselves with David (2 Sam. 10:19). (3) When Hadadezer then went to reassert his control over his former vassals to the north (2 Sam. 8:3), David attacked him to prevent him from regaining his former power. The Arameans of Damascus tried to help Hadadezer (2 Sam. 8:5), but David defeated them also and placed garrisons in their territories. David plundered Hadadezer's wealth and made an alliance with the king of Hamath, which was north of Zobah, Hadadezer's capital city. While Joab was finishing the campaign against the Arameans, (4) Abishai defeated the Edomites (2 Sam. 8:13). (5) Ammon was now isolated economically and politically from her allies. A siege laid against Rabbah was then quite effective, and Ammon fell to David's forces. This sequence of events suggests that 2 Sam. 8 through 12 is a list of nations conquered by David in the order in which they were conquered. The Arameans meddled in the Ammonite dispute, and David had to deal with them decisively before turning back to the less powerful Ammonites.

The exploits of David's mighty men were mostly against foreign enemies, so they have been placed here instead of at the end of David's reign.

Note on Part Seven Chronology

The covenant God made with David in 2 Sam. 7 is one of the more important passages in the Old Testament both because of its connection to the covenant God made with Abraham and because it is the foundation of the hopes expressed in the prophets and fulfilled in Christ. In this section, two questions will be considered: First, when does chapter seven itself suggest the covenant was made? Second, how does the covenant relate in time to the wars in chapters 8, 10-12, and more particularly to the time of David's sin with Bathsheba?

The wording of chapter seven itself suggests that God made his covenant with David after he had given him "rest from all his enemies around him" (2 Sam. 7:1). Reference to this rest uses wording from Deut. 12:10-11 where God commands that when God "gives you rest from all your enemies around, so that you live in safety, then to the place that the LORD your God will choose, to make his name dwell there, there you shall bring all that I command you: your burnt offerings and your sacrifices, your tithes and the contribution that you present, and all your finest vow offerings that you vow to the LORD." David clearly felt that the time had arrived not only to designate the place but also to build a house for God, something God had not commanded. God responded to David by saying that he had never asked for a house (2 Sam. 7:4-7). Then he rehearsed the things he had already done for David and told him further what he would do for him in the future (2 Sam. 7:8-16).

Unlike English, Hebrew does not have past, present, and future tenses. It uses perfect and imperfect aspects. The perfect is used in places where English uses both past and future events. Consequently, English translations must decide where to change from past to future in verses 8-16. The ESV and NIV shift from what God had done to what he would do in the future in the middle of verse 9, and the KJV shifts at the beginning of verse 10 following the lead of the LXX because, assuming the wars in chapter 8 and 10 are future, "rest from all your enemies" in verse 11 must be a promise.

The GNB (compare with *Young's Literal Translation*) waits until verse 12 to shift from past to future. Assuming that verse 1 in the immediate context is true, this translation puts "rest from all your enemies" in the past. If the immediate context (verse 1) is given priority over the more distant context (chapters 8 and 10), verses 8 through 11 should be seen as things God had already done for David, and verses 12 through 16 as things God would yet do for him in the future. If priority is given to the immediate context, and it should, then the English should delay using the future tense until after the reference to "rest from all your enemies."

If this reading of the text is correct, then the text itself also suggests that the covenant was made before David's heir to the throne was born. Verse 12 says, "When your days are fulfilled and you lie down with your fathers, I will raise up your offspring after you, who shall come from your body, and I will establish his kingdom." The wording of this promise to David reflects the wording of God's promise to Abraham who had waited for many years for an heir and was nearly ready to name a servant born in his household as heir (Gen. 15:4). Therefore, the covenant with David involves a promise concerning a son yet to be born who would become king after David. The son who became king and built the temple was Solomon.

The second question is now considered. When did God make the covenant with David in relation to the wars in chapters 8, 10-12, and more particularly, in relation to the time of David's sin with Bathsheba? Alter (1999, p. 231) says that the rest from his enemies in 2 Sam. 7:1 was a partial and temporary rest that preceded the wars in 2 Sam. 8 and 10-12.

Unlike Alter, most scholars admit that 2 Sam. 7 is not placed in the narrative in chronological order. J.E. Smith (2000, p. 391) says that God made the covenant with David "fairly late in David's reign" and "after some if not all" of the wars narrated in 2 Sam. 8. Youngblood (1992, pp.883-84) goes even further and places the covenant late in David's reign after his sin with Bathsheba. Crockett (1964, pp. 108-133) also places the covenant after all of David's wars and his sin with Bathsheba. The problem with placing the covenant late in David's career is that it is placed after the birth of Solomon. As noted earlier, 2 Sam. 7:12 suggests God made the covenant with David before his heir, Solomon, was born.

The chronology that best fits the wording of 2 Sam. 7 places the covenant after the wars in chapters 8 and 10 and before David's sin in chapter 11. This is the chronology adopted by Bergen (1996, p. 335). All of David's enemies would have been defeated. Only Rabbah, the capital of the Ammonites, was holding out after all of her allies had been defeated and her countryside ravaged. During a lull in the fighting with victory virtually assured when the siege of the city began in the spring (2 Sam. 11:1), David wanted to begin his next project, a house for God. He had already dedicated the plunder from his victories to the Lord (2 Sam. 8:11-12), and he was anxious to begin. However, God had different plans.

Solomon could not have been born much less than 20 years before David's death because Solomon's firstborn, Rehoboam, was one year old when Solomon took the throne (1 Kings 11:42 with 14:21). Hence, David, who died at 70, was about 50 years old when Solomon was born. The time elapsed between the making of the covenant and Solomon's birth included some time before the siege of Rabbah began and two pregnancies for Bathsheba (one for the son that died and one for

Solomon). Subtracting that time from 50 would make David about 48 years old when God made his covenant with him.

Note on Part Eight Chronology

The writer introduces the story of Amnon and Tamar in 2 Sam. 13 with the phrase "In the course of time," which apparently means that this story took place after David's repentance and Solomon's birth recorded in the previous chapter. As noted earlier, Solomon must have been born about halfway through David's forty-year reign.

The time of Amnon's birth confirms that Amnon's actions must have been after the halfway point in David's reign. Amnon, David's firstborn son, was born after David began reigning in Hebron (2 Sam. 3:2). Twenty years, give or take a few, likely passed before Amnon would have raped his sister. From this point on, the writer gives us time intervals between the major events.

Absalom murdered Amnon two years after his sister was raped (2 Sam. 13:23). Absalom fled to Geshur where he remained until David recalled him three years later (2 Sam 13:38). Absalom lived in Jerusalem two years before he saw David, his father (2 Sam. 14:28). Finally, Absalom stole the hearts of the people over a period of four years (2 Sam 15:7) before declaring himself king in Hebron. (The Hebrew text in this verse actually reads "forty years," but forty years is not possible unless one counts from the very beginning of David's reign to the end of his reign. Accordingly, the ESV and NIV use "four years," which is found in the Syriac, a few LXX manuscripts, and Josephus.)

When these intervals are added together (2+3+2+4), the total time from Amnon's rape of Tamar until Absalom's rebellion and death amounts to eleven years. We have estimated that this interval would have been from David's 51st year until his 63rd year. It might be possible to move the interval up to about four years later in David's life.

Note on Part Nine Chronology

Sheba's rebellion began immediately after the death of Absalom when David was about 63 years old.

David's census took most of a year to complete (2 Sam. 24:8). It is assumed that the census was completed at least three years before the end of David's reign because one of the possible punishments was a three-year famine (see 1 Chron. 21:12). Therefore, David would have been about 67 years old when he purchased the site where Solomon would build the temple.

Note on Part Ten Chronology

Following David's purchase of the temple site when he was about 67 years old, his health declined. A crisis arose when David did not name a successor, and Adonijah declared himself king, probably during the last year of David's life. David immediately had Solomon anointed and put on the throne. Then he called a national assembly which had three purposes. First, he introduced the heads of all government, military, and temple services to Solomon and placed them under his authority. Second, he transferred to Solomon the materials and extensive plans he had made for the building of the temple and committed Solomon and the leaders to completing the task. Finally, he had Solomon acknowledged as king by all Israel and anointed a second time before them all. Soon after that, "He died at a good old age, having enjoyed long life, wealth and honor" (1 Chron. 29:26-28). He was 70 years old at his death.

Crockett reconstructs the chronology differently. He places the national assembly that acclaimed Solomon king (1 Chron. 23-29) before Absalom's rebellion, which he found necessary because he places Absalom's rebellion in David's 40th year in accordance with 2 Sam. 15:7 (KJV and Hebrew manuscripts). Consequently, Crockett (1964, pp. 141-160) says that Solomon was made king the second time in 1 Kings 1.

Crockett's chronology creates several problems. To begin with, 1 Chron. 29:22 says that Solomon was made king the second time at the great national assembly, which would place it after 1 Kings 1. Second, the assumption in 1 Kings 1 is that there had been no national proclamation making Solomon king before Adonijah tried to seize the throne. Bathsheba did not remind David of a public proclamation but of a promise he had made her regarding Solomon. Furthermore, she said that all Israel was waiting for David to make his wishes about a successor known (1 Kings 1:20), which, if Crockett is right, David had already done. Finally, Absalom's rebellion was directed against David, not Solomon. After Absalom was killed, the people spoke of recalling David, not Solomon.

The one justification for Crockett's chronology is 2 Sam. 15:7 which says that Absalom requested permission to fulfill a vow in Hebron "at the end of forty years." This statement appears rather odd because throughout the Absalom narrative, time references relate to events within the narrative, not to the beginning of David's reign. As noted in the chronological note on part eight, the Syriac, some Septuagint manuscripts, and Josephus read "four" instead of "forty" in 2 Sam. 15:7. This reading allows ample time to call the national assembly for the second anointing after the hurried anointing at Gihon.